Language in the News

Newspaper coverage of world events is presented as the unbiased recording of 'hard facts'. In an incisive study of both the quality and the popular Press, Roger Fowler challenges this perception, arguing that news is a practice, a product of the social and political world on which it reports. Writing from the perspective of a critical linguistics, Fowler examines the crucial role of language in mediating reality.

Starting with a general account of news values and the processes of selection and transformation which go to make up the news, Fowler goes on to consider newspaper representations of gender, power, authority and law and order. He discusses stereotyping, terms of abuse and endearment, the editorial voice and the formation of consensus. Fowler's analysis takes in some of the major news stories of the Thatcher decade – the American bombing of Libya in 1986, the salmonella-in-eggs affair, the problems of the National Health Service and the controversy over contraception and the young.

Laying bare the ideologies at work in newspaper language, Fowler challenges both readers and students of the media and journalists involved in producing the news to become aware of how language can shape, rather than mirror, the world.

Roger Fowler is Professor of English and Linguistics at the University of East Anglia. He is the author of a number of books, including *Linguistics and the Novel* and *Linguistic Criticism*, and has edited *A Dictionary of Modern Critical Terms*.

Language in the News

Discourse and Ideology in the Press

ROGER FOWLER

Routledge
Taylor & Francis Group

LONDON AND NEW YORK

First published in 1991
by Routledge
2 Park Square, Milton Park, Abingdon, Oxon OX14 4RN

Simultaneously published in the USA and Canada
by Routledge
270 Madison Ave, New York, NY 10016

Reprinted 1992, 1994. 1996, 1998, 1999, 2001, 2003, 2004, 2005, 2007

Routledge is an imprint of the Taylor & Francis Group, an informa business

© 1991 ROGER FOWLER

Phototypeset in 10/12pt Bembo by
Input Typesetting Ltd, London
Printed in Great Britain by
TJ International Ltd, Padstow, Cornwall

British Library Cataloguing in Publication Data
Fowler, Roger
  Language in the news : discourse and ideology in the Press.
  1. Mass media. Linguistic aspects
  I. Title
  302.2322

Library of Congress Cataloging in Publication Data
Fowler, Roger.
   Language in the news : discourse and ideology in the Press
   / Roger Fowler.
      p. cm.
   1. English newspapers—Language. 2. Journalism—Great Britain—
   Language. 3. English language—Discourse analysis. 4. English
   language—Social aspects—Great Britain. I. Title.
   PE1474.F69 1991
   302.23′22′0941—dc20
                                              90–40794
                                                   CIP

ISBN10: 0-415-01418-2 (hb)   ISBN13: 978-0-415-01418-2 (hb)
ISBN10: 0-415-01419-0 (pb)   ISBN13: 978-0-415-01419-9 (pb)

That's a load of old squit.
Norfolk saying

Contents

Acknowledgements

Academic Press, for permission to use material which first appeared in T. A. Van Dijk, (ed.), *Handbook of Discourse Analysis*, Vol. IV, *Discourse Analysis in Society* (New York, 1985), pp. 61–82.

Open University Press, for permission to use material which first appeared in M. MacLure, T. Phillips and A. Wilkinson, (eds), *Oracy Matters* (Milton Keynes, 1988), pp. 135–46.

News International, for permission·to reproduce two pages from the *Sun*, 13 February 1989.

Express Newspapers plc for permission to reproduce the *Daily Express* opinion article of 18 April 1986.

Times Newspapers Limited, for permission to reproduce 'Scandal of hospital queues' by Garron Baines, from the *Sunday Times*, 5 February 1978.

I am grateful to colleagues who have encouraged this project, advised me on its general bearings and commented on some of the analysis; particularly to Jon Cook, Bill Downes, Martin Montgomery, Roger Sales and Teun A. Van Dijk; also to students at the University of East Anglia, Norwich, who have offered many illuminations while working on these materials with me.

A writer is a hermit in a family. Thanks to Paddy, Bridget and our border(line) collie Jess for their patience.

Chapter 1

Introduction: the importance of language in the news

This is a study of how language is used in newspapers to form ideas and beliefs. I take the view that the 'content' of newspapers is not facts about the world, but in a very general sense 'ideas'. I will use other terms as appropriate: 'beliefs', 'values', 'theories', 'propositions', 'ideology'. My major concern is with the role of linguistic structure in the construction of ideas in the Press; I will show that language is not neutral, but a highly constructive mediator.

The journalist takes a different view. He or she collects facts, reports them objectively, and the newspaper presents them fairly and without bias, in language which is designed to be unambiguous, undistorting and agreeable to readers. This professional ethos is common to all the news media, Press, radio and television, and it is certainly what the journalist claims in any general statement on the matter. For example, the following statement by Andrew Neil, the editor of the *Sunday Times*, introducing a book on the 1984–5 miners' strike written by that paper's journalists, asserts that though a newspaper may have a clear editorial position on some topic reported, that is reserved for the leader column, while the news reporting itself, on other pages, is factual and unbiased:

From the start, *The Sunday Times* took a firm editorial line: for the sake of liberal democracy, economic recovery and the rolling back of union power, and for the sake of the sensible voices in the Labour Party and the TUC, Scargill and his forces had to be defeated, and would be. It was a position from which we never wavered throughout this long, brutal dispute. Our views, however, were kept to where they belong in a quality newspaper: the editorial column. For us the miners' strike was above all a massive reporting and analysing task to give our readers an impartial and well-informed picture of what was really happening.[1]

In recent years, the professional journalist's self-image on this question of impartiality has come under strong challenge from students of the media. Notably the Glasgow University Media Group, and the University of Birmingham Centre for Contemporary Cultural Studies, have in their various research publications elaborated an alternative picture of news practices; a picture which is current generally among sociologists and other students of the media.[2] On this model, news is socially constructed. What events are reported is not a reflection of the intrinsic importance of those events, but reveals the operation of a complex and artificial set of criteria for selection. Then, the news that has been thus selected is subject to processes of transformation as it is encoded for publication; the technical properties of the medium – television or newsprint, for example – and the ways in which they are used, are strongly effective in this transformation. Both 'selection' and 'transformation' are guided by reference, generally unconscious, to ideas and beliefs. Analysis of output can reveal abstract propositions which are not necessarily stated, and are usually unquestioned, and which dominate the structure of presentation. One such was the proposition 'wage increases cause inflation' which the Glasgow Group discovered dominated the television presentation of industrial news in the first half of 1975. It is further claimed by students of the media that such propositions tend to be consonant with the ideas of the controlling groups in an industrial-capitalist society, because news is an industry with its own commercial self-interest. Thus news is a *practice*: a discourse which, far from neutrally reflecting social reality and empirical facts, intervenes in what Berger and Luckmann call 'the social construction of reality'.[3] (I hasten to assure readers that one can believe that news is a practice without also believing that news is a conspiracy.)

This argument – which I will report in more detail in chapter 2 – is not peculiar to media studies, but has its counterparts in the sociology of knowledge (hence my reference to Berger and Luckmann's book), semiotics and linguistics, the major branch of semiotics. In his book *Understanding News*, John Hartley very constructively places the usual contemporary account of news as a social and ideological produce within the framework of general semiotic theory, and this seems to me the proper intellectual context for the analysis of media.[4] The foundations of semiotics were laid by the early-twentieth-century Swiss linguist Ferdinand de Saussure. In the form of their contemporary acceptance, these principles are roughly as follows. Between human beings and the world they experience, there exist systems of signs which are the product of society. Signs acquire meaning through being structured into codes, the principal code being language. Other codes abound; they are language-like in their structural properties, but more transient, less stable. The analyses offered by Roland Barthes in his book *Mythologies* are very suggestive of the power of coding in such areas as fashion, architecture, cuisine and sport.[5] Codes endow the world with meaning or significance by organizing it into categories and relationships which are not there 'naturally', but which represent the interests, values and behaviours of human communities. So, for example, the distinction between 'plants' and 'weeds' is a semiotic, not botanical, difference: it stems from the tastes and fashions of a gardening culture, and is coded in the vocabulary of their language. The existence of these two words, with their conventionally opposed meanings, allows us to communicate about the objects concerned. But communication between people is not the only function of the language code. Language and other codes, most importantly language, have a cognitive role: they provide an organized mental representation for our experience. Whatever the 'natural' structure of the world, whether indeterminate flux, as Saussure seems to have believed, or some other structure (from a semiotic point of view it does not matter), we handle it mentally, and in discourse, in terms of the conventional meaning-categories embodied in our society's codes.

In chapters 3 to 5 I will give a fuller exposition of the linguistic model which supports this theory and analysis, but here I will just anticipate, briefly, the further linguistic apparatus that will be brought into play. It is clear that the argument needs greater *psychological* and *social* refinement than is found in Saussure and in the more recent French semioticians. We need, first, to say something more about the relationship between the semantic (meaning) structure of the language code, and the mental organization of experience. On this question, I will refer to the ideas of the American linguists Edward Sapir and Benjamin Lee Whorf, and of the British linguist M. A. K. Halliday.[6] These theoreticians maintain that there is a causal relationship between semantic structure and cognition: that language influences thought, in the sense that its structure channels our mental experience of the world. This claim, which is expressed by its proponents in various terms and with varying degrees of force, is impossible of empirical proof, and has to be handled cautiously, treated as a working hypothesis rather than a finding. There is, however, some relevant psycholinguistic research.[7]

The social dimension of this theory is more secure, because it is easy to see correlations between differences of code and differences of social setting. The style of the *Sun* newspaper is very different from that of the *Independent*, and the readerships of the two papers are very distinct socioeconomically. Presumably, this linguistic and social co-variation is significant. Many aspects of the correlation between linguistic form and social setting have been studied by sociolinguists,[8] and here again Halliday is extremely helpful. He draws attention to the tremendous range of sociolinguistic variety to be found within a single whole language such as English, and he enquires into the functions of this variety both in delimiting social groups and also in encoding the different ideologies of those groups.

My accounts of language in newspapers, and, I believe, the analyses of news media offered by the authorities I have cited, can be regarded as merely specific instances of the general principles I have just sketched. News is a representation of the world in language; because language is a semiotic code, it imposes a structure of values, social and economic in origin, on whatever is represented; and so inevitably news, like every discourse, constructively patterns that of which it speaks. News is a representation in this sense of construction; it is not a value-free reflection of 'facts'. The final theoretical point to make here is that I assume as a working principle that each particular form of linguistic expression in a text – wording, syntactic option, etc. – has its reason. There are always different ways of saying the same thing, and they are not random, accidental alternatives. Differences in expression carry ideological distinctions (and thus differences in representation). The point is sometimes obvious: clearly it is significant whether a political leader is referred to as 'Gorby' or 'Mr Gorbachev', whether the opening of the borders in Eastern

Europe is headlined 'REDS HEAD WEST' or 'Thousands cross border into West Germany'. But these grossly visible alternatives, their meanings on open display, are only a small part of the ideological working of linguistic expression. Many other aspects of language, less dramatic but equally forceful in shaping representation, can be brought to the surface for observation. This book is concerned primarily with the analysis of those linguistic features which work subliminally in the newspapers' ideological practice of representation.

The prevailing orthodoxy of linguistics is that it is a *descriptive* discipline which has no business passing comments on materials which it analyses; neither *prescribing* usage nor negatively evaluating the substance of its enquiries. But I see no reason why there should not be branches of linguistics with different goals and procedures, and since values are so thoroughly implicated in linguistic usage, it seems justifiable to practise a kind of linguistics directed towards understanding such values, and this is the branch which has become known as critical linguistics.[9] That is the method followed in this book. Now, the word 'critical' could be intended, or taken to be intended, to denote negative evaluation, but this negativity is not necessarily the aim of critical linguistics. As far as I am concerned, critical linguistics simply means an enquiry into the relations between signs, meanings and the social and historical conditions which govern the semiotic structure of discourse, using a particular kind of linguistic analysis.[10] This activity requires a very specific model of linguistics. The model has not only to identify, and to label reliably, certain key linguistic constructions; it has to relate them to context in a special way. The familiar transformational-generative linguistics invented by Noam Chomsky[11] provides my eclectic model with some descriptive terminology, but is in general terms unsuitable, because its aim is to refer linguistic structures to the set of structural possibilities that are available to human language as a universal phenomenon, presumably genetically programmed in the human brain; Chomsky is not interested in the role of language in real use (and indeed will not allow such matters to be a valid concern of linguistics). Halliday's systemic-functional linguistics, on the other hand, is specifically geared to relating structure to communicative function, and this model provides most of my descriptive apparatus. Chapters 3 to 5 elaborate the detail.

Several lines of interest converged to cause me to write this book. I was keen to develop the critical linguistics model, first sketched in Fowler, Hodge, Kress and Trew, *Language and Control* (1979) and then used in a scatter of studies by the original authors and by other colleagues. I wanted more experience of this analysis, in order to improve the technical details, and to discover what kinds of construction could be relied on to reward critical readers with insights; and I wanted to clarify the general theory, which was, and is, abstract and controversial. But my enthusiasm was not only a matter of technical interest in the model. I reflected that my work in the early 1980s, in a series of occasional lectures and articles, had become increasingly focused on the British Press – which was not my field in *Language and Control*, but a topic brilliantly explored by Tony Trew in two pioneering chapters. The newspapers became compulsive reading in this period of major and distressing events and processes: the Falklands War, escalating unemployment, disorder and violence, bombings, the miners' strike, the deployment of cruise missiles, nuclear accidents culminating in the Chernobyl disaster, the American bombing of Libya, the privatization of basic services such as water, the reduction of public funding for health and education, and so on. A number of political factors in this period seemed to me to have important and analysable implications for a reader's experience of newspaper language. I will just refer to three major problems by way of brief examples.

First, the paradoxical ideology of conflict and consensus. As has been pointed out by many political commentators, the Conservative government under Mrs Thatcher from 1979 to 1990 theorized social and international relationships in terms of conflict: striking versus non-striking miners; metropolitan councils versus central government; 'state-sponsored terrorism' versus 'self-defence'; 'appeasement' (and its advocates, such as CND) versus 'peace through defence'; and so on. I felt that public discourse, both political and media utterances, played a powerful role in establishing the categories which were sorted into these conflictual oppositions, and that the sorting could be directly observed in the details of linguistic construction (see chapters 6 to 8). But while the practice was to segregate and marginalize threatening and undesirable elements, the official discourse of government and media spoke of national unity of interest and common purpose: consensus. In a hypocritical attempt to resolve contradiction, the division between 'us' and 'them' was discursively reprocessed as 'we': 'just about every person in the land' as the *Sun* expressed it.

A second change, and problem, in the 1980s was the centraliz-ation and monetarization of power and authority. People in the best position to manage public affairs were stripped of their authority to do so. For example, local councils, and professionals such as doctors and teachers, were deprived of the ability to practise properly, and to work in the interests of the people, by a combination of strategies: legislative changes which withdrew local powers in favour of the authority of Westminster; reductions of public funding in many spheres, far below the levels needed to run a university, say, or a hospital; and discursive strategies working to reorganize conventional expectations of authority towards new, rigid and impractical hierarchies. In chapter 6, pp. 105–9, I analyse one set of newspaper materials which works in part to establish doctors as very low down in the medical ladder of power.

The third change of the 1980s is related to the second, but it was managed primarily discursively. This was the propaganda of individual responsibility or self-reliance. The government system-atically depleted the resources and protections available for those in need: unemployed, sick in mind or body, elderly, abused or deprived in whatever way. Psychiatric hospitals and wards were closed down, and their clients pushed out to 'community care'; old-age pensions were allowed to fall in value, while tax con-cessions were offered to pensioners who were willing to work or to insure for their own medical treatment; food research was deprived of funding, at a time of an alleged food poisoning 'epidemic', on the grounds that the food industry should pay for research which benefits it. In every case, the saving of central funds resulting from these moves was justified in terms of peo-ple's wish to look after themselves, not to be 'nannied'. The media played a major role in promulgating the argument of indi-vidual responsibility: see, for example, the attempt to shift the food poisoning scare from the industry to 'the housewife', chapter 10.

I end this Introduction with a simple point about method. The 'standard position' of current students of the media is that news is a construct which is to be understood in social and semiotic terms; and everyone acknowledges the importance of language in this process of construction. But in practice, language gets relatively meagre treatment, when it comes to analysis: the Glasgow Group, and Hartley, for example, are more interested in, and better equipped technically to analyse, visual techniques in television. *More Bad News* does devote three chapters to language, but the analysis is anecdotal and lacking in detail (from a linguist's point of view). In the present study, language is given fundamental importance, not only as an analytic instrument, but also as the way of expressing a general theory of representation which is entirely congruent with the theory assumed by other, non-linguistic researchers.

This book, then, offers a dimension of analysis which is skimpily or unsystematically treated in current media studies, the linguistic dimension; I approach it using the tools of one specific linguistic model, 'critical linguistics'. In order to give a full treatment of one level, I have of course had to pay little attention to other dimensions of analysis. For example, I have largely ignored the graphic format of the page, a dimension which is crucially important to the organization of newspaper text. I am well aware that typographical choices (style and size of print), composition and the deployment of photographs, drawings, cartoons, tables, maps, captions, etc., are of immense significance in newspaper representation, and that these factors interact dynamically with language proper, the words considered as linguistic structures. Newspaper discourse is so complex that concentration on one aspect inevitably leads to neglect of others, if one wants a book of this kind to remain readable – not inordinately long or methodologically over-complex.

I would like to make it clear that my intention is not simply to expose 'bias', certainly not to maintain that newspapers are especially 'biased'. My reliance on a general linguistic theory which maintains that (nearly) all meanings are socially constructed, that all discourse is a social product and a social practice – and my contention that all discourse is better understood if subjected to critical linguistic analysis – will, I hope, help to forestall a misunderstanding similar to that which marred the reception of *Bad News*. News has not been singled out as a unique instance of deliberate or negligent partiality; it is analysed as a particularly important example of the power of *all* language in the social construction of reality. I am not gunning for the Press, but looking at the linguistics of representation in newspaper discourse, which is a major element in our daily experience of language.

That said, it remains true that I have chosen to analyse in this book Press treatments of matters which are of intense concern in contemporary life: inequality, discrimination, inhumanity, war. I am often angered and distressed by what the papers say. I hope this book will give other concerned readers some practical help in decoding newspaper discourse, and in thinking about and discussing life issues and their representation.

Chapter 2

The social construction of news

BIAS OR REPRESENTATION

In this chapter, I want to outline, quite briefly, what has emerged in recent media studies, for example the Glasgow and the Birmingham research,[1] as a sort of 'standard position' on the question of partiality in news presentation. A vulgar synopsis of this standard position might be that 'all news is biased': that is how journalists and lay people have construed what the media theorists have claimed. But in fact the standard media analysis aims to be descriptive, not destructive. What is being said is that, because the institutions of news reporting and presentation are socially, economically and politically situated, all news is always reported from some particular angle. The structure of the medium encodes significances which derive from the respective positions within society of the publishing or broadcasting organizations.

In fact, what is being claimed about news can equally be claimed about *any* representational discourse. Anything that is said or written about the world is articulated from a particular ideological position: language is not a clear window but a refracting, structuring medium. If we can acknowledge this as a positive, productive principle, we can go on to show by analysis how it operates in texts. My interest is in the contribution of detailed linguistic structure – syntax, vocabulary structure, and so on – to moulding a representation of the world in news text. The standard account, though acknowledging that language has a role in mediation, has little to say about the specifics of how the process works.

As readers of newspapers, and viewers of television, we readily assume that the *Nine O'Clock News*, or the front page of the *Daily Express* or the *Guardian*, consists of faithful reports of events that happened 'out there', in the world beyond our immediate experience. At a certain level, that is of course a realistic assumption: real events do occur and are reported – a coach crashes on the autobahn, a postman wins the pools, a cabinet minister resigns. But real events are subject to conventional processes of selection: they are not intrinsically newsworthy, but only become 'news' when selected for inclusion in news reports. The vast majority of events are not mentioned, and so selection immediately gives us a partial view of the world. We know also that different newspapers report differently, in both content and presentation. The pools win is more likely to be reported in the *Mirror* than in *The Times*, whereas a crop failure in Meghalaya may be reported in *The Times* but almost certainly not in the *Mirror*. Selection is accompanied by transformation, differential treatment in presentation according to numerous political, economic and social factors. As far as differences in presentation are concerned, most people would admit the possibility of 'bias': the *Sun* is known to be consistently hostile in its treatment of trades unions, and of what it calls 'the loony Left'; the *Guardian* is generous in its reporting of the affairs of CND. Such disaffections and affiliations are obvious when one starts reading carefully, and discussing the news media with other people. The world of the Press is not the real world, but a world skewed and judged.

Now, what attitude might one take towards the 'bias'? A number of possibilities are evident. There might be, for example, an optimistic response, based on the ideology of democracy and individual responsibility: biases exist because this is a free country, with an elected, representative government, and we have a free Press putting forward various points of views, so the individual has to read carefully and comparatively in order to discount the biases and see through to the truth. Such a view would be reasonable if as much money were spent on education as on the show of parliamentary conduct, but people are not in general trained to see through the veils of media representation, and massive educational advances would be necessary in order to produce significant numbers of critical readers who could discount the bias. On the Left, by contrast, there is an even more Utopian view, which says that bias is endemic because of the ties between media production and industrial-speculative capitalism, and can be countered only by radical changes in the financing and procedures of news production, and by the provision of alternative news sources: I take it that this is the message of the important article 'Bias in the media' by Greg Philo, a member of the Glasgow team.[2] Whilst I sympathize with the analysis, it seems obvious to me that bias, on this theory, could not be eliminated by tinkering with the media, but only by altering the economic base on which the media are grounded; thus, this point of view merely reflects the spirit of revolutionary idealism. Third, there is an argument to the effect that biases do exist as a matter of fact, but not everywhere. The *Daily Express* is biased, the *Socialist Worker* not (or the other way round). In a good world, all newspapers and television channels would report the unmediated truth. This view seems to me to be drastically and dangerously false. It allows a person to believe, and to assert, complacently, that *their* newspaper is unbiased, whereas all the others are in the pocket of the Tories or the Trotskyites; or that newspapers are biased, while TV news is not (because 'the camera cannot lie'). The danger with this position is that it assumes the possibility of genuine neutrality, of *some* news medium being a clear undistorting window. And that can never be.

I think we will make progress if we follow the current standard academic account of news mediation, but dispense with the word 'bias' as a central theoretical term. 'Mediation' or 'representation' will less provocatively cover the processes which lead to 'skewing' and 'judgement'. ('Bias' could, if required, serve in a much more restricted sense of deliberate distortion for some ulterior motive. In this book I am not much concerned with cynical distortion, but would not of course wish to rule it out.)

NEWS VALUES

There are two excellent succinct accounts, by Stuart Hall and by Greg Philo, of the processes of selection and transformation which are the causes of news mediation; this is essentially the theory which underpins the larger research projects which have been reported in the last ten years. Hall begins as follows:

> The media do not simply and transparently report events which are 'naturally' newsworthy *in themselves*. 'News' is the end-product of a complex process which begins with a systematic sorting and selecting of events and topics according to a socially constructed set of categories.[3]

And Philo puts it this way: ' "News" on television and in the Press is not self-defining. News is not "found" or even "gathered" so much as made. It is a *creation* of a journalistic process, an artifact, a commodity even.'[4]

The news media select events for reporting according to a complex set of criteria of newsworthiness; so news is not simply that which happens, but that which can be regarded and presented as newsworthy. These criteria, which are probably more or less unconscious in editorial practice, are referred to by students of the media as 'news values'; and they are said to perform a 'gate-keeping' role, filtering and restricting news input. The more newsworthiness criteria an event satisfies, the more likely it is to be reported. Catastrophically negative events such as the assassination of Mrs Gandhi, the Chernobyl nuclear accident, the sinking of the ferry '*Herald of Free Enterprise*' and the destruction by a bomb of the Pan Am airliner near Lockerbie in Scotland in December 1988, score high on most criteria, so receive massive newspaper and television coverage. The origins of news values are complex and diverse: they include general values about society such as 'consensus' and 'hierarchy'; journalistic conventions; nature of sources; publication frequency and schedule; and so on.

A widely accepted analysis of news values is the following list of criterial factors (referred to as $F_1 - F_{12}$ below) formulated by Johann Galtung and Mari Ruge; they are worth studying in detail, and in particular it is worth reflecting on the great extent to which the factors are 'cultural' rather than 'natural':

(F_1) frequency
(F_2) threshold
   ($F_{2.1}$) absolute intensity
   ($F_{2.2}$) intensity increase
(F_3) unambiguity
(F_4) meaningfulness
   ($F_{4.1}$) cultural proximity
   ($F_{4.2}$) relevance
(F_5) consonance
   ($F_{5.1}$) predictability
   ($F_{5.2}$) demand
(F_6) unexpectedness
   ($F_{6.1}$) unpredictability
   ($F_{6.2}$) scarcity

(F_7)   continuity
(F_8)   composition
(F_9)   reference to elite nations
(F_{10})   reference to elite people
(F_{11})   reference to persons
(F_{12})   reference to something negative[5]

F_1 says that an event is more likely to be reported if its duration is close to the publication frequency of the news medium. Because newspapers are generally published once a day, a single event is more likely to be reported than a long process: for example, the publication of unemployment figures on a certain day is more newsworthy than the long-term phenomenon of unemployment itself. F_2 'threshold', refers to the 'size' or 'volume' needed for an event to become newsworthy: a car crash involving ten vehicles will get more attention than one involving two. $F_3 - F_5$ relate to the reader's or viewer's facility in making sense of an event. 'Unambiguity' is self-explanatory (though it must be added that mysterious events, as well as clear ones, are newsworthy if they can be related to cultural stereotypes, as in the mass hysteria incidents of the 'Mattoon anaesthetic prowler' and the 'Seattle windscreen pitting').[6] 'Cultural proximity' means, for example, that in Great Britain news items concerning France are more commonly reported than items concerning Albania; but 'relevance' can override this – the accident at the Union Carbide chemical plant at Bhopal, India, though geographically and culturally far away, is relevant to us because similar risks exist in our own industrialized country; and the fire at the Chernobyl nuclear power station in Russia on 26 April 1986, already very newsworthy on criteria such as F_2, increased in newsworthiness after its initial reporting, because it became more *relevant* to Britain as radioactive clouds moved west. The two subsections of factor F_5, 'consonance', refer to categories of events which people either expect to happen (e.g. violence at football matches) or want to happen (royal weddings and births). Criterion F_6 says that an event is even more newsworthy if it happens without warning and/or is unusual (such as the sudden and unexpected capsizing of the car ferry *Herald of Free Enterprise* as it was leaving Zeebrugge harbour on a routine crossing in calm weather on 6 March 1987). Of F_7, 'continuity', Galtung and Ruge state that 'once something has hit the headlines and has been defined as "news", then it will *continue* to be defined as news for some time even if the amplitude is drastically reduced'.[7] This persistence can be observed not only in respect of major events of great amplitude, such as the Chernobyl explosion, which stayed in the news for weeks or even months in 1986; stories which touch public or personal daily life can be sustained for months, as we will see when examining the 'salmonella-in-eggs affair' of 1988–9 (chapters 9 and 10). The next factor, F_8, 'composition', refers to the balance or make-up of a paper or radio/television news bulletin: an item will be more or less newsworthy depending on what else is available for inclusion – it is possible to have a surplus of even bank raids or train crashes on one day, given that newspapers are committed to including a range of other kinds of item.

I hope it is becoming evident to what extent the selection criteria for newsworthiness are, in Hall's words, 'socially constructed'. If we now turn to Galtung and Ruge's last four factors, the dependence on cultural artifice is very obvious; indeed, Galtung and Ruge stress that F_9–F_{12} are 'culture-bound factors influencing the transition from events to news'. F_9, 'reference to elite nations', encodes a 'superpowers' ideology of the dominating status of North America, Japan, Europe and Russia in world political and cultural affairs. As for elite persons (F_{10}), the media's infatuation with the Princess of Wales illustrates perfectly this preoccupation with notable paradigms (in fact the media could be said to have *semiotically produced* 'Princess Diana' out of the materials provided by an obscure aristocratic teenager). F_{11}, 'reference to persons', or 'personalization', is also a socially constructed value. Its application varies a good deal from paper to paper (thus underlining its artificiality), being most striking in the popular Press. Presumably, its functions are to promote straightforward feelings of identification, empathy or disapproval; to effect a metonymic simplification of complex historical and institutional processes (Arthur Scargill 'stands for' a whole set of alleged negative values in trades unionism; WPC Yvonne Fletcher, shot dead from a window of the Libyan Embassy while policing a demonstration, is made to stand for 'Britain's moral superiority over Libya'); and to facilitate the editing of a lengthy narrative to suit the 'frequency' (F_1) of newspapers and television bulletins ('the latest news on the miners' strike' is more likely to be a report of an incident involving picketing individuals than an explanation of issues and principles). Most commentators on the media, including myself, regard personalization as dangerous. The obsession with persons, and the media's use of them as symbols, avoids serious discussion and explanation of underlying social and economic factors: the brick-throwing rioter is imaged over and over again, but unemployment and the poverty of social services are rarely documented – and then only in low-circulation newspapers like the *Guardian*, and late-night minority television programmes like BBC–2's *Newsnight*. It is clear that personalization is an aspect of ideology, and a very creative one, too.

It is also obvious that the final one of the four factors which Galtung and Ruge identify as 'culture-bound', negativity, is a value rather than anything more natural: there is no natural reason why disasters should be more newsworthy than triumphs. What is not so clear, on the surface, is that most of the first eight factors in the list are cultural, too. Let us revisit one of them, F_4, 'meaningfulness'. 'Meaningfulness', with its subsections 'cultural proximity' and 'relevance', is founded on an ideology of ethnocentrism, or what I would prefer to call, more inclusively, homocentrism: a preoccupation with countries, societies and individuals perceived to be like oneself; with boundaries; with defining 'groups' felt to be unlike oneself, alien, threatening. Presupposed is what several media specialists have helpfully identified as a consensual model of society.[8] This is the theory that a society shares all its interests in common, without division or variation. Consensus is the affirmation and the plea of all political parties, expressed in appeals for 'one nation', for people to 'pull together', and so on. In the Press, this ideology is the source of the 'consensual "we" ' pronoun which is used often in editorials that claim to speak for 'the people'. How 'we' are supposed to behave is exemplified by the regular news reports of stories which illustrate such qualities as fortitude, patriotism, sentiment, industry. But although consensus sounds like a liberal, humane and generous theory of social action and attitudes, in practice it breeds divisive and alienating attitudes, a dichotomous vision of 'us' and 'them'. In order to place a fence around 'us,' the popular papers of the Right are obsessed with stories which cast 'them' in a bad light: trades unionists, socialist council leaders, teachers, blacks, social workers, rapists, homosexuals, etc., all become stigmatized 'groups', and are then somehow all lumped together and cast beyond the pale. 'Group' is a central ideological concept today, in the domain of 'them'; opposed to 'people' in the domain of 'us'. I will examine the working of language in these discriminatory practices in chapters 6 and 8. The point to note at this stage is that Galtung and Ruge's factor F_4, 'meaningfulness', can be reanalysed as the effect of a prejudicial cultural stereotype.

STEREOTYPES

News values, then, are to be regarded as intersubjective mental categories. In determining the significance of events, the papers and their readers make reference, explicit or more usually implicit, to what are variously called, in cognitive psychology and in semantics, 'frames', 'paradigms', 'stereotypes', 'schemata' and 'general propositions'.[9] In loose terms, this principle means that people work with tacit mental categories for the sorting of experience: let us just call these stereotypes for the moment. A stereotype is a socially-constructed mental pigeon-hole into which events and individuals can be sorted, thereby making such events and individuals comprehensible: 'mother', 'patriot', 'businessman', 'neighbour', on the one hand, versus 'hooligan', 'terrorist', 'foreigner', 'wet [Tory]', on the other, are some specific instances of stereotypical categories which give substance to the homocentric F_4 as I have just interpreted it. Now, it is of fundamental importance to realize that stereotypes are *creative*: they are categories which we project on to the world in order to make sense of it. We construct the world in this way. And our relationship with newspapers makes a major contribution to this process of construction.

The formation of news events, and the formation of news values, is in fact a reciprocal, dialectical process in which stereotypes are the currency of negotiation. The occurrence of a striking event will reinforce a stereotype, and, reciprocally, the firmer the stereotype, the more likely are relevant events to become news. An excellent example of this process was revealed while I was writing the first draft of this chapter, in May 1986. A fortnight before, on 26 April, a catastrophic accident had destroyed the Chernobyl nuclear power station in the Soviet Union, releasing a radiocative cloud over northern and western Europe, which killed and contaminated livestock and vegetation on a wide scale. In itself this event scored high on most of Galtung and Ruge's criteria, or in my terms, it satisfied many news stereotypes: an extremely negative sudden event of great intensity, unusual yet in a sense 'expected' despite official assurances, involving an elite nation, highly relevant to Great Britain on two counts – that it poisoned our food, and that it increased our anxiety about our own nuclear industries. Of course, Chernobyl was highly news-worthy, but the point to note here is that it consolidated the stereotype 'nuclear accident' in public consciousness, thus increasing the number of relevant events which were to figure in the news. The Chernobyl disaster became known to a British public which had for several years been increasingly aware of nuclear issues. In 1983, following months of argument and protest, American cruise missiles were installed (or 'deployed', in the jargon) in Britain, while at the same time renewal of Britain's nuclear submarines force was a widely debated political issue.[10] Other 'nuclear issues' in the air included the Central Electricity Generating Board's plan to build a new reactor, Sizewell B, to a design alleged to be unsafe on American experience; a review of sites for the dumping of 'low-level' nuclear waste; the possible connection between the nuclear reprocessing plant at Sellafield (tastefully renamed from the grimly evocative 'Windscale') and the high incidence of cancers such as childhood leukaemias in neighbouring communities; and the suspicion that such plants were responsible for radioactive spillages.

The Chernobyl accident confirmed worst fears about the dangers associated with nuclear arms and nuclear power, and quickly became the paradigm for the category 'nuclear accident.' The paradigm then quickly collected other instances, and generated a heightened perception of danger. Diverse events such as leakages, fires, explosions, temperature increases and excess waste disposals at various nuclear locations started to be reported, because they fell under a newly sharpened stereotype: 'nuclear accident'. The following report from the *Guardian*, 15 May 1986, shows the stereotype in action:

(1) **"Routine' and 'bodge' faults in N-plants**
  One of the two reactors at the Sizewell A nuclear power station in Suffolk had to be shut down yesterday when a fuel can failed, releasing radioactivity into the gas cooling circuit.

  The Central Electricity Generating Board said that although it was only a small, routine incident which did not have to be reported to government departments under existing procedures it felt obliged to make an announcement because of heightened public interest after the Chernobyl disaster.

At Hinckley Point near Bristol, the board's officials were meanwhile under fire for not publishing all the evidence its inquiry team gathered about the accidental release of slightly radioactive cooling gas from the B station on November 29 last year.

This is a particularly clear example of the productive interaction between the news media, the public, and official agencies in the formation and application of stereotypes. A comparable productive stereotype is 'food poisoning' as examined in chapters 9 and 10.

If at first the set of news values was thought of as a check-list of features of events which is referred to (consciously or not) in order to decide whether or not to report an event, my discussion of stereotypes now makes it clear that this is not the whole story. News values are rather to be seen as qualities of (potential) reports. That is to say, they are not simply features of selection but, more importantly, features of representation; and so the distinction between 'selection' and 'transformation' ceases to be absolute: an item can only be selected if it can be seen in a certain light of representation, and so selection involves an ideological act of interpretation.

SOCIAL AND ECONOMIC FACTORS IN NEWS SELECTION

So far, my explication of the notion of 'socially constructed' news has been by way of a *cognitive* commentary on Galtung and Ruge's selection factors. This commentary proposes that news stories are constructed on the basis of mental categories which are present in readers and built on by the media. This cognitive account suits the purpose of the present book, because it fits with the linguistic concern of the later chapters: to present the formation of ideas as governed by choices of language. However, it says little about the social, economic and historical determinants of the stereotypes in terms of which the news is to be understood. Other dimensions need to be added. Since they are not my main business, and anyway have been dealt with often by other writers, I will just briefly list some of them, but that is not to undervalue their overwhelming importance in an overall account of the media.[11] If we turn back to the quotation from Philo's article (p. 13), we find that he stresses the manufactured nature of news; cf. the title of Cohen and Young's book, *The Manufacture of News*. There is the question, of course, of what exactly is the product: arguably the product, in a commercial sense, is not news or newspapers (though both are clearly *made*), but rather *readers* – the profit, if any, coming from advertising revenue – or even *votes*, if the aim of the owners of newspapers is to maintain a government which will favour their other commercial ventures. It seems reasonable to assume that newspapers are involved in both of those productive aims, but, in any case, it is immaterial to my argument what exactly is the correct answer. What is overwhelmingly important is the fact that newspaper publication is an industry and a business, with a definite place in the nation's and the world's economic affairs. It is to be expected, then, that the activities and the output of the Press will be partially determined by considerations related to this fact: by the need to make a profit; by the economic organization of the industry; by its external relations with other industries, with financial institutions and with official agencies; by conventional journalistic practices; by production schedules; by relations with labour, dramatically illustrated by the troubled dealings of News International and the printers' unions over (ostensibly) the introduction of new technology and revision of printing practices. All of these commercial and industrial structures and relationships are bound to have an effect on what is published as news, and on how it is presented. For example, the Press is bound to be preoccupied with money, hence the prominence of financial pages even in the popular papers, even though stocks and shares and exchange rates cannot be of much interest to the bulk of the population. The newspapers are bound to be interested in royalty, because the Royals symbolize hierarchy and privilege, and because emphasizing the 'naturalness' of hierarchy and privilege serves the interests of capitalism, in which the newspaper industry participates. The Press is bound to be preoccupied with the ogres of socialism and trades unionism, and to condemn them, because the interests of socialism and of organized labour are experienced as antagonistic to the business of making money. It is not surprising that the British Press is almost without exception strongly Tory in its political views, and that there is no successful socialist newspaper: the latter would be a contradiction in terms.

Stuart Hall and others have shown how production schedules, and conventions for access to sources, affect the content and presentation of news stories.[12] Because newspapers have to be written and produced very quickly, steps are taken in advance, as a matter of routine, to ensure a regular and plentiful supply of daily copy. News cannot be relied upon to come in spontaneously, but has to be 'gathered': by paying professional news agencies to send in stories, and by employing journalists to regularly monitor proven sources of news. Functionally speaking, these news-gathering strategies ensure economy of time and effort. But they are also very selective, in that only certain kinds of sources are worth tapping consistently. Brian Whitaker offers the following handy list of the kinds of institutions and events which are constantly attended to by journalists:

1. Sources monitored routinely
   a. Parliament
   b. Councils
   c. Police (and the Army in Northern Ireland)
   d. Other emergency services
   e. Courts (including inquests and tribunals)
   f. Royalty
   g. 'Diary' events (e.g. annual events like Ascot or conferences known about in advance)
   h. Airports
   i. Other news media
2. Organizations issuing statements and holding Press conferences
   a. Government departments
   b. Local authority departments
   c. Public services (transport authorities, electricity boards, etc.)
   d. Companies
   e. Trade unions
   f. Non-commercial organizations (pressure groups, charities, etc.)
   g. Political parties
   h. Army, Navy, Air Force
3. Individuals making statements, seeking publicity, etc.

a. Prominent people (e.g. bishops and film stars)
b. Members of the public.[13]

In fact, there is no regular mechanism for capturing the activities and views of 'members of the public'; they are cited only when they enter the news arena by some other door, e.g. happening to witness an accident or being involved in a court case. It is important to the newspapers to include references to people – because of the factor of 'personalization' mentioned above – but their status as sources is accidental rather than privileged. The other sources and institutions just listed are of course highly privileged: they are *established* by official authority, by social status or by commercial success; they are *organized*, with a bureaucratic structure which embodies spokespersons, and a regular scheduling of statements; and they have the *resources* to pay for publicity and public relations. Thus, the most convenient sources for journalists to monitor are also, necessarily, institutions and persons with official authority and/or financial power. The effects of this weighting are evident in the Glasgow and Birmingham research and in the analyses offered in the present book.

Another way of looking at this is in terms of access. 'Accessed voices', as Hartley calls them, are the views and styles of a privileged body of politicians, civil servants, directors, managers, experts of various kinds (doctors, architects, accountants, professors), royals and nobles, stars, etc. Access is a reciprocal relationship between such people and the media; the media conventionally expect and receive the right of access to the statements of these individuals, because the individuals have roles in the public domain; and reciprocally these people receive access to the columns of the papers when they wish to air their views. An ordinary person, by contrast, could hardly expect to be heeded if they were to try to 'call a Press conference'. The political effect of this division between the accessed and the unaccessed hardly needs stating: an imbalance between the representation of the already privileged, on the one hand, and the already unprivileged, on the other, with the views of the official, the powerful and the rich being constantly invoked to legitimate the status quo.

From my point of view, there is an important *linguistic* consequence of the media's concentration on only one social category of accessed voice. Imbalance of access results in partiality, not only in *what* assertions and attitudes are reported – a matter of content – but also in *how* they are are reported – a matter of form or style, and therefore, I would claim, of ideological perspective. The newspapers are full of reports of statements, claims, promises and judgements which have been voiced by prominent people of the kinds mentioned above: reports of parliamentary debates; the findings of official inquiries; summings-up and judicial comments by magistrates, judges and coroners; political manifestos; statements by ministers and civil servants; statements by the chairmen of large companies; and so on. The fact that the newspapers are full of such reports means that they contain a lot of discourse in a prestigious and official public style. But the influence of imbalance in accessed voices goes further than that. Many parts of newspapers which seem to be *not* quotation of official voices, but, rather, written articles for which the editor, or a named journalist, seems to take responsibility, are tinged with an official ideology, because they are written in the formal, authoritative style which accessed figures such as politicians or experts habitually use. In a previous study, I analysed an 'investigative' article in the *Sunday Times*, which ostensibly exposed and condemned inadequate surgical provision in British hospitals.[15] It was found that, though the newspaper appeared to deplore the situation, its language so closely reproduced that of the bureaucrats, politicians and surgeons involved in this problem that the caring point of view was undermined: the paper, like the politicians and hospital administrators, depersonalized the patients, allowing them no individuality or initiative, and reserved all power to those high-ranking people who 'deal with' them. More details are given on pp. 124–34. Another related topic is the intertextuality of editorial articles: their stylistic (and therefore ideological) dependence on other texts issuing from official or other prestigious sources: for example, the reproduction in the right-wing Press of the attitudes, jargon and arguments of Conservative Party campaign and propaganda documents. A previous study illustrated how this worked in the case of arguments for nuclear weapons.[16]

So specific powerful institutions, frequently accessed (with neglect of other sections of the population, and other organizations), provide the newspapers with modes of discourse which already encode the attitudes of a powerful elite. Newspapers in part adopt this language for their own and, in deploying it, reproduce the attitudes of the powerful. This reproduction happens to be in the favour of the newspaper industry, which is part of the interests of an industrial-capitalist society, with an authoritarian, conservative government, and appropriate ideological and repressive[17] agencies. We need not regard what I have just said as a 'conspiracy theory' of media practice.[18] I do not wish to present the newspaper industry as *deliberately and cynically* working in this way in order to disseminate official ideology for commercial gain; to mystify the actions and the motives of government and industry; and to discredit opponents and silence the majority. Though these are indeed goals and effects of the media, they need not be consciously formulated and strategically planned, because their implementation takes place *automatically*, given the economic position and working practices of the Press. My concern is with the varieties of discourse that such factors cause the newspapers to employ, and with the ideological structuring that attends these linguistic varieties, and which literally *constructs* the news as it is written about. In the next chapter, I will show how language is impregnated with ideology.

Chapter 3

Language and representation

Representation, in the Press as in all other kinds of media and discourse, is a constructive practice. Events and ideas are not communicated neutrally, in their natural structure, as it were. They could not be, because they have to be transmitted through some medium with its own structural features, and these structural features are already impregnated with social values which make up a potential perspective on events. The medium is used by people working under certain economic circumstances, and following certain conventions of production, and habitual use in these circumstances gives rise to conventional significances. There are, of course, alternative choices of structure available for the news writer, and so alternative significances within a previously defined range. *How* the medium is used implies options for the producer or editor: the physical and structural characteristics of the medium, whether film, still photography, language, etc., offer choices; these choices are made with systematic regularity according to circumstances, and they become associated with conventional *meanings*. For example, the television news reader is generally shown full-face, head and shoulders almost filling the screen, from a camera position at or just below eye level: this arrangement signifies *authority*. This meaning changes when the news reader turns to the side towards an interviewee, and is seen at a greater distance, signifying a temporary diminution of status. Again, in filmed outside reports, anyone who is seen from above, or away from the centre of the frame, or at a greater distance from camera than the reporter, is represented as being of low authority.[1] These are simple but powerful examples of the conventional correlation between the handling of the technical properties of the medium, and the meanings invested in the process of representation. I am not saying that the camera lies, but that there is no ideologically neutral way of holding the camera. The same principle applies to many other aspects of the structure of visual and linguistic media – probably to every other aspect – and I now want to look at this question more closely in relation to language.

THE LINGUISTIC BACKGROUND

Let us begin by speculating on some general questions. Why does language have the structure that it does have? We might also ask, why does English, or French, have its particular structure? Or, more specifically, why is such-and-such a real text constructed as it is? Answers to these speculative questions fall into two broad categories, which we may call 'structural' versus 'functional'.

To be frank, the true structuralist would consider these to be absurd or ill-founded questions. In Saussurean or in Bloomfieldian linguistics,[2] language is an autonomous abstract system, self-contained, self-regulating and quite arbitrary in its genesis and its relations with the non-linguistic world. It makes no sense to ask any 'why?' questions: language is just the way it is, and the linguist's job is to describe it without reference to any external factors. In American linguistics of the Bloomfield tradition, say 1930–60, this proscription of external reference was more than a methodological stipulation, it was a dogma which denied language any personal or social relevance. For all the talk of a 'Chomskyan revolution' with the publication of Chomsky's book *Syntactic Structures* in 1957,[3] the intellectual heritage and goals are essentially structuralist, with the presentation of language as a self-contained system of rules existing somehow independently of meaning and context. As Chomsky developed his model during the 1960s, his emphases changed, in ways that are relevant, but not helpful, for critical linguistics. The title of his 1968 book *Language and Mind*, with the startling aside on the first page, 'the particular branch of cognitive psychology known as linguistics', indicates the shift.[4] The grammar of a language is no longer an abstract descriptive system, product of the linguist's analysis, but a property of the speaker's mind, a cognitive system: linguistic competence, as he calls it. But although Chomsky may have relocated language in the human mind, there is nothing particularly human about his conception of speakers and speech processes. Linguistics is said to be concerned, not with real people using language, but with

> an ideal speaker-listener, in a completely homogeneous speech-community, who knows its language perfectly and is unaffected by such grammatically irrelevant conditions as memory limitations, distractions, shifts of attention and interest, and errors (random or characteristic) in applying his knowledge of the language in actual performance.[5]

Not you or me! As part of this same idealizing strategy, language use is relegated to a category of linguistic performance, which is said *not* to be the business of linguistics. This is very unhelpful as far as our critical linguistics is concerned, because our central object of study, the functions of linguistic forms in communicative settings, is for Chomsky beyond the pale. Returning though to his 'linguistic competence', we may still ask the most general of our 'why?' questions: what is the character and source of this linguistic knowledge which speakers possess? Addressing themselves to the observation that very young children develop language with remarkable facility, Chomsky and his colleagues explain it as follows. Babies are innately equipped with a knowledge of linguistic universals, the structural properties which define the nature of all human language, or to put it another way, the range of possible human languages. Using this equipment, the child determines which of the possibilities is spoken around her or him, and builds the structures appropriate to French, say, but not those which would be appropriate to English or to Hindi. On this theory, linguistic competence is a selection from what was innately in the mind (or the genes) in the first place. It is obvious that this account excludes a great deal of what is genuinely linguistic knowledge: everything that is learned ('learn' is a taboo word in Chomskyan linguistics) concerning the values and beliefs of the culture in the lifelong process of socialization. For all the talk of cognition, Chomsky's theory of language development remains a formal, structuralist account of an abstract system which is cut off from communicative interaction.

Mainstream structural linguistics in America shared a common origin with anthropology in their devotion, in the early 1900s, to the study of the indigenous ('Indian') languages of America.[6] But linguistics drew away from anthropology in the 1930s, driven by an urge to establish itself as an 'empirical science', which is to say an empiric*ist* science on the model of the natural sciences of the time. No 'external' reference was to be made; language was to be described on its own terms alone, and thus cultural references were prohibited; and because 'unobservables' could not (until much later, with Chomsky) be considered, mentalistic concepts and explanations were eschewed.

ANTHROPOLOGICAL LINGUISTICS: LANGUAGE, CULTURE AND THOUGHT

However, while the mainstream flowed on in the structuralist channel, alternative linguistic traditions maintaining contact with studies of culture, society and thought survived. The anthropological linguists Edward Sapir and Benjamin Lee Whorf advanced a strong series of claims concerning the variable effects of the structures of different languages on the conceptions of reality peculiar to different speech-communities. Here are some characteristic statements by the two linguists. Sapir:

> The birth of a new concept is invariably foreshadowed by a more or less strained or extended use of old linguistic material; the concept does not attain to individual and independent life until it has found a distinctive linguistic embodiment. . . . As soon as the word is at hand, we instinctively feel, with something of a sigh of relief, that the concept is ours for the handling. Not until we own the symbol do we feel that we hold a key to the immediate knowledge or understanding of the concept. Would we be so ready to die for 'liberty', to struggle for 'ideals', if the words themselves were not ringing within us? And the word, as we know, is not only a key; it may also be a fetter.[7]

Whorf:

> We dissect nature along lines laid down by our native languages. The categories and types that we isolate from the world of phenomena we do not find there because they stare every observer in the face; on the contrary, the world is presented in a kaleidoscopic flux of impressions which has to be organized by our minds – and this means largely by the linguistic systems in our minds. We cut nature up, organize it into concepts, and ascribe significances as we do, largely because

we are parties to an agreement to organize it in this way – an agreement that holds through our speech community and is codified in the patterns of our language. The agreement is, of course, an implicit and unstated one, but *its terms are absolutely obligatory;* we cannot talk at all except by subscribing to the organization and classification of data which the agreement decrees.[8]

And a modern structural anthropologist, Edmund Leach, puts forward a similar view:

> I postulate that the physical and social environment of a young child is perceived as a continuum. It does not contain any intrinsically separate 'things'. The child, in due course, is taught to impose upon this environment a kind of discriminating grid which serves to distinguish the world as being composed of a large number of separate things, each labelled with a name. This world is a representation of our language categories, not vice versa. Because my mother tongue is English, it seems self-evident that *bushes* and *trees* are different kinds of things. I would not think this unless I had been taught that it was the case.[9]

The 'Sapir-Whorf hypothesis', as it has come to be called, combines the twin assumptions of linguistic relativity and linguistic determinism. *Relativity* hypothesizes that languages differ radically in their structures – this hypothesis squares with common experience, of course, but is challenged by the Chomskyan theory of universality of structure. Now, relativity would extend to any aspect of linguistic structure, including particularly vocabulary, and it is well known that different languages possess different vocabulary systems relating to roughly comparable conceptual areas: the prolific Eskimo vocabulary for 'snow', or English 'home' and 'house' to be compared with French *maison*, or English 'chair', 'seat', 'armchair', 'stool', 'sofa', etc., to be compared with French *fauteuil, siège, chaise, tabouret, canapé*, etc., or French *mouton* doing the work of both 'sheep' and 'mutton' in English. The point is that different languages not only possess different vocabularies (and other aspects of structure, but vocabulary is the clearest illustration of this point), but also, by means of these linguistic differences, they map the world of experience in different ways. To give notice of a later stage in this argument: critical linguistics extends the principle of relativity to variable structure *within* a single language as well as *between* different languages.

Whereas relativity, in the above sense, is easy enough to document by simply looking at languages, the second strand to the Sapir-Whorf hypothesis, linguistic *determinism*, is an unprovably strong, or non-disprovable, claim. The theory of linguistic determinism maintains that differences of linguistic structure cause the speakers of different languages in some sense to 'see the world' in different ways. In the most extreme version, it is said that people speaking one language cannot perceive the world any other way than in the terms provided by the mental 'map' constructed by their language: the terms of the 'agreement' which Whorf speaks of are 'absolutely obligatory', he says. He gives many examples, contrasting grammatical and lexical systems in English and in American Indian languages, particularly Hopi, which he claims show that the languages have very different ways of coding such fundamental concepts as time and movement; and on this 'evidence', he maintains that speakers of Hopi enjoy a radically different 'world-view' from speakers of English, or as he generalizes, 'Standard Average European'. The force of such examples is inevitably undermined by the fact that the stratagem of translation allows Whorf to explain the example to his readers: if the example can be explicated using paraphrase in another language, then the theory must be false in its strongest form. (Non-Hopi-speaking English speakers would not be able to understand the example, because the equivalent concepts could not be constructed in circumlocutions in their own language; yet English speakers *do* understand Whorf's examples.) But it is probable that determinism holds good in a weaker version, which ought to be called by another name, perhaps predisposition. On the weaker theory, language users are predisposed to categorize their experience according to the mental map engraved in the semantic structure of their habitual linguistic usage: language helps people to sort things, encourages them to think of the world in terms of certain artificial categories tacitly felt to be 'common sense'.[10] These categories are not, despite Sapir, 'a fetter'. Even though, if we are unselfcritical, they may guide us into disreputable routes of thought and action (as George Orwell passionately maintained),[11] they do not absolutely inhibit alternative perceptions. The British linguist M. A. K. Halliday puts it well:

We shall in no sense be adopting an extreme pseudo-Whorfian position (I say 'pseudo-Whorfian' because Whorf himself never was extreme) if we add that . . . language lends structure to [a speaker's or writer's] experience and helps to determine his way of looking at things. The speaker can see through and around the settings of his semantic system; but he is aware that, in doing so, he is seeing reality in a new light, like Alice in Looking-glass House.[12]

How can the speaker 'see through and around the settings of his [sic] semantic system'? The fact is that speakers (using the term as a shorthand for speakers, writers, listeners, readers) have access to more than one set of semantic settings, more than one 'discriminating grid'. The devices of paraphrase, circumlocution, neologism and interlingual translation are all available, the first three to all, the fourth to many, speakers: they allow rephrasing, recoding of experience, critical questioning of the categories which are ingrained in habitual usage. Explaining to someone some remark or expression that they do not immediately comprehend, we often resort to a strategy of putting it in other words: using a synonym, or a roundabout expression, or an invented word, or words of another dialect or language, we allow the person we are speaking to to regard the concept from a different linguistic perspective, casting new light on it. Literature is said to be another mechanism for getting readers to see through and around the conventional grids of meaning. In one prominent aesthetic theory, the goal of literature is defamiliarization: unsettling and querying the reader's familiar perceptions by the use of linguistic devices such as metaphor, which interrogate habitual codings of experience.[13] And though many users of English do not read novels or poems (though they do consume quantities of other fiction in the mass media), or know a second language, there is another mechanism which makes it possible to query habitual categories, and that is stylistic or sociolinguistic variety, to be discussed below. The fact is that a language like English, associated with a technologically, socially and economically various culture, is internally extremely diverse. Everyone has access, passively if not actively, to many varieties of English, and thus to numerous alternative semantic grids. (The materials are at least present, but are not consciously exploited sufficiently; hence the need for critical linguistics or linguistic critique.) Given the fact of relativity of construction, not only between, but also within, languages, it would seem perverse to claim that variants of structure all have some universal origin in the properties of the human mind. Whatever 'natural categories' happen to be coded universally in languages – the concepts designated by terms in the fields of colour, geometrical configurations and logical relationships have been suggested as candidates for semantic universals[14] – it is obvious that the majority of structures that make up our 'semantic settings' are social in origin.

FUNCTIONAL LINGUISTICS, VARIATION, SOCIAL SEMIOTIC

In one paper, Halliday gives a thoroughgoing functionalist explanation of linguistic structure in terms of social structure:

> Why is language as it is? The nature of language is closely related to the demands that we make on it, the functions it has to serve. In the most concrete terms, these functions are specific to a culture. . . . The particular form taken by the grammatical system of language is closely related to the social and personal needs that language is required to serve.[15]

This statement is not at all controversial if we interpret it in terms of the findings of modern sociolinguistics (but we will need to go further, below): for example, the well-known research by William Labov, and the development of Labov's model in a British context by Peter Trudgill.[16] Focusing on small but clear details of linguistic form, Labov demonstrated that variants in pronunciation correlated systematically with the socioeconomic class of speakers, and with other contextual variables. For example, he determined whether speakers in a sample population from the Lower East Side in New York City did or did not pronounce the phoneme /r/ after vowels and before consonants, i.e. in words like 'car' and 'card'. He noted the social class of speaker according to an official scale, so that was one contextual parameter; a second was the style of speech, on a scale from very casual to very formal. On the basis of a large sampling, involving several ingenious data-collection techniques, and a statistical analysis of the relations between the variant pronunciations and the contextual parameters, he concluded that the higher the social class of speaker, the more /r/s were produced in the positions studied (with one kink in the curve), and the more formal the speech, again the more /r/s. Thus the presence of an /r/ sound in words like 'car' and 'card' is associated with prestige, formality, conservatism. (Interestingly, the values are inverted in British English, post-vocalic /r/ being a stigmatized, rustic or Irish pronunciation. This observation bears out the semiotic principle that the values associated with forms are arbitrary rather than inevitable or natural.) The findings can be corroborated by studying other variables in the same fashion, e.g. the *th* sound at the beginnings of words like 'think', the *ng* at the end of 'speaking', and so on. Moreover, other contextual variables can be added, such as the age and the sex of speakers. In this way, profiles can be built up of the pronunciations of groups of individuals of different classes, generations and sexes, talking with different degrees of formality. The results are (one kind of) direct illustration of Halliday's principle, namely that linguistic form is affected systematically by social circumstances.

But is it justifiable to speak of these results in terms of 'function', of 'social and personal needs'? Don't these results merely show *correlations* of a mechanical kind, as one would observe in dialect studies? Labov's research has been criticized in such terms. He writes in a very quantitative way, and is extremely cautious in interpreting his findings. But a more inquisitive scrutiny of his work, and Trudgill's, reveals that functional values are at issue, and that the phonetic variables examined are implicated in the representation and the construction of social reality. Let me refer to two details of these Labovian studies. First, the 'kink' I mentioned in the curve for /r/ in the Lower East Side. This concerns the quantity of /r/s in the speech of what Labov calls the 'lower middle class', and the point is that this class uses the sound much more than the class above, his 'upper middle', in formal speech styles, yet one would expect the 'lower middle' to use *fewer* /r/s than the 'upper middle'. Labov calls this phenomenon 'hypercorrection', pitching one's pronunciation at a higher-than-expected level. Now, since hypercorrection is found in the treatment of other phonetic variables by members of this group, it is clearly not an accident, and one is entitled to look for social motivation. Labov suggests that this is an insecure, upwardly mobile social class, consciously or unconsciously 'improving' its pronunciation as one means towards the end of climbing the social ladder. This process is comprehensible in terms of one's British experience of, for instance, young people shifting their regional accents in the direction of the 'Received Pronunciation' of the South-East, when they go off to improve their social chances through a college education. The second set of compatible data emerges from Trudgill's studies of speech habits, and attitudes to speech, among working-class men and women in Norwich. Women hypercorrected, and also subjectively believed that they had a higher proportion of the prestige pronunciations than they actually produced (i.e. /tyun/ for the word 'tune'); the men *hypo*corrected, using the low-prestige form /tun/ for 'tune' more often than might have been expected, and they also thought that they said /tun/ more often than they actually did. It seems that the women's social values were different from the men's, identifying with a more middle-class world while the men wanted to express their commitment to the more macho image of the rough working-class male.[17]

From these studies, it appears then that the phonetic structure of people's speech not only reflects their social position and the circumstances in which they are speaking, but also *expresses* their view of the way society is organized, and of their own position within the social network. Accent may also be 'functional' in a more practical way, with speakers using their manner of speech to consolidate or to change their status and roles. Similar conclusions may be drawn from sociolinguistic research in models other than Labov's. I cannot review the other traditions extensively here, but will mention a few famous examples in order to show that these principles apply generally, and to other dimensions of language than phonology.

Blom and Gumperz studied 'code-switching' in the small Norwegian town of Hemnesberget.[18] They found that people possessed two dialects, the local form Ranamål, and Bokmål, a Norwegian standard. The circumstances in which each was used differed, and people switched freely – but systematically – between the two. Ranamål was used for discourse on local and domestic topics. Bokmål for formal, official, pan-Norwegian business. Thus, the choice expressed a view of the world, an ideology dividing local from external values. Other studies have found that, in bilingual communities, one of the languages signifies solidarity and local identity, and the other embodies an official, outward-looking view of the world: Spanish and English among Puerto Ricans in America, Guaraní and Spanish in Paraguay.

Ferguson studied a related phenomenon which he called 'diglossia': speakers in some communities, such as Switzerland, Egypt, Haiti and Greece, have command of 'high' and 'low' varieties of a language – High German and Swiss German, Classical and Egyptian Arabic, and so on – which are used in formal and casual situations respectively, and which therefore carry different social values.[19]

Another illuminating branch of sociolinguistic research concerns conventions of naming and address, including personal pronouns. In a pioneering study, 'The pronouns of power and solidarity', Brown and Gilman looked at those languages where a choice of second personal singular pronoun is available: *tu* and *vous* in French, *du* and *Sie* in German, etc.[20] The first of these, the 'T' form, is used by adults to address children, superiors to address subordinates; this address is answered by the other member of the dyad with 'V': the situation is asymmetrical. But T is used reciprocally by lovers, siblings and other close associates. On the other hand, V is the reciprocal address form between people meeting for the first time, or people in formal situations, or people behaving distantly to one another. 'Power' and 'solidarity' are the ideological constructs which give meaning to the pronoun usages. In these terms, the pronoun systems are a representation of social relations, and they are part of the mechanisms for reproducing the orders of power. Similar findings have emerged for variations in personal names. The ideological systems underlying choices of name and/or pronoun are of great interest in media studies, and will be considered several times in the analytic chapters below. It makes a great deal of difference whether one says 'Sir Robin', 'Robin' or 'Mr Day'; 'Mrs Thatcher', 'Margaret Thatcher', 'The Prime Minister' or 'Maggie'.

In an early publication, Halliday introduced the term 'register' in contrast with 'dialect'. Dialect was variation of language according to *user*, register variation according to *use*.[21] Examples such as the ones just referred to suggest that the distinction is not clear-cut – e.g. in code-switching, speakers change dialects in different circumstances of use – but register is still an instructive concept which underlines the semantic implications of consistent variations in linguistic form. According to Halliday, three types of circumstance determine which register is used: these he calls *field* (the activity referred to, and/or ongoing, at the time of discourse), *tenor* (the social relations between participants) and *mode* (the medium, e.g. spoken, written or scripted). These criteria allow us to distinguish registers such as scientific writing, advertising, legal language, news broadcasting, reviewing and informal conversation. The registers are differentiated by the formal linguistic features which typically occur. So, for example, scientific writing is marked by, among other features, technical vocabulary (governed by field), syntactic complexity and completeness of sentences (a property of the printed mode of publication), and impersonal constructions such as passive and nominalization (resulting from conventions of tenor which stipulate that scientific writing should be formal and impersonal).

I am not particularly wedded to the notion that a language consists of a set of registers: there are considerable procedural difficulties in drawing the boundaries between them, and, significantly, few 'registers' have been defined with any precision. (For a further comment on 'register', see chapter 4, p. 60.) But the central insights of the concept are very important for the theory of representation which I employ here. These are as follows:

(1) The linguistic construction of discourse – all the minutiae of formal structure – relates systematically and predictably to the contextual circumstances of discourse. This of course is the major finding of sociolinguistics in general. Several useful schemes for classifying the contextual forces influencing linguistic variation have been proposed; it is clear that one needs something more delicate than Halliday's 'field', 'mode' and 'tenor', and the more complex set of criteria proposed by the ethnographer Dell Hymes is one possibility (it is unnecessary to go into the details here).[22]

A most important emphasis, when we are thinking about the causes of linguistic variation (equivalently, the causes of linguistic structure in actual use), is that they are *fundamentally* social, political and economic, outside the speaker's control, and not *ad hoc* features of the immediate context. Reflection on Brown and Gilman's pronoun study will convince the reader that the choice between T and V is not a trivial matter of etiquette (as French and German speakers know very well!), but a highly symbolic obligation with deep causes. The semantics of power and solidarity emerge from a hierarchical society traditionally built on massively unequal divisions of power, wealth and privilege between groups of people; the asymmetrical usage of T and V which is forced on the speakers concerned is part of the mechanism for maintaining this inequality. The solidary reciprocal use of T among associates, on the other hand, expresses the need of less powerful people to band together in order to protect their beleaguered interests and their identity. Thus, the explanation of the pronoun system is basically historical; and this historical substantiality of linguistic function is a reminder to critical linguistics generally: it is a discipline which must make continuous reference to historical analysis.

(2) Part of the communicative ability of speakers is the facility to recognize linguistic forms as appropriate to certain circumstances. We have daily experience of this facility, in overhearing radio or television programmes without knowing in advance what they are: we can rapidly classify what we hear as a football commentary, a talk on science, a political interview or whatever it may be. It is not a matter of content, or of recognizing an individual journalist's voice; the *form* of language – lexical and syntactic choices, intonation, pace, and so on – identifies a kind of discourse and its context. And as Halliday has indicated, even a short fragment can be very informative: 'In the Commons today . . .', 'Oh! a brilliant catch on the leg side . . .', 'The outlook is for further showers . . .' In such ways, linguistic form signifies the circumstances of its utterance.

(3) A third basic assumption is most clearly indicated in the way Halliday reformulated his idea of register in the 1970s. Initially, registers were regarded as contextually determined variations in linguistic form: differences of vocabulary, syntax and often pronunciation in different circumstances of use. Ten years later, Halliday defined registers in semantic terms: 'A register is a set of meanings that is appropriate to a particular function of language, together with the words and structures which express these meanings'; or more formally: 'A register can be defined as the configuration of semantic resources that the member of a culture typically associates with a situation type. It is the meaning potential that is accessible in a given social context.'[23]

So, forms of expression within a language answer, not just to social and economic circumstances, characteristics of speech situations, etc., but to the *meanings* a culture assigns to itself and its components. This is what Halliday means by his title *Language as Social Semiotic*: the forms of language encode a socially constructed representation of the world.

SOCIAL SEMIOTIC IN NEWS DISCOURSE: AN EXAMPLE

How does the theory of language as social semiotic relate to the process of representation when a particular reader is reading a particular newspaper text, which has been written by a specific journalist? While this question is still part of the *theoretical* discussion of the present chapter, I will concretize it a little by quoting a text; the text is used for illustrative reference, not proper analysis.

(1) **THE SUN SAYS**

Wot, no Bob on the list?

Who, of all possible contenders, most deserved an award for his achievements in 1985?

Just about every person in the land would put forward one name.

Pop star Bob Geldof aroused the conscience of the world over the heartbreaking plight of the starving peoples of Ethiopia and the Sudan.

Floodgates

He was responsible for releasing the floodgates of charity that meant the difference between life and death for millions of men, women and children.

Yet there is no mention of Bob Geldof in the dreary New Year Honours List.

No mention, either, of any of the helpers who made Band Aid the most uplifting story of the year.

Instead, we have the usual plague of ever so worthy politicians and ageing members of the showbusiness fraternity.

Bob has this consolation.

The whole honours system has become so discredited that men and women who really matter ought not to give a damn whether they are on the list or not.

Fairy tale

Just look whom radio listeners have chosen in a landslide vote as their Woman of the Year.

Princess Anne.

Only a short time ago that would have seemed as unlikely as Australia winning a Test.

The Princess was best known for her temper and for slagging off her husband in public.

Dedicated

She has earned the award by her marvellous, dedicated work for hungry children all over the world.

Maybe there is a lesson here for another royal ugly duckling.

Instead of constantly complaining that she is misunderstood, why does not Princess Michael find herself a good cause?

Join the club

Since days before Christmas, paralysis seems to have swept over Britain.

If you were at work yesterday you qualified for the most exclusive club in the land.

We were working, too.

Wasn't it fun?

(*Sun*, 31 December 1985)

Although this editorial must have been written, or at least drafted, by an individual staff member of the *Sun*, the individuality and the identity of the writer are irrelevant to the communicative situation. The piece is constructed according to the stylistic and ideological conventions for editorials in this newspaper: in origin, the voice is institutional rather than personal. No more are the *functions* of this voice personal: they are economic and political, having to do with the *Sun*'s place in the industrial and political arenas of contemporary Britain. But to say that the voice is an institutional construct, and therefore impersonal in origin, is not to say that it is not personal in style: through the use of colloquialisms, incomplete sentences, questions and a varied typography suggesting variations of emphasis, the written text mimics a speaking voice, as of a person talking informally but with passionate indignation. Of course, the style is recognizable as tabloid commentary. To say this is to assume, surely realistically, that in order to understand the text, a reader brings to it a mental model of the expected style, must recognize the style intuitively, through prior learned knowledge, and be able to read into it the values it embodies. Reciprocally, from the writer's point of view, linguistic options must be taken which regularly satisfy that model (no *Telegraph* syntax or vocabulary), otherwise communication breaks down. (On this sense of 'model', and the important associated notion of 'cueing', see further, p. 44 and chapter 4 pp. 59–61.)

In this case, the model is one of direct involvement with the reader in the reader's own terms. The style is dialogic, as well as colloquial: the rhetorical questions create a space for the reader to occupy, and the reader is expected to imagine responding correctly (yes, Princess Michael *should* find herself a good cause), and in similar style – informal but emphatic. Stuart Hall's notion of a 'public idiom' for each newspaper may be mentioned here: 'The language employed will thus be the *newspaper's own version of the language of the public to whom it is principally addressed*' (his italics).[24] What this means is a question to be discussed in chapter 4 (pp. 48ff.), but, briefly, it is *not* being claimed that the newspaper copies the language which its readership does actually use in private life (such usage has not been empirically established anyway, and, conversely, it would be absurd to regard the *Sun* as a source of evidence for the structure of personal language). More accurately, the language of the editorial is a model or hypothesis being negotiated between newspaper and reader, a populist image of political discussion, implying that these things can be said in the language of ordinary people and are therefore accessible to ordinary experience, even though they concern elite individuals. The vernacular expression 'slagging off her husband in public', transplanted from local gossip, brings the public evaluation of the Royals and their responsibilities to an accessible level of mundane domesticity.

On one level, what is happening here is that the *Sun* is, through a discursive model of popular speech, consolidating a community: those who experience in the paper a kind of 'plain man's language' and who will buy it and read it because that is what the 'ordinary man' does. There is a sociolinguistically engineered group solidarity which no doubt has commercial motives: the readership will buy the paper and the products advertised within it, and in other ways behave so as to favour the interests of the proprietors of News International. Note that this cannot happen without the constructive, if unconscious, co-operation of the reader, bringing his or her knowledge of the discourse model. (On ironic reading, see pp. 44–5.)

The theory of language as social semiotic goes further than this idea of linguistic solidarity, however, in claiming that the characteristic style not only marks a group but also embodies a characteristic representation of experience. Vocabulary patterns map out the typical concerns of a register and its users ('hearbreaking', 'uplifting'), emphasizing special preoccupations, and projecting values on the subjects of discourse ('dreary', 'fun'); syntax analyzes actions and states, casting people into roles and assigning responsibility to persons mentioned (too complex to illustrate briefly here: see chapter 8); recurrent themes and generalizations are stated or implied (charity is the duty of the great; work is the duty of ordinary people; the adjacent headlines are *HARD WORK GIVES PITS A BRIGHT FUTURE . . . 20,000 fewer miners are digging MORE coal'*). These processes are amply illustrated in the following chapters, and I do not propose to analyse the *Sun* editorial in detail here. In broad terms, the reader of this editorial is expected at least to entertain the beliefs that the behaviour of elite persons is inherently interesting; that such people are to be publicly and bluntly judged; that vulgarity and cliché vouch for a robust honesty; that things are either 'dreary' or 'fun'; that work is a pleasant duty. If newspaper readers find the colloquial mode of discourse affected by this editorial familiar and comfortable, they may also regard the ideology which its structures embody as 'common sense'.

DISCOURSE AND THE READER

It should be clear that linguistically constructed representation is by no means a deliberate process, entirely under the control of the newspaper. The newspaper does not select events to be reported and then consciously wrap them in value-laden language which the reader passively absorbs, ideology and all. Such a 'conspiracy theory' would give the newspaper too much, and the reader too little, power. As we saw in the previous chapter, the practices of news selection and presentation are habitual and conventional as much as they are deliberate and controlled. And as for value-laden language, the crucial point is that the values are in the language already, independent of the journalist and of the reader. Ideology is already imprinted in the available discourse (all discourse). It is obligatory to select a style of discourse which is communicatively appropriate in the particular setting – here, tabloid editorial – and the accompanying ideas follow automatically. In selecting the required style, the journalist ceases to be an individual subject, and is constituted as something more impersonal, a writer. The fundamental principle is that, to repeat, *the writer is constituted by the discourse*. Discourse, in the present usage, is socially and institutionally originating ideology, encoded in language. Another critical linguist, Gunther Kress, provides a very useful definition of the concept:

> Institutions and social groupings have specific meanings and values which are articulated in language in systematic ways. Following the work particularly of the French philosopher Michel Foucault, I refer to these systematically-organized modes of talking as DISCOURSE. Discourses are systematically-organized sets of statements which give expression to the meanings and values of an institution. Beyond that, they define, describe and delimit what it is possible to say and not possible to say (and by extension – what it is possible to do or not to do) with respect to the area of concern of that institution, whether marginally or centrally. A discourse provides a set of possible statements about a given area, and organizes and gives structure to the manner in which a particular topic, object, process is to be talked about. In that it provides descriptions, rules, permissions and prohibitions of social and individual actions.[25]

Returning to the *Sun* editorial with this definition in mind, I would want to say that the ideological paradigms which I sketchily annotated above are part of a systematic set of values which answer the economic and institutional requirements of the newspaper and its owners. The question of how and why they emerge goes beyond my aims and my brief. They are in suspension in the mode of discourse which is mandatory for the leader writer in this context, and they inevitably precipitate in the text s/he produces. Other institutional circumstances, a different newspaper, would have different institutional requirements, different ideological needs and different discursive imperatives; but the process would be analogous.

Where does this theory of socially constructed, ideology-laden discourse leave the reader? In another recent paper,[26] Kress has made the very good point that the early model of critical linguistics gave too little power to readers, so that (as in the conspiracy theory of news distortion) they seemed to be passive vessels or sponges, absorbing an ideology which the source of the text imposed on them. This pessimistic conception needs to be eradicated, if only for the reason that it seems to prohibit on principle the possibility of critical readers understanding and taking issue with the implicit values of a newspaper text; or the possibility of any classroom strategies for educating critical readers. But a passive view of the practice of readership can be countered on more academic, less strategic, grounds.

There is every reason to propose that being a reader is an active, creative practice. In general terms, it is now believed that perception and understanding involve the active deployment (not necessarily conscious, of course) of mental schemes and processing strategies which the subject knows in advance of his or her encounter with the object being processed: these are projected on to the perceptual data in a trial at 'making sense'; their relevance, their success, is confirmed by structural or contextual clues. In understanding a painting which s/he has never seen before, for example, a viewer brings to bear a prior knowledge of compositional codes: the convention of perspective is known to viewers, as well as practised by post-medieval illusionist artists, and allows viewers to reconstruct a two-dimensional medium as a three-dimensional representation. Perspective is a cultural, historically delimited schema; the art historian E. H. Gombrich makes such schemata the theoretical foundation of his whole approach in his great book *Art and Illusion*.[27]

As a matter of fact, the schema is a fundamental concept in contemporary cognitive psychology, let alone art history. A schema is a chunk of unconscious knowledge, shared within a group of people and drawn upon in the process of making sense of the world. Schemata are of major importance in storage (memory), and in perception, where they are projected upon the impressions of sense to make experience coherent, meaningful. There have been many recent proposals for kinds of schemata employed in language processing. Stereotypes, as introduced in chapter 2, and invoked elsewhere in this book, are schemata; so are models of discourse as discussed in this and the following chapter. Other types of schemata include frames, scripts and prototypes, different kinds of structurings of knowledge which appear to be used in the shaping of discourse into coherent texts.[28] There is also much experimental evidence in psycholinguistics as to the role of schemata and processing strategies in the routine business of hearing and comprehending sentences (and texts, therefore). At the phonetic level, for example, hearers do not perceive the sounds of speech 'raw', and then recover the meanings from them; rather, they project structural guesses on to the acoustic signal as received, analysing speech not by taking the sounds apart and rebuilding them into significant units, but rather by hypothesizing what units occur, and then checking their tentative significances against contextual clues – a process called 'analysis by synthesis'.[29] This constructive (rather than, say, 'extractive') process is replicated at more abstract levels of linguistic structure. Just as we 'hear' by projecting phonological schemata on to the raw sounds, similarly we work out what syntactic and lexical units (sentences and words) are present by constructively and hypothetically applying our general knowledge of syntax, and our specific (schematized) knowledge of the world, to the text we tentatively hear.[30]

These generally agreed explanations of the schematic and constructive nature of speech processing, which presumably apply *mutatis mutandis* to the decoding and comprehension of written texts, make it natural to assign to the newspaper reader an active and potentially powerful role. *Sun* readers might not be able to write like a *Sun* leader writer, but in a real sense they know the discourse and its meanings in advance, predictively bringing relevant mental models or schemata which are to be confirmed in the act of reading. The newspaper and its readers share a common 'discursive competence', know the permissible statements, permissions and prohibitions of which Kress speaks (blondes are busty, work is a duty, play is a thrill, strikes are unpatriotic, and so on). Newspaper and reader negotiate the significance of the text around the stipulations of the appropriate discourse, a mode of discourse 'cued' for the reader by significant linguistic options – 'slagging off', for instance, is a cue to the model.

An intriguing feature of the *Sun*, complicating my analysis considerably, is that much of its text is, technically speaking, aesthetic.[31] That is to say, it deploys certain structural patterns which cue literary rather than colloquial discourse. Such 'poetic' features as alliteration, parallel phrase structures, metaphors and puns abound, particularly in the major news headlines, headlines for 'saucy' stories, the text accompanying the Page Three nude and the 'editorial' **'The Sun Says'**. Even the expression 'slagging off' could be experienced as literary rather than colloquial, since it is a highly unusual lexical choice for the printed page, and thus, in Mukařovský's term, 'foregrounded'.[32] If textual cues are foregrounded, the effect of defamiliarization can occur (cf. p. 31): the reader experiences a heightened awareness of what is being said, and becomes freshly critical of it. Interestingly, the *Sun* indulges in 'poetic' structures in places where it is being at its most outrageous about politics or sex. Cues are foregrounded to the point of self-parody. Deplorable values are openly displayed, pointedly highlighted; even a critical reader can be disarmed by pleasure in the awfulness of the discourse.

Chapter 4

Conversation and consensus

THE 'PUBLIC IDIOM' AND THE FORMATION OF CONSENSUS

In this chapter, I want to develop some lines of enquiry which were raised at the end of chapter 3. There are a number of questions to consider in the area of 'Who is saying this? What is the source, the authority?'. An anonymous journalist writes a report or an editorial, s/he adopts, with experience more or less automatically, a certain style befitting the genre of article (editorial, television review, foreign news report, etc.), a style appropriate to the particular paper and, more generally still, reflecting the social and economic processes in which the paper participates. The style, I have suggested, encodes an ideology which is already embodied in the language, implanted there by existing social and discursive practices. The journalist has little control over the values and beliefs which are found in the language. For one thing, s/he is employed to write for an organization which is governed by the very same institutional constraints which build the ideology. Also, the reader is not without power, having a constructive role to play in 'finding' the values and beliefs. Readers may not possess the writing crafts of the professional journalist, but in a sense they 'know' the significance of the various journalistic codes already, through living within the society which has moulded the institution of the Press, and through habitual exposure to the discourse. Unconsciously, readers 'read in' – a more active process than 'reading off' – the ideology which shapes the newspaper's representation of reality. Thus, values which already exist – ideas about sex, about patriotism, about class, hierarchy, money, leisure, family life, and so on – are reproduced in this discursive interaction between the newspaper text and the reader.

Such an analysis, feeling like a deterministic kind of sociology and socialism blended, will no doubt be received gloomily or indignantly, especially by those who write for the newspapers, and those who enjoy reading them. The actual experience of reading newspapers is nothing like as impersonal, mechanical, uncreative and restrictive as this picture would suggest. What we actually perceive when we read a paper are stylistic diversity, vitality, individuality. These qualities or effects are the fruits of the brilliant technical skills which many journalists possess. I do not, however, see them as evidence of personal creativity, but as a necessary linguistic virtuosity which is still framed by the institutional forces which newspapers serve. It would be death to a newspaper if it read like a Social Security booklet. Newspapers have to be lively, because they offer themselves as a brand of entertainment, and because they must disguise the fact that they are actually a form of institutional discourse. The personal voice is a necessary, but accepted, illusion. In this chapter, I want to look at how the illusion is formed, and speculate on its functions.

The basic task for the writer is to word institutional statements (those of the newspaper, and those of its sources) in a style appropriate to interpersonal communication, because the reader is an individual and must be addressed as such. The task is not only stylistic, but also ideological: institutional concepts have to be translated into personal thoughts. The process can be seen in terms of the *narrowing of a gap* between bureaucratic and personal discourse. The gap once narrowed, a discursive norm is achieved for the particular paper as a whole, a sense of a 'neutral' language embodying 'normal' values. The norm is actually a band of styles: each newspaper accommodates a range of similar voices to accompany the diversity of topics and formats within each day's edition. As we will see, the fundamental device in narrowing the discursive gap is the promotion of oral models within the printed newspaper text, giving an illusion of conversation in which common sense is spoken about matters on which there is consensus.

I will relate my linguistic account of these processes and relationships to existing discussions in media studies, by considering the well-known account of 'modes of address' proposed by Stuart Hall; this was excerpted briefly on p. 40:

An even more significant aspect of 'media work' [that is, more significant than selectivity in content] is the activity of transforming an event into a finished news item. This has to do with the way an item is *coded* by the media into a particular language form. Just as each paper, as we have just argued, has a particular organizational framework, sense of news and readership, so each will also develop a regular and characteristic *mode of address*. This means that the same topic, sources and inferential structures will appear differently even in papers with a similar outlook, since the different rhetorics of address will have an important effect in inflecting the original item. Of special importance in determining the particular mode of address adopted will be the particular part of the readership spectrum the paper sees itself as customarily addressing. The language employed will thus be the *newspaper's own version of the language of the public to whom it is principally addressed*: its version of the rhetoric, imagery and underlying common stock of knowledge which it assumes its audience shares and which thus forms the basis of the reciprocity of producer/reader. For this reason we want to call this form of address – different for each news outlet – the *public idiom* of the media [Hall's emphases].[1]

I have already pointed out that this does not mean that the idiom of a newspaper is an objective rendering of the speech of its readers; and, of course, Hall does not intend this. A key notion here is 'reciprocity' between writers and readers, the negotiation of a style with which targeted readers feel comfortable, and which allows writers the band of flexibility mentioned above. The familiarity of an habitual style has ideological consequences: it allows the unnoticed expression of familiar thoughts. The establishment of this 'normal' style is fundamental to the building of an assumption of consensus, which has been identified by media analysts as central to the ideological practice of newspapers.[2]

CONSENSUS AND CONTRADICTION

The ideology of consensus – 'Everyone agrees that . . .' – has already been mentioned. It is political and economic in origin; it springs from the need of government and business to relate to a population which (a) in general terms accepts the rightness of the status quo (so people will not wish to disrupt the existing order), and (b) holds certain specific beliefs, for instance a model of family life as self-reliant and materially well provided (so people will both make minimal demands on state resources, and also purchase consumer goods extensively). In so far as the Press is a business, it has commercial interests in fostering agreement on a range of consumer-oriented values; in so far as its interests coincide with those of government, it has political motives for conveying approval of a stable, familiar ideology. Articulating the ideology of consensus is a crucial practice in the Press's management of its relations with government and capital, on the one hand, and with individual readers, on the other. And this is a *linguistic* practice; the details of its linguistic working have been largely neglected by writers on the media.

What is the ideology of consensus? The concept has been extensively discussed by Hall, Hartley and others,[3] so I will sketch it only briefly. Consensus assumes that, for a given grouping of people, it is a matter of fact that the interests of the whole population are undivided, held in common; and that the whole population acknowledges this 'fact' by subscribing to a certain set of beliefs: everyone agrees that *p* and that *q* and that *r*. The relevant grouping for the English national Press would be something like 'the British people' – in actuality the *English* population as governed from Westminster, for the Press ignores the distinctive characteristics of Welsh, Scottish and Ulster life or, if newsworthy, treats them as aberrant. The pronoun 'we' in the media, as in the mouths of politicians ('our economic recovery', 'our health system', 'our nuclear deterrent'), generally refers to that English grouping; but the consensual image is taken through a variable lens, and 'we' sometimes narrows to southern England, sometimes broadens to refer to 'Britain and America' or 'Europe' or 'the west'. Sometimes the referents of 'we' are collected in moral or social, rather than geographical/political, terms, e.g. the 'ordinary folk' who are terrorized by 'thugs' (p. 139), or '*Sun* readers' who are supposed to agree on a whole sheaf of beliefs. 'Consensus' assumes, and in times of crisis actually *affirms*,[4] that within the group, there is no difference or disunity in the interests and values of any of the population, or of any institution. The content of the consensual assumption could be spelt out as a long series of propositions about (in this case) contemporary Britain. For example: workers and factory-owners are equally benefited

by productivity and economic growth; class differences are a
thing of the past; there is no real division between 'North' and
'South'; elected parliamentary government reflects and unites individuals' choices; everyone can buy shares, choose their children's
schools or their health care; we have freedom of speech, and a
free Press; everyone wants firm law enforcement; everyone would
like to buy their own house and live in a family life-style; there
is 'British' food, clothes, music, literature, etc. As I pointed out in
chapter 2 (p. 16) consensus on such propositions is the ideological
underpinning of the news value which I renamed 'homocentrism'.

In so far as these propositions make empirical claims, they tend
to be untrue. Numerous unambiguous economic and demo-
graphic facts could be cited against them, e.g. regional differences
in house prices, employment, voting patterns, class differences in
leisure activities and in diet. But the empirical substance to which
the ideology of consensus alludes is a separate matter which it is
not my job to analyse; the point is that consensus is posited about
a set of *beliefs* or *values*, not *facts*. If the facts do not square with
the beliefs, then apologists for consensus must make their language work hard to suggest that reality does fit in with belief.
Whether or not (to instance one proposition) the interests of
workers and of capitalists do actually coincide, consensus stipulates that they do. Let us look briefly at a news story which
implies and is supported by this particular proposition. The belief
is central to this report in the *Sun*, published (31 December 1985)
after the collapse of the 1984–5 miners' strike (significantly, the
article is printed on the same page as the editorial I quoted on
pp. 38–9, immediately adjacent to the section applauding those
who worked during the Christmas/New Year holiday, headed
'**Join the club**'):

(1) **HARD WORK GIVES PITS A BRIGHT FUTURE**
   20,000 fewer miners are digging MORE coal
   A miracle has taken place in Britain's coal industry. Miners
   are producing more coal with fewer men and are earning
   bigger bonuses. . . . the men have come to realize that the
   harder they work the more money they can earn. And that
   meant a better Christmas and a chance to pay off debts
   left after the strike. . . .
   John Northard, NCB operations director, said of the
   three tonnes a man record: 'This is a real breakthrough

which is convincing proof of the new spirit in the industry and the new sense of realism among miners about the future.

Management are in no doubt that our business is to produce coal at costs that customers are prepared to pay.

There is now a determination throughout the industry to succeed.'

The report implies that, though the miners' immediate motive was selfish ('digging so that they could have a Merry Christmas'), they are at one with management in their 'new realism' that 'Hard work [by the miners] gives pits a bright future [for both the miners and the industry]'. The unity of goal and effort of workers and management is repeatedly implied in phrases like 'determination throughout the industry'.

So far, I have paraphrased consensus in rather discursive, contentful propositions: 'everyone believes in the right to choose health care' and the like. It would be preferable to give a 'deeper' analysis in terms of an abstract system of values. So, the *Sun* report excerpted above is to be understood, not only as a statement about the unity of interest of coal workers and coal management, but also, more deeply, as the implication of a set of more abstract values including, here, *co-operation, hard work* and *material reward*. To change the example, another value, *freedom of individual choice*, would be the ideological assumption which is assumed to legitimate the proposition about health care just cited; such an assumption would also be taken to validate more specific and problematic statements still, such as encouragements to employers to offer private medicine as a perk, and appeals to support medical facilities through charitable donation. You can see that, *mutatis mutandis*, the same consensual value of *freedom of individual choice* could be invoked to legitimate ranges of statements about education, public services such as cleaning, catering in hospitals and schools, etc. Under the Thatcher governments since 1979, a vast range of devastating decisions and proposals for cutting public spending have been cynically legitimated by appealing to a small cluster of consensual values, principally *efficient use of resources, freedom of individual choice* and *self-reliance*. The Press have had a major role in assisting the process of legitimation by citing alleged consensual values.

The exact analysis of the whole system of these values is not my concern; I am much more interested in their modes of expression. The system will of course change over time as historical expediencies change; Steve Chibnall's list published in 1977[5] will illustrate the overall dimensions of the system, but readers may care to reflect on revisions that might be needed to take account of ideological changes in the last ten years – one opposition that I would add would be *self-reliance* vs *dependence*:

Positive legitimating values	Negative, illegitimate values
legality	illegality
moderation	extremism
compromise	dogmatism
co-operation	confrontation
order	chaos
peacefulness	violence
tolerance	intolerance
constructiveness	destructiveness
openness	secrecy
honesty	corruption
realism	ideology
rationality	irrationality
impartiality	bias
responsibility	irresponsibility
fairness	unfairness
firmness	weakness
industriousness	idleness
freedom of choice	monopoly/uniformity
equality	inequality

Chibnall's right-hand (negative) column displays a central contradiction in the consensual ideology: if, as the theory claims, everyone accepts the list of positive values, how is it that the negatives exist, not just as abstract possibilities, but as actual happenings and states of affairs? Corruption, murder, rape, malpractice, bigotry . . . these are the stuff of newspaper report. The apologist for consensus can cope with this problem in two ways. If departures from the norm are not too extreme, s/he affects a kind of tolerant pluralism: 'everyone is entitled to their own opinion'; 'it takes all sorts to make a world'. So the contradiction is resolved by accommodating variety within consensus: 'we agree to differ'. A second strategy is the dichotomizing practice mentioned on p. 16: the construction of 'them' and 'us'. Law and public opinion stipulate that there are many ideas and behaviours which are to be condemned as outside the pale of consensus: people who practise such behaviours are branded as 'subversives', 'perverts', 'deviants', 'dissidents', 'trouble-makers', etc. Such people are subjected to marginalization or repression; and the contradiction returns, because consensus decrees that there are some people outside the consensus. The 'we' of consensus narrows and hardens into a population which sees its interests as culturally and economically valid, but as threatened by a 'them' comprising a motley of antagonistic sectional groups: not only criminals but also trade unionists, homosexuals, teachers, blacks, foreigners, northerners, and so on.

The problematic nature of 'consensus' is exacerbated for the Press by its relation to the news values, criteria for newsworthiness, described in chapter 2. Galtung and Ruge's F_4, 'meaningfulness', coincides with 'consensus' in what I called 'homocentrism': a leaning towards topics which are meaningful to readers because they display interests and experiences which 'we' share in 'our' lives. However, the list of beliefs defining the positive side of consensus – legality, moderation, compromise, etc. – is hardly a good source for captivating news stories! A more powerful set of news values dictate preferences for the event which is of large scale rather than of modest proportions (F_2), unusual rather than mundane (F_6), elite rather than ordinary ($F_{9, 10}$), negative rather than positive (F_{12}). More newsworthy than everyday stories of ordinary folk are stories which exemplify the negative attitudes and behaviours thought to be characteristic of 'them'; so the newspapers fill their columns with murder, rape, fraud, espionage, riot, natural disaster, freaks: stories of 'the other', 'them', rather than 'the familiar', 'us'.

We are now working in the area of the ideological source of the double standards which are so distastefully and distressing displayed in the popular Press. The ostensible morality of the consensual model is denied by a *desire* for the negative on the part of the newspapers and their readers: rapes are newsworthy not for the reason that rape has been made a serious issue in sexual politics in recent years, but because they gratify a prurient voyeurism. Why did a newspaper which every day publishes pictures of naked women, publish on its front page the photograph of a young rape victim? Why are photographs of the victims of a mass murderer printed all in a row? Is it to express the pathos and horror of the crime, or to feed a fantasy experience of the attacks? Why do the papers affirm a united Britain, while daily vilifying large numbers of its population? These questions are not my primary concern. I am trying to emphasize the multiply problematic nature of the notion of consensus in relation to the public and commercial values inscribed in the Press.

CATEGORIZATION AND CONVERSATION

Because consensus is so problematic – peculiarly so for the popular Press, but also for other commercial and governmental institutions which have to pretend 'one nation', but are devoted to controlling and profiting from the unprivileged – an immense amount of discursive work has to be devoted to the maintenance of the illusion. I mean the word 'discursive' to recall the notion of discourse towards which chapter 3 led. Human communication is laden with systems of beliefs, systems of categories, 'discriminating grids', which represent the world according to the needs of the societies within which communication takes place. Language, among the many human media, is a highly effective form for encoding representations of experience and values. The lexicon (the 'mental dictionary') stores ideas in sets structured around certain formal, logical relationships such as oppositeness, complementarity, inclusion, equivalence: 'man: woman', 'bull: cow', 'parent: child', 'wet: dry', 'flower: tulip . . . rose . . . daffodil', 'tall: short', 'legality: illegality', 'moderation: extremism', etc. The vocabulary of a particular language *sorts* concepts into strictly defined categorial relationships, and this is the basic resource through which some field of experience or activity is kept stable, and transmitted from person to person, from generation to generation. Terminologies are developed for key concepts and relationships, and the terms are mentioned in a systematic way in linguistic usage. It is not just the taxonomic structure of the key vocabulary which is important – for categorizing clearly; it is also vital that the systems of meanings are kept alive and familiar, by being uttered regularly in appropriate contexts. This is where conversation has a major function.

These principles are hard to discern in a system so abstract, and so well camouflaged, as a cluster of political ideas like 'consensus' or 'law and order'. They are very much clearer if we think about some technical field, where the referents of a terminology, the associated objects and processes, are visible and practical. For illustration, let us look briefly at a segment of the vocabulary which is fundamental to the practice of *carpentry*.

Carpenters have taxonomies (hierarchial classifications) for tools, for timber, for fixings, adhesives, joints, woodworking processes, etc. The diagram below shows part of the carpenter's lexicon for tools, expanded into some of the sub-categories and sub-sub-categories for one branch, *saws*.

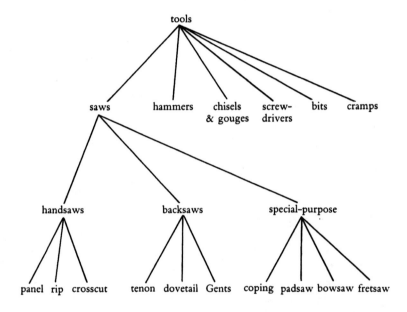

Similar hierarchical trees could be drawn for hammers, for planes, etc., and for higher categories – particularly complex in the case of *timber*, divided on various dimensions into planed and sawn, softwood and hardwood (many different kinds), boards (chipboard, blockboard, ply, hardboard), mouldings (architrave, dowel, quadrant, scotia, etc.)

A point to notice is how simple and common the fundamental terms are: 'saw', 'drill'. These are called basic-level terms; and they are usually short, native in origin, frequently used.[6] It appears to be cognitively important for each section of a lexicon to possess a clear set of basic-level terms: the meanings are more easily taught, learned and remembered, the objects and their relationships more readily recognized. Lower down the hierarchy, the terms may be more exotic or structurally more complex: 'architrave', 'scotia', 'dovetail saw'. Basic-level terms extend throughout a language's vocabulary: 'tree', 'fruit', 'bird', 'meat', 'car', 'house'; they are the cornerstones in the coding of a community's experience.

The technical lexicon for woodworking exists not only in the minds of carpenters, as an abstract resource. It is also *used*: regularly uttered in builders' merchants' catalogues, in DIY stores, in the workshop, in books and magazines. Thus, the validity of the system of nomenclature is constantly reaffirmed by usage. Note that, in use, the terms are not only handled as single items from a list: relationships are mentioned; the structure of the whole system is thereby constantly checked, and users' knowledge of it adjusted and systematized. You can see how organized each system of categories is by inspecting a textbook on the field. I checked my knowledge of woodworking terminology by consulting *The Reader's Digest Complete Do-It-Yourself Manual*, pp. 54–87 and 107–47. The accounts of tools and materials are set out in a regular, formal sequence, with lots of drawings and tables; the discourse is full of categorizing and relational propositions: 'saws . . . can be divided into three main groups: 'the Gents saw is . . . the smallest member of the backsaw family'; 'the combination plane does anything that the rebate or plough plane can do, and the work of many moulding planes as well'. This is a pedagogic discourse, a very explicit exposition of a technical field; newspaper discourse handling political ideas works in a less direct way. But the principle is the same: there exists a system of ideas which can be regarded as categories and relationships, and its existence is maintained by utterance.

Let us return to 'consensus'. Each of the oppositions listed in Chibnall's table reproduced above has associated with it a set of propositions, the truth of which is assumed to be generally agreed. It is 'common sense' that pickets should abide by the law, that management and workers should co-operate, that 'all men are equal', that everyone should be free (to buy their council house, vote without coercion, etc.), that political leaders should be fair and firm, and so on. Such general propositions will sometimes be directly affirmed in editorials or in the quotation of 'accessed voices' (p. 22), but on the whole they are not directly

stated, but implied or presupposed. A glance at extract (1)
'HARD WORK . . .', pp. 50–1) will show that it is based on a
set of underlying propositions about 'industry', 'realism' and 'co-
operation' as manifested in the post-miners'-strike 'miracle'. The
actual statements which do occur in the newspaper texts are
phrased in terms of a vocabulary of categories. Newspapers and
politicians use a recognizable vocabulary of key terms which are
mentioned as if they are basic-level terms, natural categories.
Many examples are given in the analyses in this book: for a quick
illustration, see the lists of types of person given in chapter 6,
pp. 92, 102 and 103, and the table in chapter 8, p. 143. Just like
the carpentry terms, these words fall into systems and are offered as
natural commonplaces: a picket is a picket just as a saw is a saw.

At the beginning of this chapter, I drew attention to the role
of conversational style in closing a 'discursive gap' between the
newspapers and their institutional sources, on the one hand, and
their readers, on the other. The reasons for adopting a conversational style have partly to do with the construction of an illusion
of informality, familiarity, friendliness. But there is a more important ideological reason. The ideological function of conversation is to naturalize the terms in which reality is represented,
and the categories those terms represent. Conversation implies
co-operation, agreement, symmetry of power and knowledge
between participants (contrast classroom discourse or textbook
language). If you address someone in a conversational mode, you
are assuming – unconsciously – agreement between the two of
you concerning the basic reference points to which the conversation is anchored. Conversation implies a commonly held view
of the world, a shared subjective reality that is taken for granted
and does not have to be proved.

Berger and Luckmann, in their pioneering study in the sociology of knowledge, *The Social Construction of Reality*, offer a mem-
orable and convincing account of the 'reality-maintaining' function of conversation,[7] an account which has been noticed and
discussed by the linguist Michael Halliday.[8] Their account is so
clear and sophisticated that I am bound to follow Halliday in
quoting it at length:

> The most important vehicle of reality-maintenance is conver-
> sation. One may view the individual's everyday life in terms of
> the working away of a conversational apparatus that ongoingly

maintains, modifies and reconstructs his subjective reality. . . .
It is important to stress, however, that the greater part of
reality-maintenance in conversation is implicit, not explicit.
Most conversation does not in so many words define the nature
of the world. Rather, it takes place against the background of
a world that is silently taken for granted. . . .

If this is understood, one will readily see that the great part,
if not all, of everyday conversation maintains subjective reality.
Indeed, its massivity is achieved by the accumulation and consistency of casual conversation – conversation that can *afford to
be casual* precisely because it refers to the routines of a taken-
for-granted world. The loss of casualness signals a break in
the routines and, at least potentially, a threat to the taken-for-
granted reality. . . .

Generally speaking, the conversational apparatus maintains
reality by 'talking through' various elements of experience and
allocating them a definite place in the real world.

This reality-generating potency of conversation is already
given in the fact of linguistic objectification. We have seen
how language objectifies the world, transforming the *panta rhei*
of experience into a cohesive order. In the establishment of
this order language *realizes* a world, in the double sense of
apprehending and producing it. Conversation is the actualizing
of this realizing efficacy of language in the face-to-face situations of individual existence. In conversation the objectifi-
cations of language become objects of individual consciousness.
Thus the fundamental reality-maintaining fact is the continuing
use of the same language to objectify unfolding biographical
experience.[9]

'Linguistic objectification' in this sense of 'allocation of a definite
place' is the process I have referred to as 'categorization'. Experience is sorted into agreed categories in conversational exchange,
and these categories are then the 'taken-for-granted' background
in ongoing conversation. Conversation is 'casual', or as Halliday
puts it, not 'didactic':[10] experience is referred to implicitly, not
pointedly. It is 'continuous', uninterrupted by challenges, or by
intrusions of marked or 'alien' styles.[11]

We have now seen the ideological reasons why newspapers
affect a conversational style. Let us now look at the technical
measures that are taken to construct this illusion.

ORAL MODELS IN THE PRESS[12]

A newspaper is an institution, a reader is a person. The characteristic mode of an institution is print, and its typical 'utterances'
include memoranda, reports, manuals, etc.; a person's characteristic mode is speech, and their typical utterance is conversation.
Between the two modes there is an exclusive distinction of physical medium, and a difference of communicative context (face-to-
face or not). Socioculturally, the two modes mean different
things, print connoting formality and authority, speech suggesting informality and solidarity. These are the basic dimensions of
the 'discursive gap' which I proposed at the beginning of this
chapter.

The difference between the modes is not in other respects
absolute, however, and so the newspapers are able to narrow the
gap. There exist, for a start, mixed-mode utterances, for example
subtitled films, or television news presentations in which a voice-
over expands on a series of summary statements displayed on the
screen. And there are are texts in one physical medium which
claim the characteristics of the other mode, or some of them:
scripts to be performed orally as if they were speech, bookish
speeches borrowing the formality and authority of the print which
they mimic, and so on. In such cases, we may say that one mode
adopts a model of the other mode, and that is how newspapers
proceed in order to narrow the communicative gap. The procedure is possible because, notwithstanding the absoluteness, in
some senses, of the distinction between print and speech, the
actual substantive differences in linguistic structure (syntax,
vocabulary, etc.) are only relative, a matter of tendency. No
doubt vulgarisms like the *Sun*'s 'slag off' are rare in print, but
the expression does occur, as we have seen; conversely, formal
words like 'masticate' or 'equilibrium' are not debarred from
speech, but will be rare – occurring in formal, didactic styles but
not in everyday conversation where 'chew' and 'balance' would
be preferred.

Conventional linguistics would regard a language as consisting
of a set of 'varieties' of three different sorts: a set of registers
such as scientific English or classroom English (different *uses*), a
set of dialects such as Norfolk or Brooklynese (different *regions*)
and a set of modes, namely printed and spoken (different *channels*). Furthermore, conventional linguistics would want to

stipulate that each text or utterance was in a certain register, and a certain dialect, and a certain mode. We are beginning to see that the situation is not as cut-and-dried as that. Texts are actually often heterogeneous, and they also contain segments that are either ambiguous or neutral as to variety. The traditional way of looking at this matter seems to me to put the cart before the horse. I would prefer to say, not that a text is in a certain mode (or register, or dialect), but that modes and registers and dialects are 'in' texts. I have put 'in' in quotation marks because modes are not actually present in the linguistic structure, but rather, they are perceived in texts by hearers/readers. To make sense of this notion of potential rather than actual structure in texts, we need an idea of the text which is less formalistic, less literal, than that usually employed by linguists; a concept which allows the reader to be active in assigning structure and significance. The idea of text and reader found in poststructuralist literary theory[13] suits the purposes of the argument I have been developing in this book: the text is co-produced by writer and reader, negotiating the nature and significance of a piece of language, on the basis of their more or less shared knowledge of the world, society and language itself. Assigning a mode or modes to a text is part of this practice of co-production. So a mode is not an objective structure (which is why 'mode' has to be distinguished from 'physical medium'), but an idea in the minds of language users: this is what I refer to as a *model*. So an oral model is an example of a schema.

I use the term 'schema' as a general term for representation of background knowledge, a topic which has been extensively discussed in recent years in cognitive psychology.[14] Schemas are units of tacit knowledge which are shared by people in a community (they are 'intersubjective'), which permit external phenomena and other experience to be perceived as coherent and to be understood as significant. Readers of novels, for example, acquire – through their reading of fiction, through education, through reading reviews and hearing critical discussions on arts programmes – quite precise expectations about story line, the treatment of characters, the significances of different atmospheres and styles. Readers of newspapers come to know what to expect in news reports, what sequence of exposition, where generalization or moralization is to be expected, and so on.[15] These expected properties of texts are, as I said, not 'in' the texts; they are projected on to them by readers on the basis of cues. In language and other media, cues consist of technical properties or devices, which are objective in a way that the schemata they promote are not: in perspective drawing (cf. p. 43), techniques such as convergent lines and variable shading are cues to the illusion of three-dimensionality; in newspaper writing, the illusion of orality, the oral model, is analogously cued by devices such as slang words, syntactic contractions and fragmented layout – see below for more details.

The idea of cueing implies that a model of register or dialect or mode can be assigned to a text even on the basis of some very small segment(s) within its total language: it does not have to be saturated with markers of the variety, or structured with tyrannical consistency. The cueing effectiveness of small details has occasionally been acknowledged in sociolinguistics and dialectology. Halliday, in his earliest treatment of 'register', maintains that just one sentence from a sports commentary, a church service or a school lesson 'would enable us to identify [the situation type] correctly'; and he gives plausible examples of single expressions which conjure up a particular kind of usage.[16] R. A. Hudson's textbook *Sociolinguistics* maintains an uncommon scepticism about 'varieties', giving priority to the concept of 'linguistic item' and so providing a sympathetic theoretical framework for the present approach.[17] The research of Labov and of Trudgill in urban dialectology is suggestive from this point of view, too. They do not attempt to give a complete profile of any dialect, but focus on small phonetic details which are characteristic of an accent. Some of these, called by Labov *stereotypes*, have, as he puts it, 'risen to full social consciousness', and can be regarded as symbolic of an accent and the social values associated with it. So for example, the pronunciation /toyd/ for 'third' in New York symbolizes Brooklynese by synecdoche; it concentrates in one item three highly significant features: /t/ for 'th', the highly recognizable diphthong /oy/ and the lack of the prestigious (in the New York area) postvocalic /r/.[18] What I am proposing is that the principle that a variety can be cued by a stereotypical details is as valid for models of mode – in this case 'oral', suggesting conversation – as it is for models of dialect and register.

It will be useful at this stage to list some of the features of language which may be used to make a printed medium suggest the presence of speech. My aim is to help my readers recognize these markers in their own critical reading of newspapers; after this chapter, I will pay little further attention to oral mode, having established its significance and its techniques.

Typography and orthography

Typography The typographical devices include anything that can be done to break up the monologic uniformity, the greyness, of conventional print. The tabloids employ many different typefaces on the same page to suggest variations of stress, tone and pace, the middle-class papers in a lower key use dots and dashes to break up their sentences and to trail off reflectively at pregnant points.

Phonemes Deliberate misspellings and simplications of spellings ('wot') draw attention to pronunciation; there is a literary model here in the techniques of representation of dialect speech employed by novelists such as Mrs Gaskell and D. H. Lawrence. This is not a matter of phonetic transcription, merely a suggestive disturbance of the spelling in order to connote orality.

Contrastive stress Italics or underlining indicate contrastive stress, a device proper to speech and discouraged at school for writing: 'Don't vote for *him* [that is, vote rather for some other person]'.

Intonation and paralanguage Printing tricks may suggest the pitch movement of a voice or other vocal gestures (paralanguage) such as slurring or hesitancy.

Information structure Halliday maintains that speech and writing chop up the flow of language into units of information in quite separate ways.[19] In writing, information units are coterminous with traditional grammatical units such as the clause, and the implication is that intonation curves would also be congruent with such units if a written text were read aloud. Speech, he says, is fragmented into shorter sections of information by shorter intonation curves which are more independent of conventional syntax. In newspapers, this effect is cued by a fragmented format and typography, and by short, incomplete sentences.

Register

Lexis or vocabulary This tends towards the informal, colloquial. Slang, idioms, clichés, proverbs and catch-words are all used to cue the illusion of oral mode; learned or official words are avoided by the popular Press (unless they are to be derided).[20]

Naming and address First names ('Charles'), diminutives ('Di') and nicknames ('Rambo Ronnie', 'Hurricane') are all used to connote the informality and intimacy of face-to-face discourse.

Syntax and morphology

Contractions of auxiliaries and negatives A standard cue to oral mode, of major importance not only in newspapers but also in, for example, academic writing that tries to sound chatty and user-friendly: 'he'll', 'don't', etc.

Elisions; short or incomplete sentences Again, a very important technique in the Press: 'The BBC asked him. Nobody stopped him. Why not?' (*Guardian*, 22 May 1987).

Deixis

Deixis in language (from the Greek, meaning 'pointing') consists of the devices which link a text with the time and place of communication and with the participants; which 'orient' speaker and addressee in relation to the content of the discourse. Briefly, these devices consist of:

Indicators of *person* – chiefly the personal pronouns, especially the ones which refer to speaker and addressee either separately – 'I' and 'you' – or 'together' – one of the two meanings of 'we', the 'inclusive "we"'.

Indicators of *time* – 'today', 'now', 'then', etc., and the tense forms of verbs.

Indicators of *place* – above all, 'here' and 'there' and the demonstratives 'this' and 'that'.

The deictic characteristics of speech and print are quite different. In face-to-face conversation speaker and addressee are together in the here and now; they can identify one another; the things they are talking about may well be physically present, or going on around them. None of these circumstances apply in the case of normal printed texts. It is not surprising that deictic markers such as 'I', 'you', 'here', 'now' and 'this' are prominent in speech, but much less frequent, and with different meanings, in print and writing. In newspaper discourse, deixis provides important cues to the oral mode. From the *Sun* editorial quoted in chapter 3:

> If you were at work yesterday you qualified for the most exclusive club in the land.
> We were working, too.

The last two types of cue to an oral model are explained in chapter 5, so need only be identified briefly here.

Modality

Modal expressions signify judgements as to truth ('correct'), likelihood ('certainly', 'might'), desirability ('regrettable'); other modal usages stipulate obligations ('should', 'ought to') and grant permission ('may'). The significance of modality as far as the cueing of an oral model is concerned is that it suggests the presence of an individual subjectivity behind the printed text, who is qualified with the knowledge required to pass judgement, the status to grant leave or assign responsibility. If modal expressions are frequent and highlighted, subjectivity is enhanced, the illusion of a 'person' with a voice and opinions; conversely, writing which strives to give an impression of objectivity, such as scientific reporting or certain traditions of 'realistic' fiction, tends to minimize modal expressions.

Speech acts

To consider an utterance as a speech act is to acknowledge that the speaker, in uttering words and sentences, not only *says* something (the propositional function, referring to objects and assigning actions, qualities, etc., to them), but also thereby *does* something: this is the illocutionary function of language, through which speakers make promises and requests, issue commands and warnings, etc.[21] It has been pointed out that even making a statement is an action, but when we talk about speech acts we usually mean the more explicit and interactional kinds such as ordering and questioning.

If these kinds of speech acts are frequent and prominent in a printed text, the sense of personal interaction is heightened. That this effect is sought for, and by these means, in newspapers can be confirmed by simply referring to the *Sun* leader reproduced in chapter 3 (pp. 38–9), which is full of very noticeable speech acts of questioning and commanding.

The linguistic features just listed are the principal ones which contribute to an illusion of conversational style. In the next chapter, I survey a broader range of linguistic structures which are important for the representation of reality in the Press; more detail is supplied on some of the linguistic features dealt with very briefly in this chapter, particularly speech acts and modality.

Chapter 5

Analytic tools: critical linguistics

In this chapter, we penetrate further into the details of linguistic structure. So far, I have maintained that the structure of a news text, under the pressure of the social circumstances of communication, embodies values and beliefs; that representation of experience, of events and concepts, is patterned by the structure of the medium, so inevitably that the very notion of 'representation' carries within it the qualification of representation *from a specific ideological point of view*, that values, or ideology, differ systematically in different forms of expression, as for example in the characteristically different choices of words and grammatical phrasings found in the Press. Like Halliday, I reject the extreme Whorfian position of 'linguistic determinism': it is implausible, and deeply pessimistic about the abilities of human beings, to believe that people's world-views are fettered by their language. The fact is that everyone has access to numerous kinds of discourse within their own language, because of the multiple roles they perform, and the manifold roles and situations they encounter. This diversity of sociolinguistic experience allows the possibility of people enjoying different views of the world as they move from one mode of discourse to another.

Habit and inertia, however, inhibit this comparative process. People are not terribly conscious of linguistic variety, or if they are, they are normative about it: they tend to believe that there is a 'correct' mode of discourse for a given type of situation, either their own, or that of some kind of prestige speaker. Thus speakers are prone not to learn from the plurality of different voices around them. As far as news media are concerned, most people read only one daily newspaper, and watch the news on only one television channel. Readership or audience research has shown that people have set ideas about the 'reliability' of the news, regarding television as less biased than the Press, BBC more impartial than ITV.[1] I mention this only to stress how narrow and normative people's attitudes to the media are. The result of these limitations is that people experience a much more restricted range of mental models than their society affords in potential. They project on to their reading and listening a relatively narrow range of schemata, and because their experience is limited, it is this same small set of schemata that is constantly confirmed in the papers they read. This situation can only lead to complacency and intolerance, and must favour the economic and social status quo.

The method of applied language analysis known as critical linguistics (chapter 1, p. 5) was devised in response to such problems of fixed, invisible ideology permeating language. One of two books written by colleagues at the University of East Anglia, Norwich, and published in 1979, was *Language and Control*; the last chapter of that book coined the expression 'critical linguistics', and gave details of some of the analytic tools that exponents of this model were finding to be illuminating.[2] Critical linguistics seeks, by studying the minute details of linguistic structure in the light of the social and historical situation of the text, to display to consciousness the patterns of belief and value which are encoded in the language – and which are below the threshold of notice for anyone who accepts the discourse as 'natural'. We took the view that *any* aspect of linguistic structure, whether phonological, syntactic, lexical, semantic, pragmatic or textual, can carry ideological significance: and that is the position I adopt here, as indicated by my discussion of the sociolinguistic examples in chapter 3.

Even if, in principle, any aspect of structure could be ideologically significant, as a matter of fact it is predicted by theory, and confirmed by experience, that certain areas of language are particularly implicated in coding social values. The main purpose of this chapter is to define these highly significant areas of linguistic structure, which will be the focus of analysis in the later chapters of the book. I am simply going to give a list of structures, with definitions and illustrations. To avoid a lengthy technical chapter, which readers might find heavy going, each exposition will be quite brief. If brevity gives the chapter a cryptic feel, don't worry: each linguistic category reappears at least once

in the second part of the book, with fuller discussion and exempli-
fication. At this point I simply want to set out a 'menu' of useful
analytic categories, introducing appropriate technical terminology. I will limit the structures introduced in this chapter to just
those which involve some degree of technical unfamiliarity or
theoretical subtlety. Straightforward and accessible topics, for
example the conventions for naming and address, will not be
dealt with here, but will be discussed briefly as and when they
crop up in the following analytic chapters.

I will end the chapter with some cautionary comments on the
practice of analysis. I do not want to give the impression that
critical linguistics is a mechanical procedure which automatically
yields 'objective' interpretations. Critical interpretation requires
historical knowledge and sensitivity, which can be possessed by
human beings but not by machines.

LINGUISTIC TOOLS

As we saw in chapter 3, linguistic theory exists in several different
models, which have widely divergent goals and terminologies.
These linguistic theories simply do different jobs, and it is pointless to worry about whether linguistics is a science, or to attack
linguistics for not being a science, or for falsely claiming to be
one, just because it exists in competing versions – a situation said
to be intolerable in 'real science'. Such anxieties and controversies
merely interfere with the practical work of understanding the
complexities of linguistic structure, an enterprise in which enor-
mous progress has been made since the pioneering linguistics of
Saussure and of Bloomfield. Through the combined if discrete
efforts of linguistics working with a variety of models, we have
learned a great deal about language in general; about the structures
of the world's languages; and in the last twenty-five years, about
sociolinguistic variation within communities; and, at a final micro-
scopic level of analysis, about the details of particular texts.

My attitude to linguistic tools, then, is essentially eclectic. For
the reasons given in chapter 3, the best model for examining the
connections between linguistic structure and social values is the
functional model developed by M. A. K. Halliday and his colleagues, and that is my basis; but I will simplify and alter Halliday's rather forbidding terminology when it suits my purpose,

and add terms and concepts from other models when they will do a particular job better.

The basis of Hallidayan linguistics is a very strong notion of 'function'. It is true that language 'performs functions' in a specific practical sense, i.e. being used distinctively to write headlines, to greet, to make a will, chide the children, and so on. Halliday has in mind a more global concept of 'function', hypothesizing what *in general terms* language does. He proposes that all language performs simultaneously three functions, which he calls 'ideational', 'interpersonal' and textual':

> In the first place, language serves for the expression of content: it has a representational, or, as I would prefer to call it, an *ideational* function. . . . [I]t is through this function that the speaker or writer embodies in language his experience of the phenomena of the real world; and this includes his experience of the internal world of his own consciousness: his reactions, cognitions, and perceptions, and also his linguistic acts of speaking and understanding. . . .
>
> In the second place, language serves what we may call an *interpersonal* function. . . . Here, the speaker is using language as the means of his own intrusion into the speech event: the expression of his comments, his attitudes, and evaluations, and also of the relationship that he sets up between himself and his listener – in particular, the communication role that he adopts, of informing, questioning, greeting, persuading, and the like. . . .
>
> But there is a third function which is in turn instrumental to these two, whereby language is, as it were, enabled to meet the demands that are made on it; I shall call this the *textual* function, since it is concerned with the creation of text. . . . It is through this function that language makes links with itself and with the situation; and discourse becomes possible, because the speaker or writer can produce a text and the listener or reader can recognize one.[3]

I quote these convenient definitions because of their clarity, and for fidelity to Halliday's own position. But setting on one side for a moment the content of the distinctions that they make, it is necessary to find fault with one very unsatisfactory aspect of the way they are formulated in this early paper. Halliday writes here as if language use were a matter of the individual exercise of free will: the 'speaker' 'embodies his experience', 'sets up relationships', 'produces a text', and so on. This is very much a 'free enterprise' model of communication, unwittingly I am sure. We have already seen that the whole dynamic of interaction through language is subject to social determination: content, speaker/writers, listener/readers and roles are largely constructed through language, without much voluntary control. They are derived from the meanings of the discourses (cf. chapter 3, p. 41) associated with the institutions relevant to the production and consumption of the text. For myself, the ideational, interpersonal and textual are sets of social options, not areas of privileged personal choice. (This more social emphasis is in fact explicit in Halliday's more recent writings.[4])

The three functions provide a scheme for classifying linguistic structures according to their communicative roles; the full details do not concern us here, but they may be inspected in one of the many diagrammatic presentations that Halliday offers, or in his comprehensive textbook.[5] The positive consequence of a functional classification, from our point of view, is that all the particular subheadings, the details of syntax, vocabulary, etc., are conceived of functionally: not merely as formally different kinds of structure, but as kinds of structure which are as they are because they do particular jobs. The functions also provide a facility I mentioned above: a prediction by theory of what types of linguistic construction will be particularly revealing for critical linguistics. It is quite clear that the ideational and interpersonal functions are especially valuable for our purposes, since critical linguistics is particularly concerned with the ordering of experience and with the mediation of social relationships and values. I shall now introduce some constructions in these areas that are of particular interest to our critical study of the Press.

TRANSITIVITY

Transitivity – part of the *ideational* function – is a fundamental and powerful semantic concept in Halliday, an essential tool in the analysis of representation, which has already proved extremely illuminating in critical linguistics.[6]

The meaning of Halliday's 'transitivity' differs from the sense of the term in traditional grammar. Traditionally there is a syntactic distinction between transitive and intransitive verbs, depending on whether they take an object or not: (a) 'John kicked the ball' versus (b) 'Mary ran'. But this *syntactic* distinction oversimplifies or neglects some important differences of *meaning* between various types of verb and, therefore, various types of clause. The differences concern what kind of process the verb designates: 'kick' in (a) designates a kind of action which has an effect on another entity, 'the ball'; 'ran' in (b) refers to an action which affects only the actor, 'Mary'. If we add another example, (c) 'Jane is tall', we find a quite different state of affairs encoded, no action but a description of a physical state. A further example, (d) 'Peter meditates', offers a further contrast with (a): here we have a mental process, not a physical action. It emerges that there are many more distinctions of meaning behind transitivity than the simple syntactic distinction of transitive vs intransitive expresses. We will look at the descriptive apparatus for distinguishing some of the types of clause in a moment.

A central insight of Halliday's, made very explicit in his most recent book, is that transitivity is the foundation of representation: it is the way the clause is used to analyse events and situations as being of certain types. And transitivity has the facility to analyse the same event in different ways, a facility which is of course of great interest in newspaper analysis. If we see something, says Halliday, 'perceptually the phenomenon is all of a piece'; but when we talk of it, we must 'analyse it as a semantic configuration' – that is, we must represent it as one particular structure of meaning.[7] Since transitivity makes options available, we are always suppressing some possibilities, so the choice we make – better, the choice made by the discourse – indicates our point of view, is ideologically significant.

Newspapers provide abundant examples of the ideological significance of transitivity. Note the directness of the following three front-page headlines culled from newspapers of 1 July 1986:

(1) **PC shot boy from 9 inches**

(Eastern Daily Press)

(2) **RAID PC SHOT BOY FROM 9 INCHES**
   (a) **SHOT FROM 9 INCHES**
   [inside, next to a picture of the boy]
   (b) **Sniper PC killed tot** [below]

(Sun)

(3) **PC SHOT BOY FROM 9 INCHES**
(a) **Robber's son, five, killed in his bed**

(Daily Express)

and the more complicated form of the openings of the stories themselves:

(4) (a) CRACK police marksman Brian Chester cast aside all his training and experience when he shot dead a little boy by accident, a court heard yesterday.
(b) The jury at Stafford Crown Court was told that five-year-old John Shorthouse was hit in the heart from a distance of just nine inches during an early morning armed raid on his parents' Birmingham home.

(Eastern Daily Press)

(5) A BOY of five was shot through the heart by a police marksman from a range of just NINE INCHES, a court heard yesterday.

(Sun)

(6) A TOP police marksman shot a five-year-old boy through the heart from nine-inch range in a dawn raid on his home a jury was told yesterday.

(Daily Express)

These are prominent reports of the opening of the case against a policeman who was accused of the manslaughter of five-year-old John Shorthouse as the boy lay in bed during an armed police raid on his father's home in August 1985. There is striking agreement in transitivity between the three headlines (1), (2) and (3): all mention the policeman as agent, all assign to him the action verb 'shot', and all assign the role patient to the boy. The only circumstance mentioned is the location 'from 9 inches'. The omission from the headlines of other circumstances, liberally supplied in the sentences which open the reports ((4), (5) and (6)), highlights the basic structure of the clause, which surely amounts to a claim that the policeman did kill the boy, rather than simply that he is accused of doing so. The openings of the reports themselves mitigate the accusation by noting that this is a statement of the prosecutor ((4b) 'was told'), by the use of the passive voice ((5) 'A boy of five was shot') and by wrapping it up in syntactic complexity by mentioning other circumstances ((4a) 'by accident'; (4b) 'in the heart'; etc.). There is a transitivity variance between headline and report, and it is clear which transitivity model is dominant in these papers. (A general proposition decrying violence against young children probably causes this dominance.)

The headlines happen to illustrate in a very clear way the three basic elements in transitivity: a clause is based on a semantic nucleus consisting of an obligatory verb or adjective called a 'process' by Halliday but, following case grammar, a predicate here; the predicate designates the event or state of affairs described by the clause. The predicate is attended by one or more nouns or noun phrases referring to the participants in the event or state of affairs; and, optionally, by one or more circumstances:

(7) (= (1)) **PC** **shot** **boy** **from 9 inches**

  participant *predicate* *participant* *circumstance*

For more detailed analysis of the various kinds of predicates, participants and circumstances, a small simple terminology is needed, and I will briefly present a selection of Halliday's most important terms, borrowing in one or two cases from other models when the term seems to me more suitable or more expressive.

Types of predicate include *actions* such as 'shot' in (1) and the other examples, where the action has an effect on some other participant (classic 'transitives'), or the 'intransitive' 'struggling' in (8), where no other participant is involved:

(8) Through a porthole they will watch the crew of the sinking ship *struggling* in the oily water.

               (*Guardian*, 30 June 1986)

Actions are under the control of agents: 'struggling' is a deliberate activity. 'Sinking' in (8), however, is clearly neither deliberate nor controlled, and such verbs are better simply called *processes*.

Both actions and processes relate to changes in the world: movement, construction, destruction, etc. There are also verbs, and, more often, adjectives, which imply no change or development; we call these *states*. They are italicized in the following examples:

(9) **Irish leader *secure* despite defeat**

               (*Guardian*, 30 June 1986)

(10) ROAST Welsh lamb was given the chop by the Government yesterday because more than two million of the animals are *radioactive*.

(Sun, 21 June 1986)

(11) Choose tough hedera colchica *Paddy's Pride* [original italics] for its *deep and light green* leaves *splashed with yellow*.

(Sun, 21 June 1986)

Actions, processes and states may be *material*, as most of the above: that is to say, external, physical, perceptible. Or they may be *mental*:

(12) President Reagan and his senior advisers meet today at the White House to *decide* [mental action] whether to launch the second military strike in a month against Libya and Colonel Gadafy.

(Guardian, 14 April 1986)

(13) 'I *dream* [mental process] of Hollywood and being a great actress.'

(Daily Mirror, 19 April 1986)

(14) Despite his wounds, the *tough* [mental state] part-time paratrooper held on to the bank robber for five minutes until police arrived.

(Sun, 21 June 1986)

Or they may be verbal:

(15) Mr Richard Luce, the Minister for the Arts, has been unusually sharp in *criticizing* [verbal action] what the University has done.

(Guardian, 30 June 1986)

(16) Three appeal judges *ruled* [verbal action] yesterday that the men were not party to a conspiracy.

(Guardian, 27 June 1986)

(17) As they left for the EEC summit in The Hague yesterday Mrs Thatcher and Sir Geoffrey were still *arguing* [verbal process] about Britain's role in international action against the Pretoria regime.

(Guardian, 27 June 1986)

Politics and the law, which provide a substantial amount of the newspapers' copy, rely heavily on verbal actions and verbal processes for their operation. Debates, negotiations, official statements, submissions, court-room procedures and judgments are verbal practices, and are heavily reported in the Press. Therefore there are many verbs of this kind in the newspapers, and they are an important topic for critical study. (See further, 'speech acts', pp. 87–9)

We now need a simple terminology for the roles that participants play in the transitivity structure of the clause. The doer of an action is termed an *agent*:

(18) (= (1)) **PC shot boy from 9 inches**
(19) *Graham Gooch* gave England's troubled selectors a big boost last night.

(*News of the World*, 30 July 1989)

A number of distinctions need to be drawn for those people and objects that have things done to them, or happen to them, called, as a group, *affected participants*. The most neutral is *object*, where someone or something is affected in a material way by an action or process, and is considered as a physical entity:

(20) Karen's fiance found *her body* at her flat in Church Street, Southwell.

(*Star*, 27 June 1986)

(21) *The top of a reactor* was ripped off by a huge explosion.

(*Sun*, 1 May 1986)

(What role does 'a huge explosion' perform? It causes an effect on the semantic object 'reactor', but it is clearly not an agent since it is not a sentient being. Linguists generally label this active but inanimate role *force*; cf. '*Radiation cloud* **reaches Britain**' (*Guardian*, 3 May 1986), or **More storms** to **lash Britain tonight** (*Observer*, 28 January 1990).)

Notice how in (21) the 'object' participant occurs in the syntactic subject position at the beginning of the sentence; it is not tied to the syntactic object position (after the verb, as in (20)): these semantic roles are independent of the traditional syntactic functions. The same is true of the *patient* role expressed by the italicized noun phrase in (22):

(22) *A GIRL* **DIED TO KEEP RAPE SECRET**

(*Star*, 27 June 1986;
this refers to a suicide, not a murder)

The term patient is generally used to refer to the role of an affected participant who/which is human, or at least animate, and who has something done to them. Of course, the patient role would commonly occur after the verb, as for example does 'boy' in headlines (1), (2) and (3) above, or the italicized patients in (23) and (24):

(23) **FERRET ATTACKS** *TODDLER*

(*Star*, 27 June 1986)

(24) **DID I KILL** *MY MOTHER?*

Concerning the syntactic positioning of different roles, see further 'passive', pp. 77–9.

Another kind of affected participant is one which comes into being as a result of an action or process, rather than being changed by an action or process; we may call this role *result*:

(25) Miners are producing *more coal* with fewer men and are earning bigger bonuses.

(*Sun*, 31 December 1985)

Another positive outcome is encoded in the self-explanatory role 'beneficiary'; e.g. the noun phrase 'England's troubled selectors' in example (19) above, or on one level 'miners' in

(26) (part of (25)) *Miners* . . . are earning bigger bonuses

– while in the other clause they are *agent*:

(27) (part of (25)) *Miners* are producing more coal.

These are the major participant roles which are needed for this study. Others such as *experiencer* and *instrument* will be introduced as necessary.

Finally, *circumstances* are easily dealt with: they are simply expressions indicating the time and place of the event described in the clause:

(28) (=(6)) A TOP police marksman shot a five-year-old boy *through the heart* [place] *from nine-inch range* [place] *in a dawn raid* [time] *on his home* [place] a jury was told *yesterday* [time].

SOME SYNTACTIC TRANSFORMATIONS OF THE CLAUSE

Transitivity analysis is a semantic perspective on the ideas expressed by a clause: we approach it as a proposition about the world, in which an event, situation, relation or attribute is predicated of some participant(s). But a clause is also – and essentially – a basic syntactic unit, a patterned ordering of words and phrases. Syntactic analysis is concerned with position and sequence of elements, rather than their propositional meanings and functions. This is not to say, however, that syntactic ordering is non-significant. Syntax provides for alternative phrasings, and as we have seen, wherever in language alternative variants are permitted – T or V, /r/ or no /r/ – different values come to be associated with the different variants (chapter 3, pp. 33–5). Here I want to introduce the notion of *transformation* to refer to syntactic variation of the type that is interesting to critical linguistics, and mention two specific transformations that are particularly worth looking at in critical analysis: passive and nominal. Following the convention of this chapter, other transformations will be introduced in later chapters as required.[8]

The type of syntactic variation which I am thinking about here is illustrated clearly in the first set of examples cited on pp. 71–2. Contrast (1), (2), (2b) and (3) with (2a) and (3a); for instance:

(29) (=(3)) **PC SHOT BOY FROM 9 INCHES**

versus

(30) (=(3a) **Robber's son, five, killed in his bed**

or

(31) (=(2)) **RAID PC SHOT BOY FROM 9 INCHES**

versus (taking up the story on an inside page of the same paper, and adjacent to a prominent photograph of the child)

(32) (=(2a)) **SHOT FROM 9 INCHES**

These examples illustrate the passive transformation, the main effect of which, compared with the active equivalent, is to switch the positions of the left-hand and right-hand noun phrases, so that the patient occupies the syntactic subject (left-hand) position, which is usually associated with an agent. (There are other potential changes as here, to be noted in a moment.) The process will be crystal clear if I construct an exact passive transformation of (29):

(29) **PC SHOT BOY FROM 9 INCHES**

(33) †BOY WAS SHOT BY PC FROM 9 INCHES
(34) †BOY WAS SHOT FROM 9 INCHES BY PC

(Note that the sign † is used to mark the very few fabricated examples offered in this book.)

It is usually claimed, quite reasonably it seems to me, that actives and passives share the same propositional meaning, differing only in syntactic ordering. Certainly the same predicate types and participant roles are preserved in all the examples we are looking at at the moment, with minor lexical differences which do not affect the propositional structure – 'boy' versus 'robber's son', 'shot' versus 'killed'. But even if we assume equivalence in transitivity and in propositional content, nevertheless, in a *functional* approach, there have to be reasons why the structures differ; or in general terms, why does English have the passive transformation?

A number of functional motivations for the passive will be suggested in later pages. Here, in the original headlines (1), (2) and (3), the active is chosen when the focus is to be on the agent of the action, implying clear responsibility – there seems to be a schema for English which assumes that the left-hand noun phrase refers to an agent unless or until there is evidence to the contrary.[9] The passive constructions, found in the subsidiary headlines and in the opening sentences of some of the reports of the case ((4b), (5)), reorient the story so that it is now about the boy rather than his alleged killer. The passive also allows parts of the clause to be deleted (as transformational terminology puts it). In (30) and (32) the agent is deleted, leaving responsibility unspecified so that the boy's death can be foregrounded. In (32) even the noun phrase referring to the patient is deleted, replaced by a photograph enhancing the poignancy of the boy's fate.

Passive is a common structure in headlines. It saves space, as well as immediately establishing the topic. Agency may be immaterial, or predictable from context, or unknown, and anyway if it is known and is important, it can be specified straight away in the opening of the report. Typical passive headlines, from the *Guardian*, 4 July 1986, are:

(35) **Plans to privatize water dropped**
(36) **EEC budget declared illegal**

In these headlines, it is possible that the agentless passive is chosen not only for brevity but also because of the official or bureaucratic nature of the events referred to.

We move now to the second of the two transformations to be briefly introduced here, nominalization. It has often been observed that English is a 'nominalizing' language. By this is meant that it is structurally possible, and actually common, for predicates (verbs and adjectives) to be realized syntactically as nouns: these are called derived nominals. 'Allegation' is derived from 'allege', 'development' from 'develop', etc. There are also in the basic vocabulary of English (i.e. not 'derived') very many nouns which strictly speaking designate actions and processes, not objects. Nominalization and the use of nouns for actions are in fact endemic, especially in official, bureaucratic and formal modes of discourse, once one has learned to spot these processes. Here are some typical passages from the *Guardian* of 4 July 1986; nominals derived from predicates, and nouns for actions, are italicized:

(37) The Northern Ireland Secretary, Mr Tom King, rejected a *call* in the Commons yesterday to delay the *inquiry* into the Royal Ulster Constabulary until *completion of investigations* into *allegations* against Mr John Stalker, the Greater Manchester deputy chief constable, who was originally heading the RUC *inquiry*.

(38) THE AFRICAN National Congress is bracing itself for a sustained *campaign* by the British, American, and other Western governments to 'draw its teeth' as a *liberation movement*.

As Sir Geoffrey Howe prepares to visit South Africa to try to pre-empt mounting *pressures* for *sanctions* against the white minority regime, *interviews* with senior ANC officials make it clear that the ANC is convinced that a two-pronged Western strategy is now underway.

The first prong is to try to set up some sort of process of *mediation* or *dialogue* as a *replacement* for *sanctions*, with the *argument* that any *tightening* of *sanctions* is premature as long as *talks* are going on. The second is to press the ANC to call off its armed *struggle*, or 'suspend the violence,' in order to create, it will be claimed, a better climate for government *concessions*.

These are routine passages of reporting, which I offer here simply to illustrate how densely packed with nominals the style of a middle-class newspaper is, when its writers are treating serious political topics.

Nominalization is a radical syntactic transformation of a clause, which has extensive structural consequences, and offers substantial ideological opportunities. To understand this, reflect on how much information goes unexpressed in a derived nominal, compared with a full clause: compare, for example, 'allegations' with the fully spelt-out proposition 'X has alleged against Y that Y did A and that Y did B [etc.]'. Deleted in the nominal form are the participants (who did what to whom?), any indication of time – because there is no verb to be tensed – and any indication of modality – the writer's views as the truth or the desirability of the proposition (see pp. 85–7). In *Language and Control*, we claimed that nominalization was, inherently, potentially mystificatory; that it permitted habits of concealment, particularly in the areas of power-relations and writers' attitudes.

If *mystification* is one potential with nominalization, another is *reification*. Processes and qualities assume the status of *things:* impersonal, inanimate, capable of being amassed and counted like capital, paraded like possessions. Fittingly, a self-made millionaire interviewed by the *Guardian* (5 July 1986) copes with a question about his personal qualities using a string of nouns and derived nominals:

> (39) My first question was direct. 'What have you got that fifty million other people haven't?'
> *'Ambition, imagination, drive, energy, determination, courage,'* he replied without blushing.

LEXICAL STRUCTURE

In Halliday's linguistic theory, vocabulary or lexis is a major determinant of ideational structure. Quite simply, the vocabulary of a language, or of a variety of a language, amounts to a map of the objects, concepts, processes and relationships about which the culture needs to communicate. It is usual to think of vocabulary as a 'list' of words, and that is in one sense realistic, since vocabulary inventorizes the ideas we may speak of. The image of a list is encouraged by the existence and importance in our culture of dictionaries, alphabetical compilations which claim more or less exhaustive coverage of our word-stock. The A-Z organization is of course merely a convenience for ease of reference; no one would claim that it has any semantic or cultural status as a structural principle. But vocabulary does indeed possess structure, though not readily observable on the surface (see the set of carpentry terms, p. 55). That is why I prefer to think of it as a 'map' rather than a 'list'.

There is a very useful traditional distinction in philosophical semantics which clarifies the status of word-meaning: the distinction between *reference* and *sense*.[10] Reference is a relationship between a word or phrase and some aspect of the material or mental world, between the word 'dog' and some individual canine, Rover or Fido. The relationship of reference exists only when language is being actually used; it is not an inherent part of the meaning of a word. This is a very important point: a lot of difficulties in semantics have been caused by misguided attempts to understand the notion of word-meaning in terms of the objects or concepts a word may be used to refer to. How, in terms of reference, to you explain the fact that the word 'dog' can be used equally to designate such very different phenomena as a Great Dane on the one hand and a chihuahua on the other? Disabling theoretical problems of this kind can easily be imagined, and it is unnecessary for me to go into them any further.

Sense, on the other hand, defines meaning as a relationship *between words* rather than between words and the world. We are indebted to Saussure for clarifying the basic notion of sense-relationships; but his term is *valeur*, 'value'. He uses the metaphor of currency to explain the idea. The value of a £1 coin is not determined solely by the goods for which it can be exchanged; more important is the fact that it is not £5, not 50p, not 1p, and so on, though it has a specific arithmetical relationship with each of these units. (The currency analogy also makes it clear that meaning has nothing to do with the physical characteristics of the sign: just as you could not tell that a £5 note is worth five times as much as a £1 coin by looking at them, weighing them or tasting them, so you could not tell from the size of the words that the long word 'micro-organism' designates a minute creature whereas the short word 'whale' is used to refer to a very large animal.) Returning to the relationships between elements in a system, it is with words as it is with currency units: the value or sense of a word is given by its place within a system of related terms; 'dog' is defined as not 'cat', not 'horse', not 'human', more general than 'poodle' or 'peke', more specific than 'animal' or 'mammal', and so on. Since the notion of 'sense' has been generally accepted, progress in modern lexical semantics has been largely a matter of elaborating proposals for capturing the types of sense-relationships.[11]

Sense-relations within systems explain how it is that the vocabulary of a language is a structured system, rather than just the arbitrary list that the dictionary makes it seem to be. (*Roget's Thesaurus* is a closer model.) These relations provide the structure of the 'map'. The map metaphor is worth pursuing just a little. A map is a symbolic representation of a territory. The signs it employs – systems of lines, colours, shadings, images of trees or lighthouses, letters and numbers – figure the area in terms of features which interest the consumers of the map, and in this respect different maps vary considerably. For example, maps drawn specifically for motorists generally do not represent railways, since these are thought to be irrelevant for the purpose; maps for holidaymakers include information about beauty spots and historic sites. The meaning and structure of the map are not governed by the physical characteristics of the landscape, but by the structural conventions appropriate to figuring the territory for a specific social purpose.

Vocabulary can be regarded, in the spirit of the preceding chapter, as a representation of the world *for* a culture; the world as perceived according to the ideological needs of a culture. Like the map, it works first by segmentation: by partitioning the material continuum of nature and the undifferentiated flux of thought into slices which answer to the interests of the community (recall the quotations from Edward Sapir and Edmund Leach, chapter 3, pp. 28–9). Use of each term crystallizes and normalizes the essentially artificial slices which are cut out of the cake of the world. It is an elementary, but fundamental, task for the critical analyst to note, in the discourse s/he is studying, just what terms habitually occur, what segments of the society's world enjoy constant discursive attention. Clusters of related terms are found to mark out distinct kinds of preoccupation and topic. Here are some sets taken from different articles on the front page of the *Guardian*, 4 July 1986. In each case, I have quoted the first sentence of the article with the relevant lexical items italicized, and then listed only the words which fall into the lexical sets:

(40) Cattle in Surrey, Kent and North Yorkshire have been found with *radioactivity* at more than 10 times the *danger level* for human consumption.
The *tests* . . . *thyroid glands* . . . *iodine 131* . . . *340,000 becquerels per kilo* . . . *limit* . . . *contamination* . . . *thyroid* . . . *tests* . . . *levels of iodine 131 and caesium 131* . . . *radiation.*

(41) The *Solicitor-General*, Sir Patrick Mayhew, insisted last night that *investigations* into Mr Kevin Taylor, a Manchester businessman, were separate from *inquiries* into Mr John Stalker, the *deputy chief constable* of Greater Manchester.
. . . *allegations* . . . *suspended from duty* . . . *alleged* . . . *criminal associates* . . . *police* . . . *interview* . . . *deputy chief constable* . . . *preliminary report* . . . *Director of Public Prosecutions* . . . *investigation* . . . *deputy chief constable* . . . *inquiries* . . . *preliminary report* . . . *DPP* . . . *charges* . . . *lines of inquiry* . . . *solicitors* . . . *suggestion* . . . *involved* . . . *police inquiry* . . . *inquiry* . . . *DPP* . . . *report* . . . *suggestion* . . . *report* . . . *questioned* . . . *officers* . . . *police* . . . *conducting the inquiry* . . . *ask* . . . *deputy chief constable* . . . *Royal Ulster Constabulary* . . . *suggestions* . . . *investigations* . . . *alleged* . . . *suspects* . . . *police officers* . . . *reported statements* . . . *police force.*

And from the Communist *Morning Star*, 1 May 1986:

(42) THE Morning Star sends *May Day* greetings to *working people* throughout the world. This is the 100th anniversary of *May Day* as a *labour movement* festival.
. . . *a world socialist system* . . . *the working class* . . . *state power* . . . *working people* . . . *Socialist countries* . . . *international differences* . . . *the heyday of imperialism* . . . *colonial or semi-colonial slavery* . . . *imperialism* . . . *direct colonial rule* . . . *colonies* . . . *political independence* . . . *economic domination* . . . *colonialism* . . . *neo-colonialism* . . . *the third world* . . . *imperialism* . . . *developed capitalist countries* . . . *the organized working class* . . . *multinational capitalism* . . . *capitalism* . . . *the working class* . . . *welfare state* . . . *publicly-owned industries* . . . *trade unions* . . . *reformism* . . . *class collaboration* . . . *right-wing Labour leaders* . . . *big business* . . . *the struggle* . . . *progressive left* . . . *labour movement* . . . *the left* . . . *The Communist Party* . . .

> *Marxism . . . social development . . . class struggle . . . organized working class . . . Socialism . . . disunity . . . class understanding . . . the working class . . . big business . . . class action . . . capitalism's problems . . . the road to Socialism.*

There are three distinct lexical registers in these examples: a scientific one associated with the fields of nuclear physics and pathology; a forensic one concerned with police investigative procedure; and a political register in the field of applied Marxist theory. Some of the words just quoted have a highly specific technical application in their field: 'becquerels', 'police inquiry', 'labour movement', and the like. Other words are more generally used ('ask', 'struggle'): these latter, less technical terms are coloured by their contexts, so that, cumulatively, they contribute to consolidating the register. It is presumably part of our communicative or discursive competence to recognize these registers, and to be aware that they mark off socially and ideologically distinct areas of experience: they have a categorizing function.

Categorization by lexical structure is recognized by Halliday when, diagramming the elements of ideational structure, he speaks of 'taxonomic organization of vocabulary'. Vocabulary not only sorts out experience in general terms, it makes detailed distinctions between classes of concept. This sort of structural opposition can be seen clearly in example (42), where the vocabulary dichotomizes political organizations into two groups, 'socialism' on the one hand and 'imperialism/capitalism' on the other, and predicates a 'struggle' between them. We will see that categorization by vocabulary is an integral part of the reproduction of ideology in the newspapers, and particularly, that it is the basis of discriminatory practice when dealing with such so-called 'groups' of people as women, young people, 'ethnic minorities', and so forth: see chapters 6 and 8.

The importance of basic-level terms in the practice of categorization has already been noticed (chapter 4, pp. 55–6).

Just two further lexical processes will be mentioned briefly at this point. First, there is re-lexicalization, the promotion of a new term where it is claimed that a new concept is at issue:

(43) The Labour party is preparing to jettison its commitment to traditional nationalization in favour of a new concept of 'social ownership'.

(Guardian, 7 July 1986)

Second, we must mention over-lexicalization, which is the existence of an excess of quasi-synonymous terms for entities and ideas that are a particular preoccupation or problem in the culture's discourse. The proliferation of (often pejorative) words for designating women has often been mentioned: see chapter 6 and notes.

INTERPERSONAL ELEMENTS: MODALITY

We now move from the ideational function, the representation of propositional content, to the interpersonal, the mediation of personal roles and social relationships. The boundary between these two Hallidayan functions is not impermeable, of course. On the one hand, it is the essence of representation that it is always representation from some ideological point of view, as managed through the inevitable structuring force of transitivity and lexical categorization; on the other, interpersonal practices always have some statement to make, and often work by implied propositions or presuppositions.

Even if the line between the ideational and the interpersonal is fuzzy, it is worth drawing, because there are some devices which are clearly either one thing or the other. The first clearly interpersonal feature to be mentioned is modality (a term which I use in a more traditional sense than Halliday does).[12] Modality can informally be regarded as 'comment' or 'attitude', obviously by definition ascribable to the source of the text, and explicit or implicit in the linguistic stance taken by the speaker/writer. It is useful for our purposes to distinguish four types of comment. They have technical names in modal logic, but in plain terms they have to do with (a) *truth*, with (b) *obligation*, with (c) *permission* and with (d) *desirability*. The distinctions – and some overlaps – are clearly seen in what are called in traditional grammar the modal auxiliary verbs or modal auxiliaries, italicized in the following examples.

(a) *Truth*   A speaker/writer must always indicate or imply a commitment to the truth (or otherwise) of any proposition s/he utters, or to a prediction of the degree of likelihood of an event described taking place or having taken place. Truth modality varies in strength along a scale from absolute confidence –

(44) The Tories *will not* make an election pledge to restore capital punishment for murderers and killer terrorists.

(*Daily Express*, 18 April 1986)

– down through various degrees of lesser certainty:

(45) The best bet at Edinburgh this afternoon *could be* No Restraint (4.30) in the Honest Toun Maiden Stakes.

(*Guardian*, 7 July 1986)

A straightforward truth claim does not, in fact, need any explicit modal verb; this is not to say that there is no modality, but that in the normal case, it does not need to be expressed:

(46) Since Malaysia introduced the death penalty for drug trafficking in 1975 36 people have been executed.

(*Guardian*, 7 July 1986)

Modality can also be indicated by some adverbs –

(47) The youngster is *certainly* bred to go, being by King of Spain out of Edna who was a useful speedster on soft ground.

(*Daily Express*, 18 April 1986)

– or by modal adjectives:

(48) Without [Nelson Mandela's] blessing, it is *unlikely* that any black leader in South Africa can be persuaded to meet the British Foreign Secretary apart from Chief Gatsha Buthelezi.

(*Guardian*, 7 July 1986)

(b) *Obligation*   In this case, the speaker/writer stipulates that the participants in a proposition *ought to* perform the actions specified in the proposition:

(49) The campaign against terrorism and its sponsors *must be* continuous. No single blow will be enough. Terrorist reprisals *must be* punished in their turn.

(*Daily Express*, 18 April 1986)

Other modal auxilaries used to convey this meaning are 'should' and 'ought to'.

(c) *Permission*   Here the speaker/writer bestows permission to do something on the participant(s). Interestingly, the auxiliaries used also have a more neutral usage under (a) *truth* or *prediction:* 'may', 'can':

> (50) Any time in the next ten years you *can* switch the Plan into, say, a savings scheme.
>
> (Insurance advertisment, *Guardian*, 7 February 1987)

(d) *Desirability* The speaker/writer indicates approval or disapproval of the state of affairs communicated by the proposition. Implicit in (b) and (c), this modality is explicit in a range of evaluative adjectives and adverbs. It is endemic in the Press, particularly in editorials, and especially in the tabloids and the right-wing 'qualities':

> (51) HOME SECRETARY Douglas Hurd's plan to beat the prison officers' dispute – the mass release of crooks – is *barmy*.
>
> (*Sun*, 19 April 1986)

> (52) So the question which should be asked this weekend is not whether Mrs Thatcher was *right* to authorize the American raid but whether she was right, alone among West European leaders, to continue to put the American connection above everything else. Having absolutely no faith in the capacity of Western Europe to resist the Soviet Union in the long run without the presence of American troops on this side of the Atlantic, I believe that she was [*right*].
>
> (*Sunday Telegraph*, 20 April 1986)

(The editorial from which (52) is extracted is signed 'Peregrine Worsthorne, Editor', a gesture which may have some bearing on the directness of the modality.)

INTERPERSONAL ELEMENTS: SPEECH ACTS

Whereas traditional linguistics had regarded language as primarily a channel for communicating ideas or facts about the world, modern trends emphasize that language is also a *practice*, a mode of action. As we are saying something, we are also doing something through speaking. This aspect of the interpersonal function of language has been studied particularly by linguistic philosophers, and notably by J. L. Austin – whose marvellous title *How to Do Things with Words* sums up this perspective – and, following him, J. R. Searle.[13] To Austin and Searle we owe the notion of 'illocutionary act' or (a slightly more elegant label) 'speech act'. Since newspapers both contain and report speech acts, it will be useful to describe and illustrate the concept briefly.

A speech act is a form of words which, if spoken or written in appropriate conditions, and under appropriate conventions, actually constitutes the performance of an action. Austin calls them 'performatives': classic examples include utterances such as

> (53) †I declare you man and wife.
> (54) †I name this ship *Rambo Ronnie*.
> (55) †I promise to pay you £5.

where the utterance literally effects the act referred to: Peter and Jane are thereby married, the ship is named, the speaker commits herself to pay the addressee £5. Notice that, for utterances like (53)–(55) you cannot sensibly ask, 'Is that true?' (as you can an ordinary declarative sentence of English, or logicians' favourites such as 'Snow is white'); the success of a speech act is judged according to the appropriateness or felicitousness of its performance, not its truth-value. The conventions for the felicitous performance of a speech act include some highly specific requirements, such as the following: (53) works only if the speaker is a priest, registrar or sea captain, if the parties concerned are legally marriageable, and so on; (55) constitutes a genuine act of promising only if the speaker is sincere, can afford £5, etc. Thus speech acts are integrally enmeshed with the systems of conventions that constitute a social and political world, and speech act analysis offers critical linguistics a direct point of entry into some practices through which society's ideas and rules are constructed.

Examples (53)–(55) might give the impression that speech acts are formulaic expressions to be uttered in rather routine, ceremonial settings. This is not so. Austin's enquiries led him to believe that there are no such limitations; that there are verbs naming many thousands of speech acts in English: 'request', 'stipulate', 'ban', 'declare', 'announce', 'solicit', etc. The existence of so many verbs naming acts of speech testifies to the importance of linguistic practices in human interaction, and in self-presentation; and this centrality of speech acts as *events* is borne out by the high density of speech act verbs in newspapers, society's major mode of representation of its important and habitual processes; for example:

(56) In the Commons, Mr Kinnock *indicated* deep concern about the American action [against Libya]. He *demanded* that the evidence on which the Goverment's decision was based should be *published, accused* the Foreign Secretary of possible duplicity in [?]*dealing with* European allies, and *asked* Mrs Thatcher to join him in *condemning* the raid.

(*Guardian*, 16 April 1986)

This chapter has provided some explanatory notes, and illustrations, of some aspects of linguistic structure which my experience has shown to be quite often involved in the construction of representations, in signifying beliefs and values when writers are reporting or commenting on the world. The list may seem rather formidable to a non-linguist reading straight through the chapter, but the main categories are not difficult to grasp when they are practised in the course of doing analysis, particularly in a classroom or discussion situation where several people are working together. The main ideas, like transitivity, are simple and powerful, and they are easily and memorably represented by devices such as tabular presentations of structural patterns (e.g. p. 143 and cf. p. 173). Nor are these linguistic structures arcane, highly technical concepts offering a 'new knowledge' which has to be learned by rote, as some technical concepts in science. Rather, they are systematic ways of organizing and speaking about knowledge which one already has, the intuitive knowledge of linguistic structure which one has developed as a competent speaker of a language: knowledge which is usually unconscious, and is simply brought to the surface for analysis and reflection by the practice of linguistic criticism.

Those comments were meant to be reassuring. I know for a fact that critical linguistics is not technically difficult, and that a lot of mileage can be gained from a relatively small amount of technical apparatus, even in the hands of non-specialists (I regularly teach this approach to non-linguists – sociologists, historians, literature students, and so on). The reassurance given, however, a caution must follow. No catalogue of linguistic structures such as that given in this chapter makes up a 'discovery procedure': a procedure which, applied to data, will automatically tell you something about the data that you did not know before. It is no good learning what nominalization is, say, then searching for all the nominalizations in a text and expecting the list so produced to tell you something. It won't. The reason is that there is no constant relationship between linguistic structure and its semiotic significance. A preponderance of passives, for instance, or of clauses lacking in human agents, or of generic sentences, plural nouns, or whatever, will mean one thing in one text and another in another. The significance of discourse derives only from an interaction between language structure and the context in which it is used: so the discourse analyst must always be prepared to document the circumstances in which communication takes place, and consider their relevance to the structure of the text. In the case of newspaper discourse, this means finding out what one can about the institutional and economic structure of the newspaper industry, its political relations, the political or other relevant circumstances of the events being reported, and so on. The analyst must be very well informed, and must have learned by experience how to bring the relevant knowledge to the process of interpretation. I do not know of any *procedure* for guiding this essential use of contextual knowledge. If there is any difficulty about the practice of critical linguistics, it is this contextualizing part of it, not the linguistic technique; the contextualizing is a matter of knowledge, experience and intuition. In this book we are at least dealing with familiar materials, and contemporary public life. Other kinds of discourse would be less accessible, and would require an activity of historical reconstruction.

Chapter 6

Discrimination in discourse: gender and power

PERSONALIZATION

In chapter 2, I noted personalization as an important tendency in the Press. Happenings (or fantasies) involving individual persons stand a high chance of becoming news stories: elite persons doing something spectacular or mundane, ordinary people to whom something unusual happens, even anonymous people caught up in some more general process (e.g. stranded holidaymakers, victims of an earthquake). One issue of the *Sun*, for example (11 July 1986), contains stories about Rod Stewart, Boy George, various members of Boy George's family, Ian Botham, Leon Brittan and Geoffrey Howe, Selina Scott, Goldie Hawn, Princess Diana, Ian MacGregor, Jan-Michael Vincent, Liza Minnelli, Linda Lovelace (all celebrities); and in specialized pages, hosts of pop personalities, television personalities and sports people; back on the news pages, we find obstetrician Wendy Savage, 'helicopter chief' Alan Bristow, two East German spies, a 'Page Three girl' banned from helping at a church fête, a man who fell from an office block, trades unionist John Macreadie, an 86-year-old man who has bought his council house, a solicitor accused of 'dishonestly trying to obtain shares by deception', a sick man flown to America by his friends, a man accused of supplying heroin, a man who 'shot dead his wife and then killed himself', a man who tried to jump out of a plane, two schoolteachers ridiculed by the newspaper, a 'yachtswoman' lost in the Atlantic, a man sacked for being two minutes late for work, an electrocuted angler, a woman locked into handcuffs, an American who forced a nurse to switch off his father's life-support machine, etc. While the paper is packed with items about individuals, there is almost no report of any general or extended processes.

The concreteness of individual reference is heightened, especially in the tabloids, by supplying personal details such as age, residence, job and personal appearance – with a liberal use of photographs. But this specificity on the surface is something of an illusion. The world presented by the popular Press, like the world we feel we live in, is a culturally organized set of categories, rather than a collection of unique individuals. If we imagined the world as a vast collection of individual things and people, we would be overwhelmed by detail. We manage the world, make sense of it, by categorizing phenomena, including people. Having established a person as an example of a type, our relationship with that person is simplified: we think about the person in terms of the qualities which we attribute to the category already pre-existing in our minds. In so far as we regard the category of person as displaying strongly predictable attributes or behaviour, the category may harden into a stereotype, an extremely simplified mental model which fails to see individual features, only the values that are believed to be appropriate to the type. This is, of course, a basic ideological process at work. A socially constructed model of the world is projected on to the objects of perception and cognition, so that essentially the things we see and think about are constructed according to a scheme of values, not entities directly perceived.

If we look again at our informal sample, we find that categorization is just as much present, though not so salient, as is individual reference. It is a simple analysis to pick out the words and phrases that are used to categorize people and to predicate attributes of them, and here is the beginning of a list from the first three pages of the same copy of the *Sun* newspaper:

> rock star, model, singer, cricket star, England all-rounder, friend, junkie star, junkie, pop tycoon, drugs expert, multi-millionaire, singer, senior police officer, terrorists, suicide squad, soldiers, NALGO union chiefs, white-collar workers, workers, ex-Cabinet Minister, former Trade Secretary, Foreign Secretary, man, MPs, militant, leftie, leader, red-blooded Portuguese Pedro's [*sic*], charity girl, priest, Page Three beauty, magician, charity worker, zany film star, DJ, top Radio 1 DJ, fans, bosses, spokesman, top amateur motor racing driver,

spokesman, premier, husband, BBC glamour girl, Beeb boss, US telly chiefs, newsgirl, colleague.

I don't want to analyse this particular material in any detail, having other texts to work on more thoroughly in a moment; I cite it simply as an illustration of the dense presence in newspaper discourse of category labels, and of the kinds of labels that occur.

Category labels such as these tell us a good deal about the structure of the ideological world represented by a newspaper or by a certain type of newspaper. In a simple way, they provide a list of the preoccupations of the paper, and it would be illuminating to take a large sample and note what labels occur and do not occur, and the relative frequencies of those that do occur. It would also be interesting to notice *how* categories are mentioned: most of the expressions in the small list above are in a colloquial register ('fan', etc.), a few are straight and serious ('senior police officer'), some are explicitly derogatory ('junkie', 'leftie', with the belittling suffix ' –ie') or implicitly so 'newsgirl' referring to an adult woman). Detailed analysis would reveal more structure: 'Page Three beauty' is associated with 'magician', 'BBC glamour girl' is opposed to 'Beeb boss', and so on (the syntax of the texts makes this clear in a way that the list does not). These associations and dissociations are the surface-structure outcrops of underlying abstract paradigms of the discourse, the values and relationships that underpin this particular newspaper's theory of the way the world is organized and of the way it should be.

DISCRIMINATION

I want now to make the specific point that categorization is a discursive basis for practices of *discrimination*. Discrimination is a practice which affects individual subjects, providing unequal chances of jobs, higher education, money, attention by the police and punishment by the courts, bestowing esteem unequally. But although it is the individual person who is at the sharp end of discriminatory practices, 'justification' for such practices, where offered, is given not in terms of the individual, but in terms of some assumed *group* to which the person allegedly belongs; and a stereotype which the culture has conventionally assigned to the 'group' is applied prejudicially to the individual. The stereotype might be expressed as a set of 'common-sense' propositions which the culture possesses but rarely expresses: †'We can't appoint Mrs X to this position because Mrs X, although qualified, is a young married woman and we all know that they leave to have children after a year or two when the furniture is paid for.' Mrs X is discriminated against, the job unfairly withheld because she is perceived not as her own person with her own experience and qualifications, but as the carrier of attributes which the employer has stereotypically assigned to the 'group' to which she supposedly belongs. Now I would argue that 'groups' such as 'young married women', 'immigrants', 'teachers', 'capitalists' and 'royalty' are imaginary, socially constructed concepts, almost as fictitious as trolls at bridges and princesses in towers. 'Group' is an instrument for handling discrimination, for sorting unequally, and it acquires much of its apparent solidity by being traded in discourse. (Note that these fictitious 'groups' have conceptual solidity for the culture, but typically do not display social solidarity: their members do not necessarily associate with one another – Mrs X's social affiliations, with other young married women or not, are irrelevant to the employer's categorization of her.)

The power of discourse in facilitating and maintaining discrimination against 'members' of 'groups' is tremendous. Language provides names for categories, and so helps to set their boundaries and relationships; and discourse allows these names to be spoken and written frequently, so contributing to the apparent reality and currency of the categories. I have explained that vocabulary is taxonomically organized: the sense-relations among words effect a classification of experience and ideas appropriate to the ideology of the community of the discourse. Vocabulary divides 'actress' from 'actor', the ' –ess' ending marking 'actress' as a special and unusual case; classifies 'immigrant' as a special and deviant group, just by providing a word for it (what is the opposite term, for the 'normal' case of being a citizen?); awkwardly lexicalizes 'lady doctor', making overt, in the awkwardness of the term, society's prejudicial sense of the irregularity of the idea of a woman practising a profession. In this chapter, I will be mainly looking at lexical instruments of categorization and discrimination such as these, but it is important to stress at this point that it is not only vocabulary which contributes to the reproduction of discrimination in discourse. There are also ready-made syntactic structures for stating the alleged attributes of members of categories: the proverbial style of syntax of 'gentlemen prefer blondes', the non-restrictive adjective + noun structure of 'dumb blondes'. We can use such syntactic forms to articulate the general propositions which summarize our ideology. And transitivity is of central importance in, for example, its ability to place members of a particular group consistently in subject or in object position, depending on the communicative needs of the ongoing discourse, and reproducing asymmetrical power-relations among members of a community: see chapter 8. Few of the operative linguistic structures are as blatant in asserting prejudice as 'blacks are undisciplined' (which I heard in a discussion programme on television recently); most are unnoticeable and require an activity of criticism to bring them to consciousness.

In this chapter, I am going to offer some illustration and analysis of the representation of women in the newspapers. Even a small sample, collected routinely without hunting for particularly dramatic examples, suggests that women are constituted in discourse as a special group with its own peculiar characteristics, set out from the population as a whole for exceptional evaluation. Irrationality, familial dependence, powerlessness and sexual and physical excess are some of the attributes predicated of women; these are aspects of the paradigm for this 'group' which have been found also by other writers on sexism in language.

There is now a substantial body of writings on this topic, ranging from descriptive to polemical works. Books on the subject are lively and accessible; they are the sort of book that I would expect readers of my book to enjoy reading, so I will summarize their concerns only very briefly here.[1] It has long been observed in anthropological linguistics that there are many communities which possess different varieties of language, or even different languages, used separately by men and by women; that women and men often possess different vocabularies; and that different kinds of expression are used to refer to men and to women. Contemporary writers on the subject of sexism in language take this observation much further, demonstrating that even in languages such as English which do not have obviously sex-differentiated varieties, gender is thoroughly encoded both in language used by women and, perhaps more so, in language used about women. This coding is found in almost every dimension of linguistic structure, so thoroughly ingrained is it. Linguists and feminists have been concerned with observations such as the following (not all of which are strongly documented, but the overall picture and case are overwhelmingly plausible):

- the use of male expressions generically to include reference to females, or even exclusively to refer to females: 'man', 'chairman', 'spokesman';
- similarly, the use of the masculine pronoun 'he' to refer to females in a generic context: †'a writer must ensure that *he* does not make libellous statements'; except, prejudicially, in conventionally 'female' contexts: †'a cook must keep *her* utensils scrupulously clean';
- the use of marked expressions containing extra morphemes or words to refer to females, implying deviance or irregularity or at least drawing attention gratuitously to the sex of the person referred to: 'actress', 'poetess', 'lady doctor', 'female accountant'; marked forms for men are almost non-existent, occurring only in contexts where the role is perceived as deviant: 'male nurse';
- the use of diminutive and juvenile forms to refer to or address women: 'Winnie', 'sweetie', 'girl';
- titles and address forms: the choice between 'Mrs' and 'Miss', forcing a woman to declare her marital status (sexual availability) where a man, with just 'Mr', does not have to do so; the taking of the man's name on marriage: 'Mrs Sandra Smith' or even 'Mrs John Smith';
- the over-lexicalization of women: there are many more terms for women than for men, thus indicating that the culture regards women as having an abnormal status; many of these terms are sexually abusive ('slut', 'whore'), dehumanizing ('skirt', 'piece'), trivializing ('pet', 'chick',) or signify possession by a male ('wife', 'mistress');
- some of the most offensive abusive terms, generally applied, have origins or overtones in obscene references to females: 'cunt', 'tit', 'get stuffed';
- there is said to be an asymmetry as between men and women in the terminology available to describe certain experiences, e.g. sexual intercourse: 'penetrate' but not 'enclose';
- as far as accent is concerned, women hypercorrect and over-report (cf. Trudgill's research, mentioned on p. 34);
- women's speech is said by some linguists (e.g. Robin Lakoff) to be more polite than men's (euphemistic), to contain more

emotive and aesthetic terms and to favour certain syntactic forms (e.g. tag-questions) and expressive phonetic forms (e.g. rising intonation). More empirical work needs to be done around these claims.[2]

The present chapter accepts the general claim that linguistic usage is sexist, responding to the ideological paradigms in discourse which assign women special, deviant status in certain respects.

The critical linguist has to be on the look-out for material. My usual habit is to keep track of events every day by paying attention to radio and TV news, and buying a complete set of newspapers when some event of major importance, or likely significance for my work, is brewing up. At the point when I knew I was going to write about categorization and discrimination, the 1986 New Year's Honours List was in the air, so I looked at the papers for 31 December 1985, confident at least that a large number of people were going to be mentioned, with an emphasis on roles and prestige. Besides the Honours List, I also studied some other major stories and articles on that day; they provided different but related perspectives on the topic of discrimination. In this respect, my experience of working on this set of newspapers was absolutely typical of what I found throughout this study: I selected the papers with one particular topic or story in mind, and discovered that materials elsewhere in the papers turned out to be just as revealing for the issues on which I was currently concentrating. That this happened does not seem to me to be merely attributable to coincidence; I think it shows the pervasiveness of paradigms, their persistent presence regardless of the specific content of stories. The ubiquity of paradigms is a subject to which I will refer further in chapters 9 and 10.

Turning now to the sample of 31 December 1985, let us first look briefly at clause-structure in some headlines. Recall that a clause consists of a *verb* (V) indicating the *predicate* – action, state or process – and one or more *noun phrases* (NP) designating participants; plus, optionally, noun phrases, prepositional phrases or adverbs indicating *circumstances;* thus:

(1) **Soccer-blaze heroes** [NP] **are honoured** [V]

   (Daily Express)

(2) **Zia** [NP] **repeals** [V] **martial law** [NP] **in Pakistan** [PrepP]

   (The Times)

Often, in headlines, an action is expressed with a noun rather than a verb:

(3) **Maggie's** [NP] **honours snub** [V→N] **for Geldof**

(Sun)

But this syntactic choice does not affect the semantic structure: 'snub' designates an action, 'Maggie' is clearly the agent.

Some simple analysis will reveal a lot about the categorization of participants. Three questions are particularly interesting. First of all, what kinds of participants occur in subject and object position? Characteristically, people with authority are treated as subjects (semantically, *agents*), while those with less power occur as objects (*patients, beneficiaries*), and that is indeed the case in these few random examples: President Zia and Prime Minister Thatcher are syntactic subjects and semantic agents, whereas Bob Geldof (pop star fund-raiser for African famine victims) is syntactic object and has the less powerful semantic role of beneficiary (or non-beneficiary!). The 'soccer-blaze heroes' (hospital staff who tended the injured after the fire at Bradford City football ground in May 1985) seem to occupy an intermediate position. Semantically they have the institutionally weak role of beneficiary, but they are placed in syntactic subject position, perhaps in acknowledgement of their initiative and toil at Bradford. Note that the honour-bestowing agent is not mentioned in the headline (a discreet possibility with the English passive construction), though the context of the article makes it clear that sentence (1) like (3), refers to the 1986 New Year's Honours List.

Second, with what types of verb are the various categories of participant associated? Here again, discourse distinguishes the powerful from the disfavoured. Only persons with great constitutional authority can repeal laws (2), so, on the basis of the verb selected, one would realize that Zia was a person of great power, even if one did not know who he was. And 'honour' in the other two headlines presupposes an asymmetrical relationship: bestowing honours is a function of power, receiving them implies dependency (for the occasion). So the categorization of participants is reinforced by the verbs that they attend. Those who are disfavoured and discriminated against are likely to be associated with pejorative or at least low-status verbs and adjectives: see below for examples.

Third, what kinds of expressions (names, occupational labels, etc.) are used to refer to the participants? Different styles of *naming* are conventionally associated with different social values in English, and in a systematic way; this is a highly charged sociolinguistic indicator, like the options between the second-person pronouns *tu* and *vous* in French, *du* and *Sie* in German. At issue are questions of power, distance, formality, solidarity, intimacy, casualness. However, a cautionary point must be stressed. Interpretation of such data as names and pronouns is an extremely delicate process, dependent on a precise knowledge of context (just as *using* the alternative forms is a very delicate matter). Although the forms and meanings concerned are systematic, they are not unambiguous: for example, French *tu* can signify either intimacy or authority, depending on whether it is spoken by one lover, or sibling (e.g.), to another, or by a powerful person (e.g. teacher) to a powerless one (e.g. pupil). It is a fundamental principle of critical linguistics that *there is no invariant relationship between form and meaning:* a linguistic form does not have a single, constant meaning, but rather a range of potential significances-in-context. This context-dependency is illustrated in the present materials. The diminutive form of the first name, 'Maggie', is the standard reference to the Prime Minister of the time of writing, Mrs Margaret Thatcher, in the right-wing popular Press, and in that particular context it signifies a friendly intimacy; used in the *Daily Mirror*, however, which claims to represent interests of the Left, it might connote casualness, or disrespect. Compare the use of 'Winnie' in examples (6)-(8) below, and my commentary. The possibilities with first names and diminutives are not quite the same for men. I suspect that it is more difficult to apply first names and diminutives to men than to women, though the alternative significances would be similar in the two cases; and more difficult to apply last names alone to women, with different significance. 'Zia' and 'Geldof' are formal ways of referring to male public figures. A newspaper reference to 'Thatcher' might be interpreted as indicating dissociation.

The case of the young, female, South African-born but nominally British athlete Zola Budd (sorry about the category labels, but I have to mention all the parameters) illustrates how the distinction between first and last name for women can symbolize a polarization around the issue of solidarity and dissociation. In July 1986, black African nations, incensed at the British government's refusal to impose economic sanctions on South Africa, protested against Zola Budd's participation in the 1986 Edinburgh Commonwealth Games. The Press reported the controversy extensively, generally calling her 'Zola', thereby indicating friendship and support. This is just what one might have expected, given that British newspaper proprietors had as much reason as Mrs Thatcher to oppose sanctions against South Africa, and indeed the *Daily Mail* had a direct financial stake in Zola Budd, having paid for her to come from South Africa to England. In this context the use of 'Budd' alone comes as a marked surprise, and must indicate dissociation:

(4) **Ramsamy: 'Budd deserves what she gets.'**
> (*Guardian*, 15 July 1986)

This heads a report of an interview with Sam Ramsamy, the chairman of the South African Non-Racial Olympic Committee, welcoming the official ban on Zola Budd and Annette Cowley which had just been announced. The *Guardian* tries to avoid the symbolic choice of either just first or just last name with 'Ms Budd', as I did with 'Zola Budd':

(5) After all, Ms Budd has not exactly been parading around in an Afrikaans Resistance Movement uniform.

it comments facetiously. I invite readers to reflect on the possible significances of my, and the *Guardian*'s, decisions on naming!

A major story in the newspapers of 31 December 1985 was the arrest of Winnie Mandela; here, naming conventions are definitely of interest in relation to the representation of women. From the *Guardian*:

(6) The black nationalist leader, Mrs Winnie Mandela, was arrested in Johannesburg yesterday as she made her way to Soweto in defiance of a ban.

Mrs Mandela's full name is Nomzamo Winifred Mandela, but she is always called 'Winnie Mandela', and on the evidence of her autobiography that seems to be the form which she accepts.[3] Thus the shortened form is customary, and does not have the coy force of 'Maggie'. There are certainly no belittling overtones in the *Guardian*'s full formula (T[itle] + F[irst] N[ame] + L[ast] N[ame], T + FN + LN). The *Guardian* also uses T + LN ('Mrs Mandela') regularly, and LN alone ('Mandela') once, in the main headline. This last usage is interesting: as I suggested above, LN referring to a woman could, in some contexts, indicate alienation, but that would be a highly unlikely interpretation for the *Guardian*; more likely, LN signifies the paper's acknowledgement of Mrs Mandela's entry into the male-dominated world of serious politics. Of course the *Guardian* does not use FN alone ('Winnie'), for in this seriously reported political context to do so would trivialize and degrade the subject. Finally, like the other papers which report this story, the *Guardian* specifies Mrs Mandela's relationship to her more famous husband: 'her gaoled husband, the African National Congress leader, Mr Nelson Mandela'; cf. *Express* 'wife of jailed black activist Nelson Mandela', *Sun* '50-year old wife of jailed African nationalist Nelson Mandela', etc. But the *Guardian* also gives her a political role in her own right, 'black nationalist leader'; elsewhere in the article, 'black leader'.

Of the other newspapers which report the arrest, all but two refer to Mrs Mandela as T + LN, or T + FN + LN, or FN + LN. The other two papers use FN alone at least once:

(7) **Winnie in AIDS jibe at police**

(*Sun*)

(8) **Screaming Winnie seized again after police ambush car**

(*Express*)

These two newspapers not only use the belittling (in this context) FN 'Winnie'; they also emphasize her abuse of the police: 'jibe', 'screaming', 'yelled' (*Sun*), 'screaming' (three times), 'defiant', 'yelled' (*Express*). A female stereotype of hysteria or irrationality is being appealed to; such expressions are conventionally associated with the stereotype 'woman' and can be used to undermine women's claim to be taken seriously in jobs or politics.

Marital and family relationships are often gratuitously foregrounded in the representation of women. Mrs Mandela's long-imprisoned husband, and her daughter and grandson who were in the car, are mentioned in all the reports: 'the child and his mother, Zinzi, yelled' (*Sun*). Private individuals in the news, if they happen to be women, are often wholly characterized in terms of family relationships:

(9) **Burst pipe kills wife** . . . An elderly woman . . . Mrs Lilian Arnell, 62.

(*Sun*)

(10) **Firemen in row after pipe burst granny dies** . . . A grandmother . . . Mrs Lillian Arnell . . . 'My mother' . . . her husband George, 65.

(*Express*)

(11) **Flooded gran dies after 999 snub** . . . a grandmother . . . Lillian Arnell, 62 . . . Mrs Arnell . . . her husband George.

(*Mirror*)

Or, from another story on the same day:

(12) **Lucy's New Year** . . . Heart-lung wife . . . Lucy . . . Britain's happiest lady . . . mother of three . . . Lucy Scott-Taggart, 35 . . . Mummy . . . Heart wife Lucy . . . her husband, Christopher, 48.

(*Express*)

(Sadly, Mrs Scott-Taggart died in February 1986.) Perhaps family relationships are especially relevant in such life-and-death matters, and these are not strong examples; but they illustrate the abundance of familial categorization in the case of women. Their public identity is felt to depend on their marital and kin relationships. Men, in serious stories, are not usually presented in such insistently domestic terms, but often have their professions or jobs mentioned – identity *outside* the home and family.

When women are represented from an explicitly sexual angle, there is available an immense proliferation of expressions for designating them and their attributes: this is overlexicalization (see pp. 85, 96). The *Express* has a feature on the casting of Audrey Landers as 'Val' for Richard Attenborough's film *A Chorus Line*. Women (13) and their attributes (14) are described as follows:

(13) Dallas bombshell Audrey, many hundreds of females, brazen hussies, sugar-dipped cuties, the/a girl, a lady, this blonde bombshell, aspiring cabaret singer, girl friend, a cabaret and recording artist, Miss Showbusiness, her Mom, her agent, Audrey Landers, the two women, a teenager, a wonderful dancer, another of those magical personalities, make-up girl, clever girl, graduate of Columbia University.

(14) high heels, exquisite figure, hair falling round her

shoulders, prettiest little face and laughing eyes, dainty feet, golden tresses, pretty [but not] dumb.

The women referred to are presented frivolously, and in terms of sexual stereotypes. The overlexicalization models a physical and sexual surplus, an exaggeration of the body and its expressiveness which is a central feature of the discursive representation of the female paradigm. Readers' discourse competence will tell them that very few of these expressions could be used to refer to males, and that there could probably be no equivalent list for male dancers which was not overtly offensive, suggesting effeminacy. It is a fact that society casts women, and not men, in the roles evoked by (13) and (14); a fact preceding language and independent of it. But this empirical fact about the social distribution of roles does not explain away the text: this is discriminatory discourse which, I would suggest, reinforces the stereotypes. It may not be discriminatory in intention or, strictly speaking, in linguistic form; the point is simply that the repeated use of expressions which imply one gender only reinforces the distinct gender categories by making them seem the normal thing. So the concept of women as a 'group' is reproduced by being, as I put it earlier, 'traded' in discourse.

My next examples consist of noun phrase expressions (excluding names) referring to men (15) and to women (16) taken from two items on the back page of the *Guardian* for 31 December 1985; a summary of the (presumably most newsworthy) figures in the Honours List, and a list of birthdays of public figures:

(15) image-maker, media consultant, image-builder, acting head of publicity [all the first four phrases refer to the same person], Chancellor of Sheffield University, a consultant, Labour front bench spokesman, vice-chancellor [three instances], principal, Regius Professor, Sibthorpian Professor, Professor of Radio Astronomy, chairman of Wessex Regional Health Authority, Bahamas-based millionaire, political knights, PPS [parliamentary private secretary], member for Holland, deputy speaker, arts minister, financial secretary to the Treasury, top businessmen, company chairmen, managing director, chief executive, chairman, Cornish poet, conductor, publisher, architect, president, rugby captain, jockey, goalkeeper, rugby player, trade unionist, general secretary, Labour leader,

golfer, secretary [of] the Royal and Ancient, chairman, director of music, organist, singer, songwriter, actors, chairman, captain, violinist, guitarist, President, actor, vice-chancellor and principal, Republican Senator, racing driver, spy, professor, author.

(16) Leader of the Opposition [Mrs Thatcher formerly], chairman, principal dramatic soprano, cookery writer, actress, editor-in-chief, columnist, trade unionist, actress, composer, singer, actresses.

Striking is the quantitative disproportion between (15) and (16). One would, of course, expect such a disproportion, in a society in which it is predominantly men who receive the top jobs and honours: there are few women professors, managing directors or millionaires, so few women appear in this Honours List. But the simple act of listing the sexes separately as in (15) and (16) immediately makes highly visible a disproportion on which we probably do not usually reflect. Are there significant linguistic differences, too? Well, there are some gender-specific terms in (16) ('soprano' and 'actress') which could not be applied to men, but on the other hand almost all the expressions in (15) could be used to refer to women (though feminists would, rightly, object to 'chairman' and 'spokesman', but I am just describing current conventions). The fact is that, in discourse generally, such expressions as 'managing director' *do not* designate women. Suppose we constructed a fictional but naturalistic text containing a few such terms, and then set up a simple experiment asking people what sex the terms referred to: you can predict the outcome. This is not a specifically linguistic point, but a point about *discourse*: the appearance in discourse of a large number of expressions mentioning powerful social categories and referring to men as incumbents of those categories implicitly suggests that this is the natural order of things, and so strengthens resistance to women actually being admitted to the positions concerned.

Objections to this kind of analysis would be of a 'rationalizing' nature: in an article on women dancers, there are bound to be lots of references to the physical attributes of women; in a list of public rewards, male company directors and officials are bound to bulk large. Language simply reflects the facts. This sort of objection springs largely from acceptance of the ideological status quo, but anyway it misses the point. The form of representation cannot be explained away as merely a reflex of the facts of the represented content: *discourse and its realizations in texts are themselves facts*. The samples in (7)-(16) show that women are represented in an unfavourable light, and that men are characterized by mentions of occupational and political success. The point is that such categorizations habitually saturate discourse; 'common sense' makes us fail to notice this saturation. But it is always present, and in the case of newspapers, can be readily detected in a critical reading of *any* newspaper one picks up. If the reader takes a highlighting pen – better still, a pink one and a blue one – to all noun phrases designating individuals in any front page of *The Times*, the *Telegraph*, the *Independent* or the *Guardian*, s/he will produce a male–dominated list of roles similar to (15) above; the same exercise with the popular press will produce results like (7)-(14). My readers are not meant to *compare* such sets of data (their contexts are not readily comparable anyway), but to *aggregate* them: taken all together, the discourse of the newspaper media handles men and women in terms of different sets of categories, different stereotypes. No doubt this differentiation reflects society's different ways of treating men and women (the majority of company directors are male, chorus girls are female), but it would be complacent to accept that the relationship between language and society is merely reflective. It seems very likely that discrimination in discourse helps maintain intellectual habits that promote discrimination in practice: by constantly articulating a link between a type of expression and a category of referent, discourse makes these socially constructed categories seem to be natural common sense.

DISCRIMINATION AND POWER

With reference to a new example, I now wish to explore the relationship between discriminatory categorization and power. Individuals who get placed into 'groups' that are discriminated against are by definition put into positions where they enjoy less power than other people, or other people directly exercise power over them. 'Power' can mean many things, including money, knowledge and status, but here I am thinking specifically of an asymmetrical relationship between people such that one person has the ascribed authority to control the other's actions and liberties, and not vice versa. The construction of such relationships can be observed in the structure of texts, and newspapers are not exempt from the reproduction of asymmetrical power relationships.

The 'group' in question are young people, particularly but not necessarily exclusively young women; it is interesting that the discourse *assumes* that the matter concerns women, although legally either sex is concerned. The issue here is the availability of contraceptive advice and treatment to those under the age of 16 (the legal age of sexual consent in Britain), a right tirelessly attacked by 'mother of ten' Mrs Victoria Gillick. In December 1984, Mrs Gillick won a judgement in the Appeal Court to the effect that a doctor should not give such advice or treatment to a patient under 16 without parental consent, except in an emergency. This problematic ruling placed doctors in considerable difficulty, since it conflicted with their traditional practice of treating all patients in confidence. In February 1985, the General Medical Council (the doctors' professional body) advised its members to conform with this decision, but left a loophole by declining to define what constituted an 'emergency'. The newspapers reported the GMC's advice in the following headlines:

(17) **GMC amends rules on under-16 contraception**
(*Guardian*)

(18) **Doctors get guidelines on pill for under-16s**
(*The Times*)

(19) **Doctors put ban on Pill for under-16s**
(*Daily Telegraph*)

(20) **Doctors' ban on Pill**
(*Telegraph*, back-page continuation)

(21) **Don't give girls Pill doctors warned**
(*Express*)

(22) **Wisely vague**
(*Daily Mail* editorial, referring to the wisdom of leaving 'emergency' undefined)

There is interesting variation in the ways in which structures of authority are represented in these headlines: how the participants are treated, and how the ruling – which relates to those participants – is expressed. The *Guardian* is the most impersonal, mentioning neither the doctors who will be guided by the GMC's rules, nor the young people who may be denied contraceptive advice. Note that the nominal 'rules on under-16 contraception' leaves open the possibility that this medical service might still be available. The same presupposition holds for *The Times* headline (18), strengthened by the beneficiary preposition 'for' and the designation of the potential beneficiaries by the noun phrase 'under-16s'. 'Guidelines' in (18) are of course more permissive than 'rules' in (17), but headline (18) is clearer about the chain of authority: prescribing doctors make the contraceptive pill available to the under-16s, but only under guidelines from some unspecified higher authority; and the strength of that authority is emphasized by the blunt first sentence of *The Times*'s article: 'Doctors were told yesterday that they must not . . .'; cf. elsewhere in the article the modals 'must', 'must not', and the words of authority 'permission' (twice), 'ruling', 'consent'. The *Express* (21) is stronger still: a no-nonsense negative imperative is thematized by being positioned at the front of the sentence. The speech-act verb 'warn' implies that someone has the authority to impose a sanction if the warning is disobeyed. (The *Telegraph* explains: 'Doctors who break the Council's guidelines put themselves at risk of being summoned before its disciplinary committee, which has power to reprimand them, suspend them or strike them off the medical register.') The threat is carried into the *Express*'s first sentence: 'Doctors were told yesterday to toe the line over the ban on giving under-age girls the Pill behind their parents' backs.' Note the colloquial register, consistent with the oral tone of the headline, and thereby adding to a feeling of the *presence* of a threatening authority.

So far, the headlines have assumed a three-level hierarchy of power: the GMC makes a ruling, individual doctors abide by it, and at the bottom of the ladder of power, the young patients receive contraception or not, more likely not. But there are in fact five levels if the Court of Appeal, and the parents, both cited in the newspaper texts below the headlines, are included:

(A) *Court of Appeal* – made the legal decision which has to be obeyed by everyone below.
(B) *General Medical Council* – interprets the decision in a ruling which determines individual doctors' practice.
(C) *Parents* – can veto doctors' treatment of their offspring in the case of contraception.
(D) *Doctors* – that is to say, individual family doctors, may not give people under 16 contraceptive advice, or prescribe con-

traceptives for them; they are constrained by the authority of (A), (B) and (C) unless they decide that the situation is an 'emergency' (in which case, they might have to face the problem of justifying their decision afterwards).

(E) *Patients under 16* – seem to have no authority whatsoever in a matter of personal behaviour which, whatever one might think of 'under-age sex', is at least intensely private for them.

If you look again at the headlines, you will see that the word 'doctors' differs in reference, referring to (B) (as 'agent') in (19) and (20), and (D) (as 'patient' in the technical semantic sense) in (18) and (21). Perhaps more accurately, (19) and (20) conflate the interests of (B) and (D); they seem to be very strong statements about power, and likely to be alarming for young readers of the newspapers, who might well already find their family doctor intimidating. But (18) and (21) encode the situation very differently, placing individual doctors in a position of very low authority; note particularly the bullying tone of (21). This positioning seems to me to indicate an attitude to the professions which was very common in the 1980s in those newspapers with strong Conservative allegiance. The Conservative government of the time was concerned to contain and marginalize a range of 'groups' felt to be a threat to power: among them civil servants, the medical profession, social workers, social scientists and all kinds of teachers. In some cases the alignment of the Press with this policy is blatant, as in the *Sun's* routine publication of stories likely to compromise or ridicule local government officers, social workers and teachers. In other cases, as in (18) and (21) here, the attack is made by the implicit role-assigning mechanism of transitivity and, in the more authoritarian (21) by tone.

We have seen that young people requiring contraception, the people most directly affected by the legal decision, occupy the lowest, least privileged position in the pyramid of power. Is there anything else to notice about their representation in these news reports?

The sexuality of young women is a salacious obsession in the media (amply evidenced, for example, by a prurient attention in some newspapers to the holiday activities of one of Mrs Gillick's teenage daughters in July 1986).[4] Mrs Gillick's campaign against the unchecked supply of contraceptives to young people, with its suggestion that there was a problem of juvenile sex to be dealt with, attracted a lot of media curiosity for two or three years; and in accordance with the double standards generally found in the Press on sexual matters (titillating nude photographs of young women alongside expressions of outrage against the abuse of children), the Gillick case became a focus for repressive and self-righteous attitudes. Predictably, then, in response to this obsession in the newspaper discourse, the young people concerned are treated to overlexicalization. Even in the very short reports of my sample, there is an abundance of alternative expressions designating the young people; and these expressions unnecessarily and tendentiously specify them as female, and exaggerate their youth:

> under-16s [four times], girls under 16 [twice], children, a minor, under-age girls [three times], a girl, girls, youngsters [twice], young girls, under-age children.

Quotations from the GMC's ruling and from comments on it include:

> child, patient, daughter, girl under 16, young woman [this last from a female member of the GMC opposed to the ruling].

It should now be clear what is going on here: young women seeking contraceptive advice or supplies are being discriminated for special attention, located at the bottom of a ladder of power relations and implicitly told, like the doctors, to 'toe the line'. Consciously or unconsciously, the newspapers support the return to Victorian values which was so clear a feature of Mrs Thatcher's theory of social ethics. The newspaper accounts of this General Medical Council ruling mediate it through a grid of hierarchical assumptions, a finely stratified model of the chain of authority relevant to this matter. Only the *Express* is at all polemical in its support of the chain; the others accept it as 'common sense', and that unquestioning and undemonstrative acceptance by the news media is a massive advantage to an authoritarian government.

The Appeal Court decision was later reversed, returning some of their traditional freedoms to doctors and their patients.

Chapter 7

Terms of abuse and of endearment

In the previous chapter, we noticed the preoccupation of the newspapers with sorting people into categories, and placing discriminatory values on them. This discrimination is generally achieved through a range of linguistic strategies that are so unobtrusive that their effect must be subliminal. Men and women are labelled 'managing directors' and 'actresses' in contexts which make the usage seem natural, and so the labels are unnoticed; young women are referred to as 'under-age girls', and we might not see the slur, because 'under-age' relates to the legal definition of the age of sexual consent; in the next chapter, we will look at a text in which doctors and patients are placed in different semantic roles in sentences, so that the former are consistently doing something and the latter having things done to them: patients are known, impersonally and one could say inhumanely, as 'cases'. We should not assume that newspaper writers are doing these things consciously: they probably accept without question that the contexts make the usages 'natural', to the extent that they are not even aware of the choices of phrase. I hope this book serves to encourage both writers and readers to see that 'normal usage' can encode prejudice, and so requires critical reflection.

In this chapter, I want to record, quite briefly, the fact that newspapers also give voice to explicit judgements on people, by terms of abuse and – much less prominently – terms of endearment. This is well known to any reader of the popular Press, so I am not revealing anything here; I simply notice these judgements, for completeness.

Two small but typical examples. The first list of expressions is taken from a series of articles in the *Star* newspaper of 9 August 1986, condemning the behaviour of English soccer fans who went on the rampage aboard a Dutch ferry taking them to 'friendly' matches on the Continent. To be fair, this was an explosive topic for the British popular press, which had taken a strong line against football hooliganism since the deaths of thirty-nine spectators in crowd violence at a match between Liverpool and Juventus at Heysel Stadium, Brussels, in May 1985. The reaction is heightened because the behaviour is seen as not only 'violent' but also 'uncivilized', 'unpatriotic', 'letting England down', i.e. for the Press it is all of a piece with the drunken rowdyism of British holidaymakers in Benidorm. Anyway, the epithets are direct enough:

> (1) **SCUM**, the mad dogs of English football, the cancer that is destroying [English football], football vermin, rioting British soccer louts, idiots, rioting fans, rival gangs of drunken soccer fans, youths, well-heeled thugs, self-styled 'elite' of soccer hardmen, thugs 'elite'; 'villains', 'idiot', 'their behaviour was worse than pigs' [the last three are attributed quotations].

Such abuse is common in the popular press, consistently focused on certain classes of person, notably soccer hooligans, vandals, blacks, demonstrators, 'the loony Left' in politics and local government, male sex offenders, spies, homosexuals, teachers, and foreigners, particularly foreigners coming from countries which are perceived as culturally very alien from Western Europe (Arabs, Africans, Russians).

On the converse, explicit praise or implicit approval can sometimes be attached to individuals who are felt in some way to express 'paradigms' or emulative models. The two girls who became 'princesses' on marrying into the British Royal Family in 1981 and 1986 have provided copious illustration of how individuals can be set up to collect and express the many features of an elite paradigm. The backgrounding of the older royal women by Diana Spencer, and then by Sarah Ferguson, the use of Sarah Ferguson as a way of commenting on Princess Diana, the invention of a 'bad princess' (Michael) to complicate the judgements further and the rehabilitation of a previously disfavoured princess (Anne) constitute a spectacular public myth-making, if you are interested in this particular area. The princesses are hardly ever out of the news, and each time they appear they are endowed with characteristic properties. On any occasion, the applause may be sparing, but cumulatively over the months a positive model is built up. Here is a typical set of applaudatory epithets bestowed on Sarah Ferguson by the *Sun* on her wedding day, 23 July 1986:

(2) Fergie, Royal bride [both numerous times], the bubbly bride, a very special girl, full-figured Fergie, fun-loving Fergie.

RAMBO AND THE MAD DOG

Let us now look at a more serious set of evaluative materials: explicitly negative and, to a lesser extent (as is usual), positive valuations, as they emerge in a quite brief but complicated news story of mid-April 1986, centred on the bombing of Libya by the United States on 15 April. For months, tension between the United States and Libya had been rising, the two leaders trading insults and threats, against the background of world-wide 'terrorist attacks', for instance the bloody assaults on Rome and Vienna airports on 27 December 1985. President Reagan's position through all of this was that Libya, and Colonel Gadafy personally, was the chief agency world-wide in sponsoring, aiding and giving sanctuary to terrorists. Provocatively, US aircraft-carriers began 'exercises' off the Libyan coast on 22 March 1986; on 24 March, Libyan forces fired on US planes, and on the same day the US retaliated, and did so again on 25 March. Two further 'terrorist attacks' soon afterwards were read as Libyan retaliation: an explosion in an American TWA airliner over Greece on 2 April, and a bomb in a West German nightclub on 5 April. Americans were killed in both incidents. Now it was starting to be alleged that 'there is indisputable evidence that the nightclub bombing can be linked to a worldwide network of terrorists set up by Colonel Gadafy' (General Bernard Rogers, Supreme Allied Commander, Europe). From this point in early April, the US put dual pressure on Europe to support measures against Libya: by sanctions, and by military action. As it turned out, while sanctions were being debated publicly, behind the scenes President Reagan had privately secured the agreement of Mrs Thatcher (the then British Prime Minister) for air bases in Britain to be used to launch bombing attacks against Libya. The press coverage of the lead-up to the bombardment reflects the confusion of the

time: here are the relevant headlines from the *Guardian*, 14–16
April; remember that the bombing took place on 15 April:

(3) (a) **Reagan's fever for war cools**

(14 April)

(b) **EEC fails to back action against Libya**

(15 April)

(c) **World angered by revenge attack**

(16 April)

(The local dailies, with their compact distribution, are best set to
capture a rapidly developing chain of events. On the crucial night,
15 April, the *Eastern Daily Press* published three editions, the first
of which (midnight) was headed '**EEC clamps on Libya**', the
second '**E. Anglia bases on standby**', the third (3 a.m.) '**US
fires on Libya**'.)

By the afternoon of 15 April, the smoke had cleared, at least
as far as the US/GB justification was concerned. Statements by
the President and by the Prime Minister invoked article 51 of the
United Nations Charter as justifying acts of 'self-defence', in this
case the bombing of Libya in 'self-defence' against Libyan terrorism against US and UK citizens. However, not only the political
opponents of Thatcher and Reagan, but also the leaders of major
states in Europe and elsewhere, refused to perceive the matter
that way: far from 'self-defence', the bombing of Libya looked
more like a cold-blooded act of revenge, carried out in an excessive fashion, and resulting in civilian casualties. Reagan and Thatcher came under fire, not only for the nature of the attack (and
of course its debatable strategic effectiveness), but also for the use
of British air bases. It was felt that Mrs Thatcher's giving permission for the planes to be launched from British bases implicated us dangerously, turning us from innocent bystanders to
prime targets for retaliation. (I can vouch for the anger and
anxiety felt in East Anglia, where United States Air Force bases
were situated at RAF Lakenheath and RAF Mildenhall.) We shall
see that although *the world* attacked Reagan and Thatcher (cf.
Guardian, (3) (16 April) above), *the Press* did not.

We now need to progress the narrative a couple of days further
on, and again will do so with headlines from the *Guardian*:

(4) (a) **US threatens new attacks against Libya**

(17 April)

(b) **Britons lie low in Beirut as hostages die**

(18 April)

(c) **Hunt on for Heathrow terrorist**

(18 April)

(d) **Arab held in bomb hunt**

(19 April)

(e) **Heartaches and dangers facing the foreigner in Beirut**

(19 April)

These headlines refer to violent acts which were widely assumed to have been undertaken in retaliation against Britain's part in the bombing. Three British hostages held in Lebanon were killed, and their bodies found in the town of Sofar, in Syrian-held territory outside Beirut. But the event which attracted the fury of the Press was the incident referred to in (4c) and (4d). The 'Arab' or 'terrorist' mentioned was a Jordanian, Nezar Hindawi. At 9.15 a.m. on 17 April, a bomb was found packed into a suitcase being taken on board an Israeli El Al jumbo jet. The person carrying the bag was a young woman, Irish, pregnant; it emerged that she was Ann-Marie Murphy, Hindawi's girl-friend. Hindawi himself took the woman to the gate, then unexpectedly departed after saying that as an Arab he could not fly El Al; that he would change his ticket and join her later. As (4d) indicates, Hindawi was quickly apprehended. (Brought to trial in October 1986, he was 'sentenced to a record 45 years for trying to use Miss Ann Murphy, his pregnant girlfriend, as a human bomb to destroy an El Al flight carrying 375 people' – *The Times* 25 October 1986.)

The immediate importance of the Hindawi affair, from my point of view, is that, whether or not it was connected with the bombing of Libya, it could be associated with Libya, it provided another villain to set beside Gadafy, and the outrageous and callous nature of Hindawi's intentions implicitly demonstrated the rightness of President Reagan's action against 'Arab terrorists'.

Four principals, then, figured in the news treatment of the bombing and its aftermath: Reagan, Thatcher, Gadafy and Hindawi. If we compare newspapers, the styles of reference to these individuals differ considerably. We may contrast the *Guardian* (5) with the *Sun* (6); quotations from other sources are in inverted commas, and it is to be noted that the expression 'mad dog' originates with President Reagan himself, in a statement of 9 April 1986:

(5) (a) Gadafy, Colonel Gadafy, the Colonel, Colonel Muammar Gadafy, deranged ruler, 'mad dog', 'martyr', 'a tyrant'.

(b) President Reagan, the President, the President of the United States, President, Mr Ronald Reagan, Ronald Reagan, Mr Reagan, the US President.

(c) Mrs Thatcher, Thatcher, Mrs Margaret Thatcher, (the) Prime Minister, 'Rambo's daughter'.

(d) Nezar Hindawi, Hindawi, Mr Nezar Hindawi, Mr Hindawi, the/an Arab.

(6) (a) Gaddafi, Colonel Gaddafi, Libyan leader Colonel Gaddafi, Libya's dictator Colonel Gaddafi, the crazed dictator, madman, Mad Dog Gaddafi, mad dog, 'Mad Dog', 'mad dog' Gaddafi, 'the bastard', 'a schizo'.

(b) President Reagan, the US President, the US leader, the President, Reagan, Mr Reagan, Ronald Reagan, Ron, Ronnie, Ronnie Reagan, Rambo, Rambo Ronnie, President Ronald 'Rambo' Reagan, commander-in-chief Reagan.

(c) Mrs Thatcher, Thatcher, Margaret Thatcher, Maggie, Premier Margaret Thatcher, the Premier, the Prime Minister.

(d) Nezar Hindawi, Hindawi, the terrorist, rat, ruthless rat, Arab rat, Arab terrorist, smooth-talking Jordanian, cold-blooded fanatic, suspected terrorist assassin, Jumbo bomb suspect, suspect bomber, bomb suspect.

A little continuous text will illustrate the different tones of the two newspapers:

(7) **Libya strikes back at US signals base**

Libya yesterday claimed to have destroyed an American-manned communication station on the Italian island of Lampedusa in retaliation for the US raids here and in Benghazi.

But for an authoritative indication of where their country is headed the Libyans depend entirely on Colonel Gadafy, who, though apparently unscathed, has yet to make a public appearance.

His 15-month-old adopted daughter, Hanna, died in the bombing of Azizya barracks where the Libyan leader lives. Two of his sons, Khamisd and Sief al-Ardab, were seriously injured and were last night receiving treatment in an intensive care unit. Gadafy's mother was being treated for shock.

One report last night estimated that about 100 people had been killed in Tripoli alone, but there was no official confirmation.

(Guardian, 16 April 1986)

(8) **THRILLED TO BLITZ!**

Bombing Gaddafi was my greatest day says US airman

Jubilant American bomber pilots were walking on air last night after the revenge mission aimed at wiping out Libya's 'Mad Dog' Colonel Gaddafi.

One airman described the hit-and-run raid as 'the greatest thrill of my life'. But another crewman said he regretted the crazed dictator had escaped with his life and that 'we didn't nail the bastard'.

The raid early yesterday was spearheaded by 18 F–111 bombers based in Britain – backed by 15 jets from US carriers in the Mediterranean.

The attack was ordered by President Reagan as a reprisal against outrages by Libyan bomb squads.

One airman, relaxing in a bar near his base at Mildenhall, Suffolk said: 'We were not told until the last minute we were taking part.'

The fuel tanker flier added: 'Gaddafi is a schizo. How else do you deal with a guy like him?'

Gaddafi's 15-month-old adopted daughter Hanna died in his Tripoli HQ, Libyan doctors claimed. His two youngest sons were also injured.

Another 13 people are said to have been killed with about 100 injured.

Two F–111s failed to return from the strike – the biggest by the Americans since Vietnam.

A search was going on for one lost in the Mediterranean last night. A second landed in Spain with engine trouble.

In the *Guardian* ((5) and (7)) the protagonists are referred to by

name and/or title in formal style. Evaluative terms are attributed
to others ('mad dog' to President Reagan or to 'American opinion') or otherwise distanced, e.g. 'martyr' and 'a tyrant' refer to
how Gadafy might be perceived under certain conditions. The
only exception is the sarcastic appellation 'Rambo's daughter'
which is applied to Mrs Thatcher in a signed 'Commentary'
article by Hugo Young (17 April), not in a news report. The
newspaper dislikes the US/GB action (though its editorial on 16
April seems to be saying that 'something had to be done') but
does not indicate its values by abusive or laudatory references.
The *Sun*, on the other hand, is ecstatic in its praise of President
Reagan and Mrs Thatcher ('***Right, Ron! Right, Maggie!***' is the
heading of the editorial on 16 April), and strident in vilifying
Colonel Gadafy and Nazem Hindawi. The front-page article on
16 April, (8), cleverly transfers the strongest expressions of
excitement and of abuse to purported interviews with US airmen
returned from the attack, but the list of expressions in (6) (most
of them repeated many times) shows that the abuse and the praise
are also pervasive in the *Sun*'s own language, too. On the one
hand, the paper doles out familiar diminutives ('Maggie', 'Ron',
'Ronnie') and honorific titles ('the Premier'), while the villains
are treated to extreme insults ('madman', 'rat'). While many of
the insults are trite, and meaningless in their conventionality,
others are supported by more complex, and disturbing, systems
of values. Consider the term 'rat', applied to Nazem Hindawi.
This is on the surface merely the trace of a conventional saying:
proverbially, rats leave sinking ships, and he was a rat to leave
his girl-friend carrying a bomb on to a doomed plane. But 'rat'
also falls into a paradigm of animal abuse, in this discourse:

(9) (a) Arab rat
    (b) Libyan mad dog
    (c) Syrian swine [applied to the Syrian ambassador,
        expelled from Britain after the Nazem Hindawi case]
                                    (*Sun*, 25 October 1986)
    (d) hunted [the search for Hindawi, 18 April]
    (e) Gaddafi has been sending out his killer packs for years
                                    (*Sun*, 18 April 1986)
    (f) monster
    (g) fiend

The first three (each of which is repeated in the texts) make quite clear the perception of 'Arabs' as non-human, bestial. 'Swine' is not semantically fortuitous, a word chosen for the alliteration; applied to a Muslim, it is a profoundly offensive insult. Then, 'hunted' is a term appropriate to humans hunting animals; Gadafy's 'packs' connote wolves; 'monster' and 'fiend', in isolation trite, reinforce the non-human in this paradigm. The paradigm of Arabs as pigs (or other taboo animals) is one expression of a deep chauvinism verging on xenophobia which can be regularly observed in this newspaper. There is a theoretical point to be emphasized, that the paradigm, the particular system of beliefs, pre-exists these news reports, being part of the general discourse of the paper and, more widely, of the culture of its production and consumption. The animal insults are not judgements formed specifically for the evaluation of Gadafy and Hindawi *on this occasion*, but expressions of a set of general prejudices.[1]

Finally, two expressions which are meant to convey approval of Mrs Thatcher and of President Reagan work by referring outside the text in a slightly different way:

(10) Falkland Maggie

(*Express*, 16 April 1986)

(11) Rambo Ronnie [see (6) above]

By intertextuality, explicit reference from one text to another or to others, these expressions call up the reader's knowledge of examples of a particular kind of paradigm which we might term a narrative model; and by this device, the values associated with the model are cited. (10), 'Falkland Maggie', appears in the headline of an account of Mrs Thatcher's parliamentary statement of 15 April, in which she defended her decision to support the strike by the United States. The narrative reference is to her conduct of the Falklands War against Argentina in 1982, a war which delighted the tabloid Press and popular opinion. The victory over Argentina's General Galtieri consolidated Mrs Thatcher's reputation as 'the Iron Lady', fearless, resolute and invincible in the defence of freedom, and so on. Paraphrasing the Prime Minister, the *Express* reminds its readers of the values which are to be associated with this model: 'And she warned that the Western world faced the choice between striking back at terrorism in self-defence, or cringing before it.' Thus a small reference which is powerfully supported outside the text economically provides readers with a whole frame of values within which the Prime Minister's role in the bombing of Libya is to be perceived. Similarly, the characterization of President Reagan as 'Rambo' appeals to readers to applaud his macho determination and power. The cutting reference to 'Rambo's daughter' cited in (5) above works well, because the American myth of Rambo and the British myth of the Iron Lady were so closely related in their values and in their functions within the ideological system of national power current in 'the West' in the 1980s.

POSTSCRIPT

This is how two of the papers recalled the event nine months later, in their end-of-the-year news review of 1986 (Sunday 28 December 1986); notice how straightforward the judgements for and against have become:

> **INTENT ON REVENGE** Colonel 'Mad Dog' Gadaffi of Libya proclaimed in January that he would 'train and equip Arab terrorists for suicide missions'. He enflamed the United States' sensibilities, shut off the Gulf of Sirte and the war of words erupted to load the guns. In March, the final straw came with the bombing of American servicemen in a West Berlin discotheque. Reagan threatened and then ordered a strike in April – making controversial use of American air bases in Britain to launch his F–111s, and diluting the concentration of American tourists venturing to holiday in the United Kingdom. Tripoli was shattered as Gadaffi's adopted daughter was killed in an explosion and his private, luxury tent was completely devastated. Colonel Gadaffi went to ground.
>
> (*Sunday Express*)

> **Ronald Reagan got tough** on terrorism when US planes bombed Libya in April. Alone of his NATO allies Britain gave direct support by allowing his F–111 bombers based at RAF Lakenheath to be used in an action which killed indiscriminately. As dead children were dug out of the rubble in Tripoli [photograph] British police massed at Lakenheath to repel protesters. Many people wondered who was the 'mad dog' and who the 'terrorists'.
>
> (*Observer*)

Chapter 8

Attitudes to power

IDEOLOGICAL ROLES OF THE PRESS

In the previous two chapters, I illustrated how language assists in the formation and reproduction of the schematic categories in terms of which a society represents itself: by providing labelling expressions which solidify concepts of 'groups', by assigning different semantic roles to the members of different groups, thus discriminating among them and, by imbalance, assisting the practice of allocating power and opportunity unequally among them. In this chapter, I want to take this topic of language, power and inequality further; and while doing so, to develop the analytic tool of transitivity (cf. p. 70).

Before going on with analysis, however, let us consider what specific roles the newspapers perform in these practices. First let us recall that, in terms of the theory of language used here, newspapers have *no* special character among representational texts (cf. p. 8). I have explained that this study, which says that the Press presents – and therefore helps constitute – reality from specific angles, is not claiming that the Press is especially biased. Of course bias does exist, different biases in different sections of the newspaper world, but that is only marginally my concern. From a theoretical point of view, the Press is an example of a process found in *all* discourse, the structured mediation of the world.

The discourses of the Press, again like all discourse, relate to its own institutional and economic position, and to the particular circumstances of the different papers. Now, it is quite clear that several cultural and economic features of the Press combine to give it a unique importance in the (re)production of ideology. In

Western countries, there is generally a wide selection of news-papers published, many of them with vast circulations running into millions of copies. Each of them is a substantial text, some (e.g. the Sunday *New York Times*) gigantic in bulk and wordage. The publication frequency (daily or weekly, morning or evening) and modes of distribution (early morning delivery to the home; sale in shops which also sell petty daily consumables such as cigarettes, sweets and pens; street vending at conventional times, particularly when people are travelling to and from work) encour-age readers to habitualize themselves to consuming newspapers as a fixed part of their daily routine. For the majority of people, reading the daily newspaper makes up their most substantial and significant consumption of printed discourse. For the majority, it is second only to television as a window on the world. These are factors of quantity and of habit which give newspaper discourse a major ideological importance.

Economic circumstances strengthen this importance, and lend shape to the ideology. The main economic purpose of newspapers appears to be to sell advertising space, and again they are second only to television as a medium for consumer advertising. And consumer advertising is based on the representation of ideal fic-tional worlds, i.e. sets of beliefs about desirable personal and social behaviour in relation to such products as cars, deodorants, coffee, hair care, washing powders and sweets. The texts of the newspapers themselves also offer fictional model worlds, for example the obsessive discussion in the tabloids of television soap operas as if real, of actors, personalities and stars, the escapism of the travel pages in the middle-class papers. From the adver-tisers' point of view, the textual content of the paper must be broadly congruent with the products to be advertised, and this is a well-known constraint on what the papers can say, or at least a problem. Another economic circumstance which relates to the papers' ideological roles is the fact that most of them are owned by people and companies which are commercial enterprises, often selling a range of diverse products and services other than news-papers. It stands to reason that a newspaper is likely to project such beliefs as are conducive to the commercial success of its proprietors generally. That is partly a political matter, in a society whose parliamentary parties divide fundamentally on economic theory and policies.

There are two factors, then, which give the Press a peculiar importance in mediating ideology for the individual. First is the scale of publication, and the success of a sales and distribution system which ensures that the bulk of the population read a newspaper as part of their daily routine. Newspapers are part of the *mass* media, and their ideological power stems from their ability to say the same thing to millions of people simultaneously. The second factor is qualitative rather than quantitative. The economic and political circumstances of the newspaper industry give it a vested interest in mediating ideas from particular perspectives, varying somewhat from paper to paper, and so the point of view, or world-view, of a particular paper has a function and an expression which need to be studied.

In chapter 6, I analysed texts which manifested a prejudicial categorization of women, and particularly young women. I made little gesture towards explaining the origins or functions of this discrimination, or distinguishing between the treatments in different papers. If we accumulate a lot of material from a wide range of papers, as I did in chapter 6, it emerges that the processes of categorization and discrimination are widespread and general: cumulatively, they make up a kind of ideological background which can be regarded as a representation of the culture's 'common-sense' views about the different positions and characteristics of women and of men. If newspapers are reproducing a discriminatory ideology, then their power and pervasiveness (the 'first factor' above) make their unexamined categorizations a matter of concern. This is so even with newspapers which make an attempt to be liberal and well intentioned. I do not think the *Guardian*, the *Independent*, *The Times* or the *Telegraph* would use phrases like 'sugar-dipped cuties' or 'black thugs' or 'gay plague' or 'the loony Left', except in ironic or heavily reported contexts, but even so, the 'quality' papers do contribute unwittingly to the background ideology by being full of phrases which refer positively and seriously to men's roles: 'a government spokesman', 'company directors', 'test pilot', etc. I am referring even to innocent contexts full of goodwill and free of any hint of conspiracy:

(1) (a) **BIRTHDAYS**
    Coral Browne, actress, 73;
    David Essex, singer, actor,
    39; **Michael Foot**, MP, 73;
    Graham Gooch, cricketer, 33;

Elspeth Huxley, author,
79; Victor Korchnoi, chess
grandmaster, 55; Richard Rogers,
architect, 53; Peter Twiss,
former Test pilot and world's
speed record holder, 65.

(b) OBITUARY
E. A. 'Ted' Ellis, the
Norfolk-based naturalist,
author and broadcaster,
who wrote the Guardian Country
Diary regularly for two decades,
died yesterday aged 77. He was
a world authority on micro–
fungi, and for some years
presented the radio programme,
Nature Postbag.

(*Guardian*, 23 July 1986)

Against the general background which these newspapers cumulatively build up, we do find marked differences. I have suggested
one in the case of the *Guardian*, namely an avoidance of frivolous
terms for women but a large number of high-status occupational
expressions for men (this whole proposition would need demonstrating in more detail, of course). The *Sun, Express* and other
popular or conservative papers are different in these respects.
Looking at the texts more closely, one could suggest, for example, specific reasons why Winnie Mandela is abused through language: she is a woman, she is black, she is a black woman
involved in politics, she is a black woman politician actively
opposing the white South African government – my series is
meant to suggest how these categories compound her offensive-
ness, or her potential threat, from the point of view of a white-
owned conservative English newspaper whose political and
economic interests agree with those of white Britain and South
Africa. I hinted at the possibility of a similar contextual explanation in the case of the 'under-age contraception' story, and,
written out in full, it would be a complex and interesting one
involving sexual voyeurism, the claim of moral authority, a desire
to contain the threat posed by the young, a multi-strata vision
of power, a fear of specialized knowledge and of individual

professional judgement (as possessed by doctors) – the ingredients all combined in different mixes according to the political needs and readership perceptions of the different papers.

To sum up the general argument so far, then, I am suggesting that the articulation of ideology in the language of the news fulfils, cumulatively and through daily reiteration, a background function of reproducing the beliefs and paradigms of the community generally: what Hall and his colleagues, and, following them, Hartley, call a 'consensual' view of society.[1] Against that background, the individual papers are involved in more particular and active engagements with the ideas of the culture; modes of engagement, and world-views, which differ according to the situation and needs of each paper. As this book progresses, I shall concentrate more on the dimension of difference, and on the discursive strategies which are called up to handle the problems of particular newspapers in relating their ideas to the national ideological consensus of the community. In the present chapter, looking at the coding of power relations, I shall examine some discursive structures which respond to the problems inherent in reporting and discussing topics which concern the unequal distribution of power.

THE DOMINANCE OF THE STATUS QUO: HOSPITAL PATIENTS AS POWERLESS

We look now at an example of a text in which a newspaper expresses sympathy with the underdog, affirms the need for reform of the system, but in which the overtly reforming aims of the article are gainsaid, in its own discourse, by the power, the ideological entrenchment, of the status quo. This is a case of a newspaper trying to say one thing, but being forced to imply, subliminally, the opposite. The topic happens to be a situation characterized by extreme power differential: the helplessness of sick people faced with inadequate state hospital provision, and with the failure of the politicians and administrators who control the system to improve the facilities.[2]

The text in question is a report in the *Sunday Times*, 5 February 1978, concerning the delays encountered by large numbers of people waiting for surgical treatment in hospital. The article first quotes a brief parliamentary statement of 22 November 1977, by the then Secretary for Social Services, David Ennals (at the time

Labour MP for Norwich North; later, Lord Ennals), to the effect that only people who do not have an urgent need for surgery have to wait, while 'urgent cases' receive prompt treatment. In a piece of 'investigative journalism', the *Sunday Times* re-analyses the statistics on the basis of which the claim was made, interviews a number of politicians, doctors and other powerful people involved (and at the end, melodramatically, one elderly patient) and suggests that the situation is nothing like as satisfactory as Mr Ennals had claimed: that there is inadequate surgical provision in general, and that patients are waiting long periods for operations, even when they are suffering from acute and painful medical conditions. The connections between this discourse and power differential are clear, once mentioned. Lord Ennals was at that time a cabinet minister; his words were uttered in the House of Commons and reported in *Hansard*, the official printed record of parliamentary proceedings; the *Sunday Times* was at that time generally regarded as a serious middle-class newspaper. Many of the protagonists mentioned in the article are also in positions of great power (and probably *Sunday Times* readers): surgeons, administrators, politicians. By contrast, the countless elderly patients who must wait years for surgery are profoundly powerless: ill within an inadequate system, they can do nothing to speed their treatment unless they have the money for private hospital care; in the state system, only the surgeons have the authority to decide which patients get early treatment, while others die or suffer years of pain.

The point I want to make about the discourse practice encountered here is that, although the newspaper is ostensibly critical of Mr Ennals's claim, and explicitly sympathizes with and appears to champion the patients' interests, its language characterizes the patients as inherently powerless, and the surgeons and politicians as inherently powerful, and so it tends to reproduce the power differential as if it were natural. These power-relations are firmly encoded in the habitual discourse of institutionalized medicine, which provides the *Sunday Times* with a ready-made language to use on this topic; the 'common sense' of the institutionalized status quo is ingrained in the discourse, and it would have been very difficult for the newspaper to avoid communicating a sense of the natural and inevitable unless it constructed some new mode of discourse. The problem with that strategy would be that the language would no longer seem 'appropriate to the topic'; the

Sunday Times's predominantly middle-class readers might well not accept such a degree of defamiliarization, and so reject the language as *in*appropriate and the arguments as ill judged.

The layout of the article foregrounds the contrast between claim and reality by putting Mr Ennals's statement in large type in a prominent 'box', two columns wide, at the head of the article:

(2) **This is how Ennals told MPs the lists are shrinking**

Mr Ennals: In the majority of cases there is little wait if the matter is urgent. That should be recognized. Most of those who are having to wait are non-urgent cases. When a case becomes urgent, it goes to the top of the list.

This report describes the reality – seen through the eyes of surgeons who must take life or death decisions .

A cold, bleak Thursday in Northampton. Inside a cramped office at the sprawling 19th century general hospital, surgeon John Chapman is deciding who shall be called in from his waiting list for operations next week. He scans through 400 or so cards – one for each patient. It is a job as grim and depressing as the weather outside.

'I couldn't even tell you if some of these are still alive,' he says. 'This chap' – pulling one card from the pile – 'he'd be 93 by now and he's been waiting for 3½ years for surgical corrections to waterworks trouble. He's probably in severe discomfort, getting out of bed several times a night to relieve himself. There's always the possibility that a complication might mean I would have to admit him as an emergency.'

In the past two or three weeks, emergency cases have squeezed out a significant number of urgent admissions to Northampton General. Even then, some of these have had to wait in casualty while a consultant found a bed by sending another patient home prematurely. 'We have literally had to throw people out of the hospital who weren't ready to go home in order to cram in another emergency sitting in casualty,' says Chapman. 'It's ridiculous.'

He pulls another card from the pile: a 70-year-old woman who had an emergency colostomy operation 18 months ago (insertion of a bowel outlet in the abdomen). She should have been readmitted 15 months ago for the operation to be reversed. Now Chapman books her down for the week after next.

'The lady hasn't been in great pain, but to cope with a colostomy at her age is quite traumatic and she has had to wait 15 months longer than necessary. She is very embarrassed, and even now I can't say categorically I will get her in the week after next.'

Chapman picks another card at random. This time it carries a red sticker, telling him that a GP believes the patient now needs 'very urgent treatment.' It is another elderly patient with a suspected tumour, who goes on to the next week's list. [© Times Newspapers Ltd. 1978. This is about the first quarter of quite a long article.]

The typographical contrast between the statement set out at the top of the article and the body of the text seems intended to signal a contrast between the official (and allegedly misleading) position on hospital waiting lists, and the true situation as revealed by the newspaper's research. To put it that way, legitimately it seems to me, is to see the difference between Mr Ennals and the *Sunday Times* in terms of the content and the truth of propositions: and no doubt that is the way the newspaper sees the relationship. But there is a more complicated relationship between the two texts, if they are regarded as discourses rather than vehicles for content. Discursively, the Ennals statement is a subtext to the *Sunday Times* text, and their relationship is one of intertextuality: the latter could not exist without the former, and finally the *Sunday Times* articulates the same ideology as the subtext. The *Sunday Times* strives to oppose, but cannot break free from, the official formulation of the powerlessness of the sick.

Mr Ennals's statement has the characteristic impersonality of official discourse, and the characteristic modality of authoritarian discourse. To note modality first, of the seven clauses of this text, five are offered as unquestioned assertions: the auxiliaries and verbs are not marked with any expression of tentativeness, or anything less than certainty: 'is', 'is', 'are', 'becomes', 'goes'.

The other two clauses contain modals indicating obligation: one an obligation on the receiver of the statement ('should be'), the other an obligation on the patients ('having to'). There is no equivocation: this is how the situation necessarily is. No space is provided for any questioning of the truth of the claim, or the satisfactoriness of the situation described.

Impersonality of style is a routine feature of official discourse, but the fact that it is a kind of institutional standard should not blind us to the facts that impersonality is indeed significant, and that the significance may be different in different contexts. In this case, the important thing to note is that it is an inappropriate way of handling medical patients, human beings who happen to have acute personal needs. Impersonality here begins with the pseudo-locative phrase 'in the majority of cases', which mystifies a set of complex relationships between patients, their illnesses and their official medical histories, by expressing these relationships in a single locative phrase, a phrase that is indeed pointless here, as far as the literal meaning of 'in' is concerned, but which serves in this register of officialese to obscure relationships that are embarrassing to the discourse. It is impossible to tell from this phrase what the patients are supposed to be doing or experiencing, for they are given no semantic role in the transitivity structure of this clause. But the main vehicle of impersonality is the use of nominal expressions (see p. 79). People and their medical predicaments are encoded in the highly abstract words 'case', 'wait', 'matter' and 'list'. The use of the word 'case' is particularly striking – but only on critical reflection. The word is specifically and conventionally associated with the context of medical records (also the courts, another context with negative connotations), so in a sense its use here is unexceptional, and perhaps unnoticeable. But this conventionality does not mitigate a fact which, on reflection, is rather unpleasant, namely that 'case' is an extremely impersonal expression for referring to an individual suffering from an illness so severe that it requires surgery; the highly general 'matter' referring to the illness works in the same way. To return to 'case', it is foregrounded by three repetitions in a text of only forty-two words, and finally replaced by the inanimate pronoun 'it', thus achieving a remarkable and dehumanizing transformation of a human individual into a depersonalized object. As far as 'wait' is concerned, this noun echoes the main predicate 'wait' associated with the sick people; the noun removes all poten-

tial of action and all suggestion of personal control. Turning
finally to 'list', presumably this is an ordering of patients according to adjudged medical priority. Put on a list, the patient loses
her or his individuality, and is subsumed in an aggregate of
people. (The constant plurals found in mentions of 'groups' efface
individuality in a similar way: 'women', 'football hooligans',
'Asians', etc.) It is a central feature of this parliamentary statement
that impersonality of style leads to depersonalization in the representation of people. Mr Ennals's assurance may or may not
correctly reflect a reality of the prompt availability of treatment,
but at any rate it is unkindly in tone, and sets an official norm
according to which patients are anonymous and powerless.

The main text, the newspaper article itself, complains that the
claim is untrue: that in reality, patients are having to wait an
intolerable length of time for vital surgical attention. The *Sunday
Times*'s ostensible attitude is that this is a bad situation, which
should be changed to provide better and more humane treatment;
and the newspaper represents the surgeon interviewed as taking
the same line. On the surface, both the paper and the surgeon
appear to be on the side of the patients. However, the article
reads rather unsympathetically, and I would want to say that
the overt socially reforming message is weakened by a covert
implication of disregard for the patients. The *Sunday Times* cannot
free itself from the official discourse available for treating this
topic, and so it comes about that the dehumanizing norm which
we found in Mr Ennals's statement persists even in the text that
challenges it.

In the main text, we find again impersonality, and an extreme
inequality of power between the patients and those who are supposed to manage their treatment. Among the linguistic structures
that communicate these ideological features are the lexical classification of participants, their characteristic roles in clause structure
and the types of predicates they accompany.

Let us look first at the ways in which the human participants
are classified lexically, what groups, and styles of reference, are
found. This is a very simple analytic exercise, involving simply
collecting nominal expressions in lists. I have taken full noun
phrases, not pronouns, since the latter are not very informative
for my present purpose, and though they *might* be, there is in
fact nothing in the main text as salient as the astonishing 'it' in
the Ennals statement. The noun phrases seem to fall into two

lists depending on who they refer to: sick people, or patients, and, marginally, their families, on the one hand ((3) below); on the other, medical, administrative and political persons to do with the hospital service (4). These lists are taken from the whole article, not just the extract quoted above. I have added another dimension by arranging each list in an order which reflects my intuition as to how *individuating* the expressions are, going from the most specific to the most general and abstract.

(3) [*Patients:*] 82-year-old Elizabeth Cooper, Miss Cooper, a 70-year-old woman, the lady, this chap, a niece, breadwinner, family, people, these, patient(s) [9 times], urgent cases waiting more than a month, non-urgent cases waiting more than a year, cases awaiting urgent treatment, those who have had to wait for urgent treatment more than a month, those who have had to wait [3 times], urgent waiting cases, urgent cases [twice], non-urgent cases, case(s) [4 times plus the complex noun phrases based on the word], urgent admissions, emergency admissions, emergency cases, emergency [twice], waiting lists, lists [3 times], waiting figures, lengthening queues, overall total, total figure, number [these quantitative expressions occur several times].

The article is in an important sense about individual persons, but it treats them in an extremely impersonal way. Only one individual is referred to by name; four other noun phrases refer to specific persons in casual, commonplace phrases such as 'the lady', 'this chap' (not entirely respectful); two refer to family roles; one speaks very generally of 'people'. The most frequent expression, 'patient(s)', places the people concerned in the category that is most relevant to the article, but note that it is a term which generalizes away from individual reference, and so contributes largely to the atmosphere of impersonality. There is an important point about 'naturalness' to be repeated here (cf. my comment on 'case' in the Ennals statement). Although it may seem natural, even inevitable, to speak repeatedly about 'patients' in this article, given the subject-matter, this does not neutralize the stylistic or ideological effect of the usage, but merely makes it less noticeable. Of course, the same point can be made in relation to the frequent references to 'case' in the main text.

Another notable feature of the word 'case', as used in this text, is the fact that it provides the basis for an extensive technical system for classifying types of patient. In *Language and Control*[3] we noted how in official discourse nominal forms readily breed systems of technical terms. What happens here is that compound noun phrases based on 'case', 'waiting', 'list' and related terms ('urgent cases waiting more than a month', etc.) proliferate to form a taxonomy of patients seen as 'waiters'. This proliferation of complex nominal expressions makes very visible the parameters of the classifying system, inserting the structure of the system between the individuals to whom the text refers and the reader's perception of those individuals. As the remainder of the list of patients (3) shows, the purpose of the system is to subject the patients to quantification, to sort them into categories for the purpose of ranking and counting: a process which is far removed from writing of the particularities of their condition – and, I would argue, discourages *thinking* about individuals and their particular ills.

The list of politicians, administrators and medical staff differs sharply from the list of patients:

(4) [*Other*:] (David) Ennals [10 times], (John) Chapman [7 times], (Maurice) McLain [twice], Dr Maurice Miller, Dr [Sir, 1986] Gerald Vaughan, Secretary for Social Services, the Hon. Gentleman, chairman, the minister, an opposition health spokesman, surgeon(s) [3 times], consultant [4 times], a GP, colleagues [twice], politicians, (health) administrators [4 times], doctors, general surgeons, orthopaedic surgeon(s) [twice], nurses, anaesthetists, back-up staff, MPs [8 times], the Commons, Parliament, health authorities, Ennals' department.

We note first of all the presence of persons of high prestige, and the fact that they are named and given their titles: an important individuating feature, virtually absent from the first list. Those who are not named at least receive a role term such as 'chairman', 'opposition health spokesman' (cf. the vague 'lady', 'chap'). There are numerous precise occupational labels: 'nurses', 'anaesthetists', and so on. Even the less personal categories, such as 'Parliament', point to sets of specific individuals in such a way that one could discover who these people are, which is not possible with, for instance, 'non-urgent cases', which is an artificial product of the classification system, with completely anonymous members.

A further differentiation between the two sets emerges when

we examine how they relate to predicates. The nouns from the 'Patients' list (I will abbreviate them as 'P' – though I apologize for diminishing them even further!) often relate to state predicates, including mental states, and characteristically have the semantic role of experiencer:

(5) P are alive, [woul]d be 93, [i]s in severe discomfort, [is]n't quite ready, [has]n't been in great pain, is very embarrassed, needs, housebound, has given up hope, relies on, could cry.

P nouns are very rarely agents of actions, and these are usually actions that affect only the patient him-/herself.

(6) P getting out, relieve himself, cope with, eases the pain.

Other apparent actions of P really refer to processes relating P to the waiting lists ((7) below) and therefore should be grouped with predicates that indicate states and changes of state of the waiting lists ((8) below):

(7) P been waiting, wait, had to wait, goes on to, waiting, having to wait, goes to, wait, on the waiting list, awaiting, had to wait, waits, have been waiting.
(8) number of P down/up/decreasing [many instances], lengthening queues of P, on his list, rise in number of P.

P nouns are also the patients (in the semantic sense) of action predicates of which individuals from the other list (surgeons, etc.) are the agents; sometimes in passive constructions:

(9) P be called in, admit P, squeezed out P, sending P home, throw P out, cram in P, P be readmitted, books P down, gets P in, take P, P marked for, cut P, reduce P, decides P, promised P, told P.

A telling list. Some of the verbs designate violent physical actions: 'squeezed out', 'cut'. Though a sympathetic reader might excuse these because they are used metaphorically, the words and their connotations *are* in the text, and some are not metaphorical: 'throw out', 'cram in'. The world-view of the *Sunday Times*, and perhaps subconsciously of the surgeons from whom these words are quoted, accepts that patients can be subjected to violent physical manipulation.

Finally, as might be expected, the predicates associated with the doctors, administrators and politicians are much more active than those associated with P quoted above; they include the actions just mentioned in (9), the physical handling by John Chapman of his card index and other activities.

(10) [*Actions:*] scans through, pulling from, admit, found, sending home, throw out, cram in, pulls from, books P down, get P in, picks, take P, set ourselves, spending, dealing with, spend, share.

(11) [*Speech acts:*] call in, says, say, answering, told, declared, added, assure, present a picture, misled, told, say, told, explained, asked, explain, told, asked, said, said, points out, guarantee, promised.

(12) [*Mental processes (rather than states) involving judgement or reflection:*] deciding, believes, inferred, was selective, chose, compared, inferred, identify, thought, expect, seek consolation, believe, decides.

Mere states (of the doctors, etc.) are few: 'quietly indignant', 'depressing'. These individuals are almost never *experiencers* or *patients*, and then self-pityingly: MPs are 'misled', surgeons are 'cajoled'.

The picture emerges of a large number of specific surgeons, politicians, administrators and the like, who are being active and vociferous, if ineffectual; and of countless anonymous patients who have no opportunity for action, or even for personal recognition. The latter are, linguistically, on the receiving end of official actions, but all that happens to them is that they get classified, quantified and ranked. I do not think that this is quite the story that the *Sunday Times* wished to tell. The writer of the article would doubtless claim that he has exposed a hospital system whose inadequate resources seriously underserve the needs of patients, and which desperately requires both more funds and also procedural reform. But in writing about the inadequacy of the system, the text uses institutional language which strongly encodes a power differential as if it were natural. I suspect that the mass publication of such discourse tends to inhibit, rather than encourage, change.

This text is no rarity as an instance of the inherent contradiction that traps a writer when s/he leans on official discourse. This conventional middle-class discourse, quite ordinary in its stylistic character, is the standard mode for discussing matters of public concern in serious media contexts. It would take a major, bold and self-conscious shift of discourse for a newspaper writer to avoid this mould. It is difficult to see how the commercial Press could tolerate such a deviation.

LAW AND ORDER

One of the most disturbing social developments of the late 1970s and the 1980s was the proliferation of violent incidents in public places, involving large numbers of people and police. For example, what the Press called 'riots' at Toxteth in Liverpool, Handsworth in Birmingham, Southall in London; mass industrial picketing at Grunwick, Warrington and Wapping, and at Orgreave and many other locations during the 1984–5 miners' strike; violence at and around football matches, including the horrific events at Heysel Stadium in Belgium in May 1985, when nearly forty people were killed as a result of fighting between Liverpool and Juventus supporters. Deaths and serious injuries were commonplace at these troubles, as was damage to and destruction of property. As the scale and violence of such events increased, so did the level of police activity, and its style changed. Larger numbers of officers were mustered on such occasions; forces were drafted from one area of the country to another, particularly during the miners' strike. The police were equipped in an increasingly military fashion, using riot shields, plastic bullets, horses and armoured vehicles. They were given special training in 'riot control'. There is ample evidence on film and other documentation of the use of military tactical procedures at locations such as Orgreave; evidence too of needless brutality on the part of individual police officers.

'Public order' or 'disorder' during this period was an extremely difficult and controversial matter to think about and discuss. A fundamental intellectual difficulty was caused by formulating the matter as a single issue in the first place, and yet this is what was done in the culture's public discourse, and we will look at some of the discursive mechanisms for generalization in a moment. In fact, the behaviours and incidents subsumed under this heading were dissimilar: urban riots in depressed areas usually with high unemployment and a high black population; crowd trouble at or around football matches caused deliberately by violent hooligans choosing the occasion; mass picketing relating to specific industrial issues; 'peace people' or 'hippies' camping on private land; assemblies or marches against nuclear weapons or apartheid or unemployment; and so on. It would have been much easier to discuss these diverse topics – and probably to tackle the problems – if they had been analysed separately, but as it happens all parties to the discussion visualized them stereotypically, as instances of a single paradigm, viewed of course from quite different angles depending on their politics and social theory. The Conservative government in office since 1979 represented public disturbances as straightforward criminality, a view which the media supported by constantly speaking of 'riots', 'mobs', 'violence'; the government's response was to strengthen the powers of the police and of the courts. The Left saw vandalism and violence as expressions of social malaise caused by government policies which brought unemployment, deterioration of health care and education, etc., and industrial and political demonstrations as legitimate exercise of the right to free speech against such policies. The Left also saw evidence of police provocation and brutality, and improper use of the courts. Finally, the Left claimed, plausibly, that the government's tough line on 'public order' had political motivations: a 'law and order' policy was a vote-catcher for Conservatives; and trades unions and political demonstrators posed political threats which could be countered partly by outlawing public assembly.[4] On this view, the police were being used as a political instrument.

At this point it would have been possible and illuminating to analyse newspaper representations of some violent public disturbance, and indeed I did consider looking at the 'battle for Orgreave' during the miners' strike in May and June 1984: the conflict between pickets and police over the delivery of coal to the British Steel Corporation's coke-making plant at Orgreave, near Sheffield. The series of incidents at Orgreave is extensively documented and discussed,[5] and television coverage provided some lingering powerful images. But other material, of a more general and inclusive kind, became available, allowing more direct access to the abstract paradigms underlying the theme of 'public order', and also making visible the interaction between the voices of the government and of the newspapers in the discussion of the powers to control behaviour in public. This opportunity came with the publication on 16 May 1985 of a White Paper, the *Review of Public*

Order Law (Command 9510), and the extensive Press coverage it received on 17 May.[6]

The White Paper reported the conclusions of a review of public order legislation, which had been initiated in 1979, and was reportedly speeded along in response to the miners' strike of 1984–5. At the time of the review, the main statutory instrument available was the Public Order Act, 1936, controlling marches, formulated against the Mosleyites, but first used against striking Derbyshire miners in 1937; common law offences were also available, and antique offences such as an 1875 offence of 'watching and besetting' were used during the 1984–5 strike. The review recommended that common law offences should be replaced by new statutory offences of riot, violent disorder and affray; that the law should be tightened up in relation to threatening words and behaviour, and incitement to racial hatred. It also sought advice on other possibilities such as an offence of 'disorderly conduct'.

In Parliament and in the Press, less attention was given to the proposed new offences than to proposals concerning police control of marches, and of static meetings and demonstrations. This latter extension of existing law to static assemblies seemed to be aimed at industrial picketing, and certain kinds of political demonstrations such as vigils outside embassies, and peace camps at weapons sites; it attracted a good deal of criticism. But perhaps the heart of the matter was the proposed powers for the police to impose conditions on meetings and marches. The police were to be empowered to make stipulations about the numbers, location and duration of marches and meetings where they felt there was a likelihood of serious public disorder, disruption of the local community or coercion or intimidation of individuals. Seven days' notice was to be required for marches and processions (a condition which, as the National Council for Civil Liberties pointed out, would inhibit spontaneous response to an immediate situation). The police would be given the authority to ban a *single* demonstration (rather than imposing a blanket ban, as was the practice). This selectivity, and the requirement of advance notice, alarmed Labour MPs; and the extension of the law to picketing would, according to the Shadow Home Secretary, Gerald Kaufman, turn the police 'into the reluctant and unwilling agents of the government's industrial and political policies' (*The Times*, 17 May 1986). Breach of police conditions would be an offence with heavy penalties, particularly for those individuals who organized non-compliance with the conditions. Among other matters offered for discussion was the possibility of the police taking legal action against the organizers to recover policing costs when conditions were breached: a possibility not too distant in potential effect from the idea floated two years earlier, during an anti-CND drive, that demonstrators should pay the costs of their own policing.

The White Paper contained a complex set of proposals, which were reported in detail only in *The Times*, the *Telegraph* and the *Guardian*. All of the papers offered revealing condensations of one sort or another, and these synopses help us to consider the question: what is this report, as mediated for us by the press, essentially *about*? Does the Press see the essence of the report as a concern with violence, or with freedom, or with the police, or with picketing, football hooliganism or what? And how does the Press's perception relate to the 'official' presentation, for example to the words of the Home Secretary?

The then Home Secretary Leon Brittan's presentation of the White paper in the House of Commons on 16 May specifies the new offences and police criteria in detail, but uses rather general terms when referring to the problems and situations which the proposed legislation is intended to cover. His speech is reported, apparently complete and verbatim, in *The Times*, from which the quotations below ((13)-(15)) are taken. In the first paragraph, he generalizes about the problems which have given rise to the report: 'we have taken into account the lessons to be learnt from the varying forms of major public disorder in recent years'. But although the report in the newspaper mentions specific recent instances of 'disorder' such as secondary picketing at the Grunwick film processing laboratory, Mr Brittan does not. He speaks frequently of 'marches', 'assemblies' and 'demonstrations', but rarely ventures the specific instance or category; but when he does approach the specific, his language becomes emotive:

(13) One of the major developments of recent years has been that the threat to public order or to the rights of the individual is nowadays often posed not by a march but by a static demonstration or assembly – whether it is a football crowd that has turned into a mob or a mass picket behaving in an intimidatory manner.

Despite the general belief that the miners' strike was the main spur to the recommendations, the word 'picket' is used only three times in Mr Brittan's speech. Questioning by Gerald Kaufman immediately forces him to confront the issue, or his anxiety about it, more directly:

(14) During the course of the strike there were criminal offences committed daily on the picket line.

One of the main purposes of the proposed new legislation was no doubt to allow this 'criminality' to be defined more enforceably. (Thousands of miners were arrested and charged during the miners' strike, but very few cases were actually brought to court or, if brought, prosecuted successfully.) Overall, Mr Brittan's speech is very delicate on the question of what the legislation refers to; it sticks to generalization in terms of a Tory model of freedom and responsibility. Here is the conclusion of the speech, considerably more rhetorical than the body of the text:

(15) The White Paper contains a set of proposals which bring up-to-date the age-old balance between fundamental but sometimes competing rights in our society. We must and shall continue to preserve the basic and crucial right to freedom of speech and freedom of assembly. These freedoms are essential to any democratic society. They must be given full and effective protection.

But people also have the right to protection against being bullied, hurt, intimidated or obstructed, whatever the motive of those responsible may be, whether they are violent demonstrators, rioters, intimidatory mass pickets or soccer hooligans. I believe these proposals will contribute in a practical way to protecting both sets of freedoms.

There is a curious mixture of styles here. In the penultimate paragraph, we find the discourse of pseudo-philosophy in the manner of Mill on Liberty, with a strong modality suggesting necessary truth, and a moral obligation on government. But in the last paragraph the hitherto almost suppressed force of violence and abuse comes to the surface: derogatory categorizations such as we have often seen in the texts discussed in this chapter ('violent demonstrators', etc.) imagined as the agents of predicates designating brutal actions ('bullied', etc.). The government 'must protect people' against these disorderly threats.

The newspapers on the whole take their cue not from the 'philosophical' apologia, nor from the technical details of the proposed legislation, but from Mr Brittan's threatening conclusion. The matter is overwhelmingly represented as a 'crackdown' or 'curb' against certain categories of violent behaviour, and welcomed as such. Here is how the *Sun* tells the story:

(16) **BRITTAN ACTS TO CRUSH TERROR OF THE THUGS**
   ● **Picket-line law is planned**
   ● **Crackdown on soccer louts**

By TREVOR KAVANAGH

Home Secretary Leon Brittan yesterday declared war on thugs who bring terror to ordinary folk.

He announced that police are to be given tough new powers to deal with soccer hooligans, picket lines, marches, and racial hatred.

Mr Brittan said people had the right to be protected from being bullied, hurt, intimidated or obstructed.

The key proposals – published in a White Paper yesterday – are:

SOCCER crowd limits will be set by police at matches where there is a serious threat of trouble.

PICKET line numbers will also come under police control when there is a danger of obstruction or intimidation.

MARCH organizers must give seven days' notice – and police will now be able to ban a single march instead of imposing a blanket ban on a whole area.

RACIAL incitement laws are to be amended to include a new offence of behaviour intended to cause race hatred.

Violent

Mr Brittan said the proposals – which will become law in the next session of Parliament – would strike a balance between protecting the right to demonstrate and protecting the public.

They follow a series of violent episodes, including the 1979 Southall riots, the 1981 riots in Brixton and Toxteth.

Labour Home Affairs spokesman Gerald Kaufman

criticized the proposals, claiming the police would become 'unwilling agents of Government policies.'

Cops back new powers

By SUN REPORTER

- POLICE Federation chairman Leslie Curtis welcomed the new proposals and said they would make the law 'more enforceable.'
- He added: 'It appears they give more discretion to senior police officers to use their common sense.'
- Charles McLachlan, Chief Constable for Nottinghamshire, said: 'We do not want more and more laws which would prove difficult to enforce.'
- 'But these plans on the whole, are very good,' he added.

The first two sentences of the main text of the article contain clauses which sort the participants into the relationships which dominate the newspaper's vision of the situation:

(17) (a) thugs who bring terror to ordinary folk
      (b) Leon Brittan declared war on thugs
      (c) police are to be given tough new powers to deal with soccer hooligans, picket lines, marches, and racial hatred.

(17a) simplifies the analysis of the existing situation that the new legislation is supposed to address: it proposes an 'us/them' dichotomy (cf. pp. 52–3) in which 'ordinary folk' have the role *patient*, terrorized by a deviant out-group of 'thugs'. Clause (b) and the main headline state how the situation is to be transformed by putting the boot on the other foot, as it were (note the violent and militaristic predicates assigned to the Home Secretary): the thugs become the patients, to be crushed as a result of Brittan's action. (17c), about instrumentality, is in fact two clauses: in the first the police have the semantic role *beneficiary*, benefiting from 'tough new powers'; in the second they become *agent*, 'dealing with' – not 'crushing', note – 'soccer hooligans, picket lines, marches, and racial hatred'. The levelling effect of the list – a standard effect of listing syntax – is noteworthy. It is not only soccer hooligans who are 'thugs', we are also meant to regard pickets, demonstrators on marches and people intending to incite racial hatred[7] as equally 'thugs'. It is quite obvious, on reflection, that these four categories are very different, but for the newspaper they belong to the same paradigm, with soccer hooligans as the extreme and typical case. This levelling under a general term of abuse is common in the other papers. The *Express* has a main headline

(18) **Brittan declares war on the nation's bully boys**

and a subsidiary

(19) **Welcome curb on the bully boys**

The *Express* also uses the listing structure, generalizing about violence

(20) on the picket line, on the streets and on the soccer terraces

and specifying 'bully boys' as associated with

(21) race riots, animal rights demos, Grunwick, Greenham Common, the miners' strike and the Libyan embassy siege

So the women at the peace camp outside the Greenham Common cruise missile base (who were the victims of much violence and abuse by the police, the military and local people – 'ordinary folk') are branded 'bully boys', such is the irrational power of this simplifying stereotype.

If we now line up all the headlines from the reports of 17 May, we will see how general the patterns so far identified are in the media coverage of the White Paper. (*Asterisked examples below are the headings of editorials.)

(16) **Brittan acts to crush terror of the thugs**

(*Sun*)

(18) **Brittan declares war on the nation's bully boys**

(*Express*)

(19) **Welcome curb on the bully boys**

(*Express*)

(22) (a) **Blitz on the mob thugs**
    (b) **Blitz on thuggery**
    (c) ***Just what the public ordered**

(*Daily Mail*)

(23) **Brittan to crack down on violence**

(*Daily Star*)

(24) **Curb on Mobs**

(Mirror)

(25) (a) **New police powers against mobs**
    (b) ***Public order review**

(Eastern Daily Press)

(26) (a) **Brittan plans law to nip mob rule in the bud**
    (b) **Brittan plans mob law**
    (c) **Anti-mob laws to let police curb demos in advance**
    (d) **'Political role' feared in control of pickets**
    (e) ***Public Order**

(Daily Telegraph)

(27) (a) **Police powers to curb crowd violence proposed**
    (b) **Powers to curb mob violence proposed**
    (c) **New powers on pickets and football crowds proposed**
    (d) **Brittan rejects Labour fears and defends powers over picketing**
    (e) ***Ordered freedom**

(The Times)

(28) (a) **Brittan gives police right to ban protests**
    (b) **Government attacked about plan to give police powers over marches**
    (c) **Ministers seek tougher police powers to combat pickets**
    (d) **Brittan proposals will mean police have to make political decisions – Labour**
    (e) ***The order of one day, and the next**

(Guardian)

There is a substantial uniformity in the way these headlines précis the White Paper and its presentation. What is being referred to, remember, is a complex set of proposals for changes in one area of the law, as presented in a just-published printed document and a parliamentary statement by the Home Secretary. However, what the dominant transitivity pattern of the headlines conveys is something quite different: a relationship between two participants in which one has an agentive role, performing a simple action affecting the other; in tabular form:

Agent	Action	Patient or affected
Brittan	crush	thugs
police	curb	demos
etc.		

Let us extend the materials by listing expressions from other relevant clauses in the texts which the headlines summarize:

| police, Brittan, government, legislation, law, powers | blitz, crack down on, deal with, tougher sentences, control, fix limits, ban, curb, cope with, plans to outlaw, declare war on, limit numbers, limit, catch up with, hit, order, move, crush, set limits, nip in the bud, combat, prevent | (1) marches, violent demonstrators, mass demonstrations, demonstrations, protest groups, violence at demos, demos, static demonstrations, open-air meetings, riotous marches, racist demonstrators, protests (2) soccer fans, soccer crowd, football hooligans, soccer hooligans, soccer thugs, soccer louts (3) picket-line numbers, picket lines, intimidatory mass pickets, picket line crowds, picket line clashes, rowdy pickets (4) mob thugs, mob violence, rioters, mobs, bully boys, thuggery, mob rule, thugs, crowd violence |

The table virtually speaks for itself. I would want to say that the dominant pattern, presented schematically here, encodes a view of the world which assumes the polarization of groups, conflict of interest and the desirability of the repression or destruction of 'them' (demonstrators, hooligans, etc.) by the legitimated agents who work on behalf of 'us' (the Home Secretary, the police). It is to be understood that the participants listed above under 'Agent' occur over and over again in texts analysed, so that the police and the government are overwhelmingly in the *agent* role in transitivity, while the marginalized and attacked groups are always *affected* or *patient* – power is distributed in just the way it is in the hospital text. There are very few clauses like (17a), 'thugs who bring terror to ordinary folk': the existence and culpability of such thugs does not need to be asserted in this context, since they are assumed to have been demonstrated adequately (to the point of consensus) by the newspapers' routine, hostile reporting of 'riots', 'clashes', 'hooliganism', day by day.

By contrast with the lexical economy of the agent column, notice that the patients are subjected to overlexicalization (many different terms are used and repeated) like the young people referred to in the articles on contraception analysed in chapter 6; we would expect this, since violence and disorder are preoccupations of the popular Press. I have categorized the 'Patients' or 'Affected' into four sub-classes, the first three answering to topics specified by branches of the new legislation; there is by the way a relative silence on the fourth topic, incitement to racial hatred, presumably because the topic is an awkward one for some newspapers, hostile to 'foreigners' and to 'racial minorities', to address (see chapter 7). Category (4) consists of abusive general terms employed largely in the headlines (except in the *Guardian*) which can be applied to any of the members of (1), (2) or (3). The blurring or levelling of these categories has already been illustrated from the *Daily Express* (see (19)-(21), and comment); it is endemic in the reports, and this fact can hardly facilitate objective discussion. Still, objective discussion is obviously not the point here; what is going on is that the 'groups' which are to be targeted by the proposed legislation are, in the newspapers, first discriminated by overlexicalization and repeated mention, and implicitly tarred with the same brush, the smear of violence.

A further point made overt by the table is the contradiction involved in the accusation of violence. Whatever the actual violence of the various groups addressed by the legislation, in these texts they are coded as patients, not agents: the recipients, not the initiators, of violent actions. What is more, the predicates relating the police and the government to the demonstrators, soccer fans and pickets are noticeably violent ('crush', 'hit'), even militaristic ('blitz', 'declare war on', 'combat').

This last observation could be a starting-point for broadening the enquiry. So far I have commented on newspaper stories about distinct topics: hospital surgery, contraception, public order. I have made the point, fleetingly, in a few cross-references, that the texts are not separate and self-contained. All of them imply an absolute difference of power between groups of people, with the lower groups always presenting a problematic crisis for the upper group. And there are common elements in the various proposals for managing the crises: force and restrictive legislation (never sympathetic social and economic change). We have seen that violent and militaristic language is common in the texts, and that is part of a more general 'atmospheric' ideological mood, the sense that a conflict model is relevant to class relations: since the Falklands, a *combat* model. An extension of our analysis would show how pervasive this ideology of aggression and warfare is. If I simply set out all the headlines from the one relevant page of the *Sun* newspaper of 17 May 1985, the point will be obvious:

(29) **Brittan acts to crush terror of the thugs**
(30) **Picket-line law is planned**
(31) **Crackdown on soccer louts**
(32) **Cops back new powers**
(33) **Duran's view to a killing**
(34) **Maggie's walloping for wets**
(35) **Sextuplet's battle**
(36) **Rev cleared in sex case**
(37) **Dearer butter**

Numbers (29)–(32) are about the public order proposals. It is the language of (33), (34) and (35) which is to be particularly noted: 'killing', 'walloping', 'battle'. Only (36) and (37) are without violent references, but that is fortuitous. I am quite sure that a study of the language used to report 'sex cases' and home economics would add to the ideological picture which I have been building up. In chapters 9 and 10, I will discuss more fully the way in which abstract paradigms or general ideas persist in texts which are superficially about quite diverse subjects, and the linguistic mechanisms which are deployed to maintain these paradigms.

Chapter 9

A Press scare: the salmonella-in-eggs affair

PRESS HYSTERIA

In the winter of 1988–9, for roughly the three months from late November to early March, an hysterical episode of massive proportions built up in the British media. There was a panic about food poisoning, and specifically about two types of bacterial poisoning the incidence of which allegedly had been increasing alarmingly: salmonella poisoning caused by the strain *Salmonella enteritidis* phage type 4, apparently newly discovered to be present in eggs (as opposed to poultry meat); and listeriosis, a flu-like illness caused by *Listeria monocytogenes*, a bacterium occurring widely in the environment and now found in pre-cooked and chilled food, and some cheeses. Food poisoning 'cases' and 'outbreaks' had apparently increased substantially in numbers over recent years and months; and during the panic of that winter, a few deaths and stillbirths specifically linked to salmonella and listeria occurred or were reported.

To have doubt cast on eggs and cheese, staple foods in Britain and inexpensive sources of protein, was alarming enough. The Press kept these products in high focus throughout the period, reporting all statements by politicians and experts, giving statistics, dispensing advice, investigating producers and retail outlets, commenting on the responsibilities and shortcomings of the government departments involved (Health and Agriculture). But the panic went far beyond eggs and cheese: it collected all kinds of problems in a wide range of areas, some quite unrelated to the two bacteria and their effects. In the sphere of food, other dangerous organisms or substances were identified (e.g. aluminium coating on sweets, pesticide residues in cereal products);

there was a general concern with hygiene in shops, restaurants and kitchens, with adulteration and with the production of food (the use of animal remains in animal feed, milk hormone, high-technology practices in food production generally). The concern broadened to include other kinds of 'poisoning' and 'infection' (hepatitis, legionnaires' disease). Widening further, it included contamination of water supplies, highlighted by illnesses caused in an area of North Cornwall by the accidental dumping of aluminium sulphate in the main supply; the concern with water was sustained by parliamentary and public discussion of the privatization of the water industry. Numerous other specific environmental hazards were reported (radon gas, methane in rubbish tips), often in articles placed adjacent to reports of the latest on the salmonella scare. By February 1989 the context was global; copious discussion in the Press of such matters as the destruction of the Amazonian rain forests, breaches in the ozone layer caused by the use of CFCs, acid rain, an oil spillage in the Antarctic and the 'greenhouse effect' gave salmonella and listeria a heightened, universal significance. They were by now instances of 'The poisoning of our world' (*Daily Express*, 13 February 1989).

I would like to explain carefully what I mean by 'hysteria'. We are told that the bacteria concerned are dangerous. For example, Dr Barbara Lund of the Institute of Food Research in Norwich was quoted by the *Eastern Evening News* on 24 February 1989:

> (1) I feel that listeria presents a health risk to the public. Listeria is life-threatening, causing quite a variety of symptoms.
>
> In pregnant women it tends to give a generalized infection like flu. This can result in the foetus being aborted, or birth of an infected baby which is very seriously diseased.

In using the word 'hysterical', I do not wish to suggest that salmonella and listeria poisoning are insignificant or illusory. Nor am I in a position to claim that the level of public alarm was out of proportion to the level of medical risk and actual illness ('the risks are exaggerated', as some contributors to the debate, notably government spokesmen, alleged): the facts about 'infection' are themselves controversial or inaccessible, so I cannot easily say that the public response was excessive. Certainly, people have died from these causes. Without meaning to contrast the facts and the newspapers' response to them, one can assert that this response was hysterical in terms of its high emotive content, the

massive scale of Press reporting and its extraordinary generalization to 'the poisoning of our world'.

Hysteria is not simply behaviour which is in excess of the
events which provoked it; it is also behaviour which attains autonomy, which sustains itself as an expressive performance, independent of its causes. People behaving hysterically 'go on and on'
(sustain) and 'shout and scream' (excess, express). Hysteria
requires an expressive system, a mode of discourse, and, established, exists within that mode of discourse independent of
empirical reality. Since expressive systems are shared among
members of a community, hysteria can be intersubjective: mass
hysteria. Such was the status of listeria hysteria/the great egg
scare: once established in the discourse of the media, it persisted
autonomously within that discourse, going on and on at an
increasing pitch independent of the factual unfolding of the
matter. The great egg scare was not a medical phenomenon, not
an epidemic; it was a construct of discourse, a formation and
transformation of ideas in the public language of the newspapers
and television.

I am speaking then, of hysteria *in the Press*. When the newspapers spoke, as they did frequently, of an 'eggs panic' or 'eggs
scare', it was not clear who was supposed to be scared. There
were occasionally interviews with individuals, for example
mothers of young children, who confessed to alarm or confusion;
and the writer of one cookery feature declared that she had not
bought eggs 'for some months' because she could not feel them
to be '100 per cent safe' (*The Times*, 4 February 1989). The letters
columns during the period I sampled contained little evidence of
panic, though there were many controlled and informed attacks
on modern food production practices, and on the failure of
government departments to control these practices in the interest
of consumers, or to manage the crisis politically. No relatives,
colleagues, acquaintances or neighbours of mine panicked, though
most exercised caution in the use of eggs. A common response,
in the rural Norfolk community where I live, was that 'it was a
load of old squit': 'they' were always telling 'us' that one food
or another was unsafe, it was all empty talk and we should just
get on and eat what we wanted. Whatever one thinks of this
attitude, it does highlight the fact that the crisis was discursive
rather than empirical. It was triggered by an outspoken pro-
nouncement in December by the Junior Health Minister Mrs

Edwina Currie (see the sections on 'Participants' and 'Chronology' below) and then maintained at a high level of stridency within the discourse of the media. In this sense the salmonella-in-eggs affair was a case of Press hysteria similar to other well-documented cases such as the 'Mattoon anaesthetic prowler' and the 'Seattle windscreen pitting' referred to in chapter 2, p. 14.

The AIDS scare is analogous, and relevant, because it afforded the Press an opportunity to practise the management of something which was dramatically negative and which could be presented as a 'public health problem', a 'social disease of our time'. Suddenly publicized in the 1980s, Acquired Immune Deficiency Syndrome escalated, in the Press, from a specific and novel catastrophic illness associated with homosexuals and drugs needle sharers, to a 'gay plague'. The discourse made much reference to statistical predictions: 'cases' or deaths in Britain by such-and-such a year, in America by the end of the century, and so on. Incidence of the illness would apparently rise geometrically. Calculations began to refer not only to homosexual relationships, but also to multiple sexual contacts, and to heterosexual transmission, said to be rising. This last factor permitted a shift in the discourse. As long as AIDS was presented as a 'gay plague', the newspapers could regard it as a deplorable product of the behaviour of 'others': those people who are 'not like us'. The discourse was about perversion, promiscuity, self-infliction. AIDS had at first been seen as threatening 'us' only as innocent bystanders: medical staff, haemophiliacs, the victims of road accidents, etc., who might receive transfusions of infected blood. Now the heterosexual dimension allowed the newspapers to talk about innocent babies infected in the womb (the discussion of listeriosis followed this model), and about the perils of *any* sexual contact. By 1989 AIDS was presented as a sign of the times, a condition of a sick 'western' society approaching the end of a millennium. As for 'us', we are all touched by it, it is for 'us' a matter of individual responsibility, as the condom campaign instructed us. This logic was followed in the discursive representation of the food poisoning scare, as we shall see.

The discursive output of the salmonella affair was massive, and astonishingly complex. My account of it is an attempt to understand it, not a definitive analysis. When Mrs Currie's statement in December triggered the furore, I considered starting to collect materials for analysis, but at the time decided against, partly because I had other topics planned for this book, and partly because I feared the problem of coping with the immense amounts of data that seemed likely. Early in February, when the topic was fully established in the Press, and indeed escalating in its daily production of new instances of danger and scandal, I could no longer ignore the importance and interest of the salmonella-in-eggs hysteria. Even so, it was impossible for a lone researcher and author to handle anything like the complete newspaper coverage. I started with reasonable samples from December and January culled from newspapers that had happened to remain in the house. From the beginning of February I bought at least two newspapers a day, varying them somewhat; more when I knew that some significant development had taken place or would take place; and I also scanned any other newspapers which I came across casually – in the village pub, in common rooms and waiting areas at the university, and so on. I stopped collecting materials in mid-March, a couple of weeks after the House of Commons Agriculture Committee published its report on the salmonella-in-eggs affair. By that time, I had obtained over three hundred cuttings of reports and features, generally substantial articles printed in prominent positions in the papers. The articles were not only about salmonella and listeria, but also about other food bacteria such as campylobacter; about farming and food production practices; about the conditions of storage, marketing and service of foods; about restaurant and kitchen hygiene; about adulterated food and meals; about water poisoning; about environmental damage – CFCs, the Amazonian rain forest, etc. – which became a major topic as February progressed, and was clearly associated with the food poisoning scare by the language used and the juxtaposition of articles on the page. I collected not only major and central stories but also minor and tangential reports, e.g. **'Toenail in MP's food'** (*Sun*, 3 February 1989), and even articles and headlines which merely used the *language* of the food scare while actually being about something else: **'Tummy trouble'** (*Sun*, 2 February 1989), which actually concerns 'stomach exercisers fitted with faulty springs', and **'Getting back to culinary basics in the Budget'**, (*Independent*, 2 February 1989), which is about the imminent March Budget but takes a metaphor from the current discourse exhorting elementary good practice in the kitchen – hygiene, fresh ingredients.

The texts are as obscure and complex as they are voluminous.

They are hysterical and confusing in tone and content, and this chapter will be largely devoted to describing the styles of hysteria. In the next chapter, I will try to answer the by-no-means simple questions, what are these texts about? And what is the subject-matter of this discursive excess? First, however, I will indicate the participants and chronology of the affair.

PARTICIPANTS

The food industry   Directly involved, though mostly silent, were *egg producers*, and at a prior stage in 'the food chain', the manufacturers of feed for hens. It was thought that the spread of salmonella was caused by the use of carcasses of infected birds in the preparation of food for laying hens. This revolting idea, which was matched by other revelations of hidden and unpleasant practices in food manufacture, contributed to the high emotive level of the discourse. Later, publicity about listeria threw the spotlight on producers of *unpasteurized milk, cheese* and *cook-chill meals*. As the crisis broadened, attention was generalized to *farmers, food producers, distributors, retailers* and *restaurants*.

Government departments   The Ministry of Agriculture, Fisheries and Food (MAFF) at that time headed by Mr John MacGregor. It was widely commented that MAFF's broad · constitution required it to represent the potentially conflicting interests of both farmers and consumers, and alleged that MAFF's handling of the salmonella affair favoured farmers rather than consumers; there were allegations of a 'cover-up' by the ministry.

The Department of Health Minister, Mr Kenneth Clarke: accused of tardily publicizing, and of playing down, the risks of salmonella and listeria; statements by the Chief Medical Officer, Sir Donald Acheson, seemed designed to allay public anxiety, rather than provide reliable information about any danger to health. But the most active participant in the Department of Health was the outspoken and photogenic Mrs Edwina Currie, Conservative MP for South Derbyshire, and at the outset of the affair Junior Minister in the Department of Health. Already well known for a series of outrageous statements about eating habits and health, Mrs Currie spoke out on 3 December 1988, claiming that 'most of the egg production in this country, sadly, is infected with salmonella'. Refusing to explain what she meant (i.e.

refusing to stick to the low profile adopted by her department), Mrs Currie was forced to resign on 16 December but maintained a high profile throughout the rest of the affair. The participation of Mrs Currie was a godsend for the newspapers, because it allowed a dimension of personalization (p. 15) in what was essentially a drably political affair. She was mythologized as a fearless champion of the people in the face of the evasions and cowardice of bureaucracy.[1]

Government and Opposition The Conservative Prime Minister, Mrs Margaret Thatcher, made little intervention until late in the process: not until mid-February did headlines such as **'Thatcher to ban unsafe food in shops'** (*Sunday Times*, 12 February 1989) and **'Thatcher moves to end muddle on food hygiene'** (*Daily Telegraph*, 15 February 1989) begin to appear. Meanwhile, the Labour leader Mr Neil Kinnock, and shadow health spokesman Mr Robin Cook, maintained a vigorous parliamentary attack over the government's handling of the crisis and of food matters generally.

The House of Commons Select Committee on Agriculture, Chairman Mr Jerry Wiggin, was charged with investigating the salmonella crisis, and reported on 1 March 1989. The committee had an important role in maintaining a stage for the drama (particularly, in allowing Mrs Currie to continue her performance), and then in helping to bring the crisis to an end; its contribution to the latter process was to blame everyone involved.

Experts For lay people, and presumably for journalists too, the salmonella affair and its relatives were highly mysterious in every aspect: experts were needed to explain the bacteriology, the medical effects, the alleged causes in the food industry and the scale of the 'epidemic' (a statistical construct). A prominent source of advice was Professor Richard Lacey, Professor of Microbiology at Leeds University, who throughout the affair took frequent opportunities to stress the reality of the two principal 'poisonings', the scale of the risk and of the 'epidemic' and the inadequacy of the government's response. Other food scientists told the same story. Their evidence and judgements were invaluable to the newspapers as justification for producing an atmosphere of alarm.

The Press The materials analysed in this chapter suggest that the newspapers were very active in constructing and developing the food poisoning scare. It was a good story: salmonella affects individuals, so the newspapers could directly address their readers, and also validly claim to speak on their behalf; in politics, the fight was led by a newsworthy champion, Mrs Currie, who could be exalted as a popular hero; it was the fault of institutions, business and government, who could be self-righteously castigated. The Press had the benefit of a story which could be maintained at a high level of coverage for several months, a story with a popular appeal; in maintaining the coverage, even to hysterical levels, the newspapers surely performed a public service, in that there is now a greater awareness of the risks presented by modern foods. Even if the gesture was opportunistic, the generalization to environmental damage also raised public consciousness in a welcome way. It is however unlikely that newspaper pressure concerning salmonella, listeria, etc., brought any changes in food legislation or practice.

People It should be clear that this affair had its being in the discourse of institutions and organizations beyond the reach of individual members of the public. People could boil their eggs for seven minutes instead of three, or choose not to buy soft cheese, but they could have no participation in the issues that were being talked about, for instance reform of the responsibilities of MAFF, provision of more veterinary inspection of abattoirs and health inspection of restaurants, banning of the use of suspect substances and practices in food production. Yet 'ordinary people', 'the consumer' and 'the housewife' are important characters in the newspapers' narrative: they are seen as affected in various medical, psychological and constitutional ways, they have various rights, and, above all, responsibilities. I should feel guilty about 'poisoning' every time I wipe down the kitchen table or use my shaving foam.

CHRONOLOGY[2]

The food poisoning hysteria in the newspapers lasted from late November 1988 to early March 1989. But certain earlier events are relevant to its content and its progression. It had long been known publicly that salmonella was generally present in poultry meat, and due precautions were taken to thaw and cook frozen birds thoroughly. The new factor was the discovery of salmonella in eggs. The newspapers took the line that the government had known about this new danger much earlier than the autumn of 1988, but had been forced by pressure from the food lobby, first to conceal the facts, and then to minimize the risks. In the summer and autumn of 1987 there had been outbreaks of egg-related salmonella poisoning in north-eastern America and in Spain; and in the latter part of that year, MAFF and the Health Ministry were allegedly aware of the existence and spread of salmonella in eggs and in the ovaries of egg-laying fowls in Britain. Apparently, intensive research, and checking of farms, went on in the winter and spring of 1987–8, but the public were not informed or warned. In April, seventeen people were poisoned by home-made ice cream in North Humberside, and in May, twenty-four members of the House of Lords were poisoned by mayonnaise.

On 19 July 1988, the Health Ministry warned hospitals not to use raw eggs; the same warning was issued to the public on 26 August. A second press release from Health, on 21 November, extended the warning from raw to soft-boiled eggs. 'It also says 26 outbreaks of egg-associated salmonella have been reported by the public health laboratories' (*Sunday Times*, 22 January 1989; the figure is forty-six in another newspaper source). On 23 November, Professor Lacey suggested on television that the number of cases was likely to be much higher; there began to be talk, denied by the government, of 'a salmonella epidemic of 2m'. This huge number is produced by a hypothetical 100x factor to compensate for under-reporting of minor stomach upsets; it is not my business to discuss the calculation, but the figure was high enough to warrant discursive panic.

On 3 December, Mrs Currie took on the egg producers with her notorious claim that 'most of the egg production in this country, sadly, is infected with salmonella'. The impending hysteria was thereby generously fuelled, and egg sales plunged. MAFF offered a £19 million compensation deal for egg producers. Mrs Currie refused to explain what she meant, and was forced to resign on 16 December. The Press kept her in the news from this date, though she made no further intervention until 25 January, when, in a letter declining to give evidence to the Agriculture Select Committee, she changed her statement to 'a significant number of the egg-laying hens in many of the egg-laying flocks in this country are infected with salmonella'. Forced however to testify two weeks later, Mrs Currie did so in an ostentatiously uncooperative and uninformative manner.[3] In the meantime, it was announced that she had contracted to write 'a wide-ranging book on the state of the nation's health' (*The Times*, 2 February 1989) or, as the *Sun* put it, 'about her adventures as a junior Minister' (6 February).

Meanwhile, in mid-January, the risks from listeria, known the previous year, erupted into a parallel crisis.[4] Perhaps more sinister than salmonella, because less familiar, listeria was said to infect milk and cheese, and convenience meals which were sold cooked and chilled. Deaths were reported, particularly deaths of babies; Professor Lacey was once again called on, to explain the illness listeriosis, and to comment on the rising incidence and the link with certain foods.

The 'revelations' and 'new threat' of listeria added significant dimensions to the food poisoning panic. First, it vastly extended the range of suspect basic foods. Second, it was extremely confusing: no reliable advice was available on which cheeses to avoid (though the finger was briefly pointed at French brie, giving an opportunity for chauvinistic posturing); or on whether pasteurization was relevant or not. Third, as far as pre-cooked meals were concerned, it was easy to deflect the blame from the manufacturer to the housewife:

> (2)   The cook–chill process was not inherently dangerous, it was stated. Contamination was a result of inadequate hygiene and storage arrangements.
>
> (*Sunday Times*, 22 January 1989)

('Blaming the housewife' is discussed further on pp. 186ff.) Finally, the fact that the word 'listeria' rhymes with 'hysteria' was a significant factor: the phrase 'listeria hysteria' soon became current, helping to reify 'the panic'.

In February, the 'Eggs row bubble[d] on' (*Observer*, 12 February) with the Select Committee continuing its deliberations, confronting Mrs Currie and preparing to report. But thanks largely to the compounding effect of listeria and to the introduction of environmental issues, the panic had become much more general. Here are some sample headlines from roughly the first two weeks of February 1989:

(3) **Fears over the toxic cocktail**
Pesticides
Risk of cancer lurks in mains
Pipes
Presence of metal in water linked to Alzheimer's
disease
Aluminium

(*Guardian*, 30 January, all on same page)
Thought for food

(*The Times*, 30 January)
Green consumers 'voting with their wallets'

(*The Times*, 1 February)
Leaking diesel freighter poses threat to Antarctic
environment
BBC fined for legion disease
Radon warning

(*Guardian*, 1 February)
Greenhouse theory after warmest recorded year
Gaps found in code protecting water lands

(*Independent*, 1 February)
Policy on pollution must be spelt out
Public to be told of nuclear accidents
Haute cuisine
Nuclear testing blamed for poisoning islanders' food
UK the dirty man of Europe, peers claim

(*The Times*, 2 February)
Ministers knew of health risk from eggs a year ago
Getting back to culinary basics in the Budget
Tap-water 'failing to meet EC standards'

(*Independent*, 2 February)
Scandal of danger 'slim' aids
Tummy trouble
Tap water beats the bottled!
Beauty creams given green light

(*Sun*, 2 February)
Currie brings salmonella-in-eggs affair to book
US tries to contain Antarctic oil spill
Warning of energy damage

(*The Times*, 3 February)

Toenail in MP's food

(*Sun*, 3 February)

'Green-top' ban
(Sun, 4 February)

Actors win hepatitis payments
Currie may get order to attend
(The Times, 4 February)

Neglected rivers die in stench of scandal
Edwina Currie on politics and health
(Sunday Times, 5 February)

Currie brought to book on eggs
(Observer, 5 February)

Fury over Eggwina's [*sic*] new book
Speak, Edwina
Chemical con is a farce
(Sun, 6 February)

Confusion and concern reign at shop counters as more
  foods go on the danger list and another industry
  faces a crisis
Poisoning scares hit sales and diet habits
Hard choice: C– I– chooses her cheese carefully at a
  Birmingham supermarket [caption to photograph of
  pregnant woman shopping]
EC probe may lead to cut in price of milk
(Sunday Times, 12 February)

End this food roulette
(Observer, 12 February)

Have a heart for housewives
20 ways to beat the killers in your kitchen
(Sun, 13 February)

The poisoning of our world
Minister in great soft cheese muddle
Farmers despair over milk shaker that threatens to
devastate their lives
Turning the heat on a hidden peril
Cheesed off!
(Express, 13 February)

Reprieve for French cheese
Pasteurization cuts risks but is no safety guarantee
'1 in 20' has listeria infection
[Cheese] producers fear hard times
Bacteria 'not so predictable'
(Guardian, 14 February)

This selection of headlines shows that, by February, a 'food poisoning' paradigm was firmly established, still largely focussed on 'the twin perils of listeria and salmonella' (*Sun*, 13 February), but also, in the productive manner of stereotypes, beginning to collect instances of other kinds of threats, broadly environmental. We can also see the high emotive level characteristic of hysteria: in the vocabulary of confusion, danger and crisis, in the obsessive punning.

To complete the chronological background, I would like to make two observations about rhetorical developments in the Press during February. First, there is an increasing stress on the responsibility of 'the consumer' or 'the housewife'. The *Sunday Times*'s representation of a woman 'choosing her cheese carefully' is typical of one strategy for the middle class; the popular papers tend to urge 'the housewife' to keep her kitchen clean; and the phrase 'food hygiene' comes into use in February. A second development during the month was a move towards addressing 'environmental' issues directly, in a sense changing the topic. The *Express*'s banner **'The poisoning of our world'** in mid-February is symptomatic of the change. This headline occurred in an issue in which the argument about cheese-related listeria was very prominent, but it was also followed up by a series of articles about threats to wildlife, etc. The 'quality' papers made a strong environmental investment, e.g. the *Guardian*, 24 February, has several pages on **'The darkening skies'**; the *Independent*, 2 March, features **'The atmosphere at risk'**. *The Times* and the *Sunday Times* went more and more green throughout February: see, for example, the colour magazine, Sunday 26 February: **'The world is dying. What are you going to do about it?'**. So did Prime Minister Thatcher, hosting an international conference on CFCs and the ozone layer: **'Thatcher hogs the green line'**, *Observer*, 26 February.

The final chapter in the salmonella-in-eggs affair properly speaking was written by the Agriculture Select Committee, which reported on 1 March. All the participants received at least criticism, more usually castigation: the egg industry for refusing to accept evidence of salmonella in eggs and for failing to have a hygiene code; MAFF for failing to police the egg industry properly; Mrs Currie for making the remark which caused public alarm, and then taking seven weeks to qualify it; Mr Clarke, the Health Minister, for mishandling the public relations crisis. The still-punning headlines of 2 March encode delight at universal condemnation: '**They all get fried**' (*Guardian*), '**Egg all over their faces**' (*Express*) '**GUILTY!**' (*Sun*), '**Bad egg-timing**' (*Telegraph*). This general condemnation released the safety-valve, reduced the pressure and temperature. The committee report also reassured consumers that the risk from eggs was minimal (the same reassurance had been given by the Health Ministry and the egg producers in November and December 1988):

(4) The report concludes normal, healthy people should **NOT** be worried about salmonella, although there is a 'slight risk' when eating raw eggs.

It adds that the 'tiny' risk of eating eggs is no greater than driving a car, smoking, or making love.

(*Sun*, 2 March)

The salmonella crisis was over. Personal, political and industrial life could return to normal. It is to be noted that no real changes were made in response to the crisis, despite clear and well-founded pleas from the Press and from experts. No mandatory code of practice was created for food producers; MAFF remained responsible for food; no government department was set up to protect consumers' food interests; no steps were taken to increase the inadequate numbers of environmental health officers, or of vets at abattoirs. One newspaper, a few days after the report was published, reported that '**Funding cuts close leading project on salmonella**'.

The *Telegraph* weekend magazine, 4 March, published a lengthy feature '**Inside the food factory**', giving a detailed and approving account of anti-bacterial precautions taken by Marks & Spencer (leading retailers of cook-chill meals and prepared salads) and their suppliers. The narrative concludes with reference to a woman 'pick[ing] two cartons of cannelloni from the shelves'. There immediately follows a two-page, graphically illustrated article '**THE HAZARDS IN YOUR KITCHEN**': 'Food inspector Tony Beeson guides Elisabeth Dunn around a domestic kitchen, identifying risks and explaining how to avoid them'. The responsibility for food poisoning is returned to 'the housewife'.

Or so it seemed, in March. But food scares continued to erupt in the late spring and summer of 1989: contaminated baby food in April, listeria in fast food in July and throughout 1990, BSE or 'mad cow disease'. Public and media concern continued at a high level, with a particular focus on food production and farming practices. In late July, the government published a White Paper, *Food Safety – Protecting the Consumer*, which was widely attacked in the Press for complacency and inadequacy; Egon Ronay condemned it as a 'whitewash' (*Sunday Times*, 13 August 1989). Clearly, the food scare had settled into a permanent critique of commercial food and of the management of food. That seemed still to be the case as I worked on my final revision of this book on 20 February 1990: an item on the BBC–2 television programme *Food and Drink* that evening investigated temperature control and safety in domestic refrigerators, a topic which obviously has the listeria scare as its sub-text. In the next chapter, I will comment on some discursive mechanisms which helped the concern about food persist.

SOME ASPECTS OF HYSTERICAL STYLE

The following extracts illustrate a range of styles of writing about the salmonella affair and its satellite topics:

(5) **Cooked food hazard 'is unchecked'**
Supermarkets are free to keep cook-chill foods in conditions which allow an astronomical increase in listeria bacteria, even though the Government has been warned of the danger by its own public health officials.

Evidence from independent sources emerged yesterday which supports claims by Professor Richard Lacey, the Leeds microbiologist, that listeria food poisoning is a serious and previously hidden health hazard which causes meningitis, still birth, and the death of up to 200 vulnerable people a year.

Supermarkets typically sell cook-chill foods which have been stored for a week or more at temperatures at over 7°C.

But these breeding conditions allow a sudden and exponential leap in the number of bacteria in infected food, according to figures from Dr Richard Gilbert, director of food hygiene at the Public Health Laboratory Service.

They show that listeria will stay virtually dormant for five days after contamination even if the food is stored at 7.5°C. But then reproduction suddenly erupts.

(*Guardian*, 24 January 1989)

(6) **Ministry knew of health risk from eggs a year ago**

The Ministry of Agriculture knew of the salmonella epidemic a year ago but was unable to persuade egg producers of the seriousness of the problem and failed to warn the public, according to confidential reports which have reached *The Independent.*

The ministry had reports 12 months ago showing that in 1987 more than 100 egg and broiler farms were infected by *Salmonella enteritidis* – a threefold increase in the number of infections over the previous year. The link between home and farm was clear because the same type *4 enteritidis* was involved in both places. But the egg industry would not accept the evidence produced by the Public Health Laboratory. . . .

The Department of Health wanted to tell the public that salmonella infection could be carried in raw egg and was not just the result of poor hygiene. But egg industry representatives wanted to put the responsibility for egg poisoning back on to the consumer by emphasizing the need for good hygiene and avoidance of cracked eggs.

So the industry decided to construct a defence that infection within eggs was a near-hypothetical risk. Later this stance was to be translated into the suggestion that the likelihood of egg poisoning was as remote as being struck by a meteorite.

(*Independent*, 2 February)

(7) **Don't delay on new food law**

Agriculture Secretary John MacGregor moves to allay public anxiety about the quality and safety of the food we eat as the 'blacklist' mounts alarmingly.

After a weekend of growing confusion he says, comfortingly, that a Food Act is being drawn up seeking to update old laws which have not kept pace with modern food production.

That's the good news. The bad news is that Mr MacGregor does not have a parliamentary slot. 'It is not for me' he says, meekly. And when it is suggested that perhaps Mr MacGregor *ought* to make it a matter for him, one of his aides replies haughtily 'We don't do things that way in Agriculture.'

The new proposals, perhaps the most urgent facing the Government, must be given top priority.

(*Express*, 13 February)

(8) **The chilling facts of safe home cooking**

Checklist of simple dos and don'ts, compiled with the help of David Edwards of the Food Hygiene Bureau:

- Don't buy cooked-chilled food outside the 'sell-by' date, and eat it by the 'use-by' date.
- Buy cooked-chilled food from reputable shops which show an awareness of hygiene.
- Buy chilled foods at the end of shopping expeditions and get them home to the fridge as soon as possible, particularly in summer.
- Check that your fridge is working properly.
- Follow the cooking instructions and ensure your reheating is thorough.

(*Sunday Times*, 22 January)

(9) **Have a heart for housewives**

What tough days these are for the poor housewife.

When she goes shopping for her family, she must feel as if she is entering a minefield about which foods are safe and which potentially dangerous.

If, in her dilemma, she is angry with the Government, who can blame her? . . .

Since Edwina Currie's famous warning about eggs it has been speaking with two voices – and sometimes with no voice at all – on matters vital to the nation's health.

Agriculture Minister John MacGregor's flirtation with a ban on non-pasteurized cheese is the latest example of fumbling indecisiveness.

He does not exactly say he will forbid imports.

And he does not exactly explain why these products have suddenly become suspect.

(*Sun*, 13 February)

(10) **Currie really got it right**

. . . It was Mrs Currie who recognized this and became the first politician, let alone government minister, to articulate it. In this she was assisted by her remarkable ability to strike a popular chord, catch the public eye and hit the headlines. For this she has been criticized frequently, and wrongly.

It is an important quality of political leadership.

What is certainly true is that in launching her attacks on northern eating habits and calling on old people to wear warm clothes, she emphasized personal responsibility while wrongly and patronizingly ignoring the impact of material deprivation. In this she was a true Thatcherite.

But she was none the less right about the importance of individual responsibility.

(Sunday Times, 29 January)

(11) **You damage the earth just by living on it**

You burn fossil fuels – petrol, oil, coal – and huge amounts more are burnt by those who supply you with goods and services.

You create waste, which has to be buried, burnt or discharged into the sea.

You accept the profits of investments which are trading on Third World poverty and putting further strain on already over-stretched resources.

You buy goods from farms and factories whose ill-effects from chemical waste range all the way from dead fish to dead people.

You are a polluter. But you are also a conservationist.

(Sunday Times Magazine, 26 February

Some brief, informal notes on the style of hysteria in these extracts. (5) and (6) highlight a vocabulary of 'hazard' and 'risk'. Note also the indications of large-scale growth: 'astronomical increase', 'increase'. Extract (6) is a typical narrative of secret dealings between government departments, and between government departments and industry; (7) and (9) are unusual in attempting to lay the blame on an individual. (7) speaks of 'public anxiety' and 'growing confusion'; cf. 'dilemma' in (10). Extract (8) encodes a strategy of educating (and therefore blaming) 'the poor housewife' (cf. (9)): (8) employs the rhetoric of *command,* also dominating extract (11). These rhetorics are distinctive, tailored for the job and linguistically specifiable. Extract (10) comes from a long article praising Mrs Currie in a style of unusual optimism and vivacity; other politicians and organizations are generally dealt with in a tone of tetchy gloom. Finally, extract (11) is an ecological tirade, raised to an apocalyptic pitch as the *Sunday Times* had by now globalized the agenda and the guilt.

Let us look in more detail at some aspects of hysterical style. In the next chapter (pp. 174–8), I will demonstrate a linguistic mechanism (formulaic phrases) which sustains the hysterical discourse and extends the range of its referents. First I will note how a high level of intensity, an excess of negative feeling, is expressed.

The most obvious source of stridency in the discourse is its permeation by terms denoting emotive reactions, always negative, clustering around the concepts of fear and confusion. A list of such words drawn from part of my materials is given on p. 179; 'scare' is the most common (at least 27 times), also 'confusion' (10 times), 'anxiety' (6 times) and a number of related terms.

Another prominent vocabulary set stresses 'danger', 'risk', 'hazard'; it includes words which connote deliberateness or malevolence such as 'threat', 'menace'. Again, the full list of such words from a selection of the data is given in another context in the next chapter: see p. 179.

There is, particularly in the 'serious' papers, a multiplicity of technical and medical terms, terms of a kind which people find difficult, unfamiliar, frightening:

- *types of bacteria, viruses*, etc.: rota virus, Norwalk virus, *Escherichia coli, Salmonella typhimurium, Salmonella enteritidis* phage type 4, *Listeria monocytogenes*, legionella bacterium, cryptosporidium, staphyloccus, campylobacter; .
- *infections and diseases*: Alzheimer's disease, cholera, typhoid fever, campylobacteriosis, septicaemia, giardisis, listeriosis, hepatitis, legionnaires' disease, pneumonia, bovine spongiform encephalopathy or 'BSE' (a horrible-sounding cattle disease);
- *chemicals, minerals*, etc.: bovine somatropin ('BST'), aluminium, aluminium sulphate, lead, nitrates, chlorofluorocarbons ('CFCs'), trichloroethylene, cytotoxic drugs, radon, methane.

This technical and medical jargon is alienating and disturbing.

The salmonella and, particularly, listeria bacteria are treated to a rhetoric of animation: they are 'germs' or, worse, 'bugs' which can be presented as deliberately harmful. The *Sun*'s melodramatic phrase 'the killer bug listeria' (28 February), or the cartoon reproduced and discussed on p. 197, captures well this aspect of the presentation of the food poisoning affair. Elsewhere we find meta-

phors of 'war' and 'battle' in the kitchen against 'a billion bugs';
cf. 'minefield' in extract (9). There are also formulations like
'keep the salmonella or listeria at bay' (*The Times*, 2 February),
'Cooked food hazard "is unchecked" ' (*Guardian*, 24 January),
connoting a struggle against wild animals threatening to go out
of control.

But the language does not have to be particularly melodramatic
or ominously metaphoric to suggest that we are threatened by a
very powerful and virulent enemy. In the nature of the case,
explanations of the bacteriological processes involved were provided for readers who, like the journalists, had never heard of
listeria. In the extracts below, I have italicized words and phrases
which animate and activate the bacteria:

(12) [L]isteria will stay virtually *dormant* for five days after
contamination even if the food is stored at 7.5°C. But
then *reproduction suddenly erupts*. . . . listeria, unlike most
bacteria, *gets even more virulent when it is threatened* by
extremes of temperature.
(*Guardian*, 24 January)

(13) The bacteria produces an enzyme, listeriolysin, which
damages human cells, allowing bacteria to *invade and multiply* inside the cells.
(*Independent*, 23 January)

(14) Campylobacters and salmonellas become much more
dangerous when, like listeria, they are *invasive, penetrate* the
gut wall and *enter* the bloodstream, *causing* septicaemia.
(Letter in *Independent*, 26 January)

Animacy is also enhanced by the use of phrases such as 'breeding
ground' and 'breeding conditions' which occur frequently but
happen not to appear in the above three extracts. And note that
it is transitivity as well as vocabulary which assists the effect of
animate and deliberate activity: noun phrases designating the
'bugs' occupy the agent role in many clauses, coupled with verbs
which designate actions having consequences for other organisms.

The meanings of the metaphor of a battle against the bugs are
available to readers by intertextuality. Horror movies and stories,
and science fantasies, supply antecedent paradigms of invasion by
little creatures, germ warfare, uncontrollably multiplying chemical and botanical threats, assault by plagues of birds and insects.
But the central meanings of this discourse of billions of hostile

bugs are recognized only when we notice that it intersects with a discourse specifically aimed at 'the housewife': extract (9) above makes the link absolutely clear. Women are supposed to be afraid of 'bugs' or 'creepy-crawlies' like spiders and ants; they are supposed to go hysterical in fear of such; and their fears are supposed to be sexual: cf. expressions like 'reproduction suddenly erupts', 'penetrate', 'invade', in extracts (12)-(14); other connotations of sexual assault may be found in a further set of hysterical terms, to be discussed in a moment (see list (18) p. 168). Furthermore, the intertext is not merely the cultural stereotype of the woman in a fright because a spider might run up her skirt. The cartoon animation of bugs and germs, and the threat they present, is a common strategy in the television advertising of disinfectants, toilet cleaners, and so on; these advertisements are aimed at women, and they articulate an important part of the culture's housewifely image. This area will be discussed in more detail in the next chapter, pp. 186ff.

Finally, a different discursive strategy for intensifying hysteria is the rhetoric of quantification; and this is really the dominant stylistic feature of the discourse. Throughout the three months' hysterical episode, there were many things to be counted, phenomena to be given statistical tags; the data I collected contain hundreds of numerical expressions, most of them indicating very large quantities indeed, and also expressions of quantitative increase. The basic proposition being debated was that Britain was experiencing ' "a new salmonella epidemic of considerable proportions", possibly affecting up to 2m people a year' (*Sunday Times*, 22 January). The dramatic figure is of course a statistical extrapolation from the numbers of reported cases, but the claimed number was so large as to make an alarming impact on public consciousness anyway, whatever the facts of the matter; and the speculation was repeated over and over again in the Press. Also mentioned many times was the number of 'reported cases' of either 'food poisoning' or 'salmonella poisoning'; the following statement is typical:

(15) More than half of salmonella isolations by the Public Health Laboratory, 24, 123 in 1988, are now *salmonella enteritidis*. The increase in this species of salmonella accounts largely for the great increase in salmonella infec-

tions which began in 1986. Total cases of salmonella are
now twice what they were in 1986.

The latest figures show there were 12,553 isolations of
salmonella enteritidis phage type 4 last year, compared with
4,962 isolations in 1987. . . .

Campylobacter is the commonest single cause of food
poisoning, responsible for 28,714 cases last year.

(Independent, 23 January)

(16) [T]he number of cases [of campylobacteriosis] in England
and Wales had risen from 12,822 in 1982 to 28,174 [*sic*]
in 1988, as against 24,123 due to salmonella.

(Letter in Independent, 26 January)

Such figures are very difficult for newspaper readers to take in
and retain, especially as they refer to counts of different entities
(food poisoning, salmonella poisoning, *Salmonella enteritidis* poisoning, campylobacter poisoning, etc.), or refer to different periods: 39,000, 28,196, 24,123, and so on. The quantities diverge –
28,174 or 28,714? – or are silently rounded: 23,000, 25,000 a year.
Inevitably the figures blur, becoming impressions rather than
facts, but what remains is the repeated mention of large quantities
in the 20,000 to 30,000 range, usually associated with 1988, and
this seems, subjectively, an alarmingly substantial number and a
solid basis for the statistic extrapolation:

(17) Last November Mr Lacey said the number of people who
fell ill with salmonella poisoning in 1988 was 24,500, but
because not all cases were reported the actual number was
probably 250,000, of which 150,000 were due to eggs.

The total figure could be as high as 2,500,000.

. . . A spokeswoman for the Health Department . . .
said that the Government report, which said there may
be as many as two million salmonella poisoning cases a
year, was based on an estimate that the actual number of
cases was 100 times the number of cases reported. . . .
'Other suggestions are that the factor might be only 10.
The fact is that nobody knows for certain.'

(Telegraph, 10 February)

The reader is bombarded with lots of very high numbers, and
will certainly remember the 2,000,000, however sceptical s/he is
about it.

Large numbers are mentioned throughout the discourse, because things other than 'salmonella infections' had to be counted, calculated, reported. Calculating the chances of someone eating an 'infected egg' produced astronomical figures: 10 billion eggs eaten per year, 30 million eggs a day. Then there were 400 million eggs and 4 million hens to be destroyed under the compensation scheme, but 'only 62 of the 40,000 egg producers in the UK, offered £1.50 per bird, had sent a total of 786,000 laying hens for slaughter' (*Guardian*, 11 January). Figures are also given for listeria infections and for the proliferation of listeria bacteria at different temperatures and in different conditions: up to 'a billion bugs'. Elsewhere, 50,000 families at risk from radon gas, 600,000 people in Oxfordshire advised to boil their drinking water, 18 million tons of rubbish dumped each year, 240,000 and 360,000 cans of reject French food, Britain producing 105,000 tonnes of CFCs each year and exporting 48,000. In addition to numerical counts, percentages are also cited: 40 per cent increase in food poisoning, 50 per cent drop in egg consumption; also doublings, treblings and even a million-fold decrease in listeria bacteria after microwaving.

There is a group of recurrent predicates – verbs, or nouns derived from verbs – designating changes in numbers:

(18) increase, rise, grow, spread, mount, expand, jump, leap, multiply, proliferation, escalation.

Some, such as 'increase' and 'rise', occur so extremely frequently that they are part of the constant background (but presumably cumulatively present to readers in a subliminal way). Others are found in dramatic, metaphoric contexts, immediately striking:

(19) astronomical increase, large and accelerating rise, rampant rise, sudden and exponential leap.

They are related to other dramatic expressions such as 'reproduction suddenly erupts' noticed earlier.

These predicates are interesting because they are multipurpose: they can go with different phenomena being quantified – cases of food poisoning, or bacteria, or types of food problem, or public fears, can all increase; different things can mount, or multiply, or proliferate, and so on. As a result, ambiguous phrases appear many times: 'the growth of listeria', 'increase in salmonella', and so on. The result is a blurring, a diminution in analytic precision; an impressionist style comes over, especially in conjunction with the ubiquitous mentions of large but constantly shifting numbers. The discourse is constantly alarming and hyperbolic, but in an obscure way: a problem of considerable proportions is always being alleged; we are bound to be concerned about it, but its outlines are indistinct, like some huge threatening shape on the horizon in a bad horror movie.

Chapter 10

The salmonella-in-eggs affair: Pandora's box

WHAT AM I?

The phrase 'the salmonella-in-eggs affair' is used repeatedly in the newspapers, with significant variants, to label an 'it' which is the subject of discourse during the period. The phrase reminds us of the original cause of the discursive hysteria back in November and December 1988, food poisoning from eggs; but I am using it, as the papers do, to designate something which had become broader and more diversified by the New Year: as a shorthand, a metonymy, for an underlying 'it' of a more abstract kind.

As a working principle in discourse analysis or critical linguistics, we assume that the ostensible subject of representation in discourse is not what it is 'really about': in semiotic terms, the signified is in turn the signifier of another, implicit but culturally recognizable meaning.[1] There have already been many examples in this book: the story concerning Winnie Mandela (pp. 100–1) is about the anomaly of women in politics, the reports concerning contraception for the under–16s (pp. 105–9) are, additionally, implicitly about hierarchical power-relations between institutions, professionals and individuals. There is always a feeling, in reading the newspaper materials about salmonella in eggs, listeria and related matters such as aluminium in baby milk (*how* are these related?), that the specific texts are 'about' something else. It is as if salmonella is to be read symbolically, and one newspaper gets close to expressing the symbolic nature of the discourse: 'the underlying public health problem which salmonella contamination presents' (*Guardian* 11 January 1989, quoting Dr Tim Lang, director of the London Food Commission). The texts suggest that there are many different topics 'underlying' the salmonella-in-eggs signifier: political, for instance the government's neglect of the consumer and of the environment; bureaucratic, e.g. the anachronistic constitution of MAFF and the lack of co-ordination between MAFF and the Health Ministry; commercial, e.g. cost-cutting but harmful agricultural practices, bad hygiene in the distribution and storage of food products; social, e.g. 'food faddism', or the use of convenience foods; personal, e.g. ignorance about cookery basics, poor hygiene in the home; global-ecological, e.g. CFCs and global warming.

In an attempt to arrive at a more precise understanding of the deep meanings of the discourse, I extracted from the materials I had collected noun phrases which designated the subject which was being discussed, either in specific terms–

(1) the salmonella outbreak, the scare over infected eggs, a major epidemic, the poisoning episode, Britain's worst water pollution case, the salmonella crisis

– or in general terms:

(2) the human food chain, mounting concern over food safety, the state of the nation's health, public confusion, the problems posed by modern food production techniques, poisoning the nation, the poisoning of our world.

The total of noun phrases collected for this part of the analysis was 560: many more could have been extracted, but this was an adequate sample, and my collecting was guided by the patterns and recurrences that the phrases fell into, rather than the principle of getting everything down.

Syntactically speaking, noun phrases (NPs) have a number of possible different structures. They may be *simple*, consisting of either just a noun like 'contamination', 'panic', or a determiner followed by a noun, like 'the organism', 'the force'. The determiner might be a definite or indefinite article, 'the' or 'a[n]', or a demonstrative such as 'this' or 'that'. One meaning of the definite article 'the' is especially significant in this material: the word means not only 'definite', 'specific', but also 'known', 'given'. The definite expression 'the salmonella-in-eggs affair' presupposes an agreement between writer and reader that they are both familiar with the matter being discussed.

It is unnecessary to go into details of all the possible variants of *complex* noun phrases. They range from 'the salmonella controversy' to much more elaborate structures such as 'the concern about the health implications of intensive and high-technology methods of food production'. In a complex noun phrase, the noun which refers to the 'it' being talked about is called the 'head': in the examples just cited, 'controversy' and 'concern'. The other parts of the NP which attend the head are known as 'modifiers': they qualify the head semantically, restricting its reference to, say, a particular category of 'controversy', 'the *salmonella* controversy'. Modifiers may follow as well as precede the head noun: 'the concern *about the health implications*'. (Note that in this complex NP, 'implications' is in turn the head to the modifier 'of intensive and high-technology methods', and 'methods' is a head modified by 'of food production'. NPs may be included within NPs to an apparently indefinite extent.)

Very prominent among these materials were two types of NP: definite article + modifier + head; and definite article + head + modifier; respectively.

(3) the salmonella outbreak, the egg crisis, the food fight

and

(4) the risk of listeria, the dangers of listeria, the growth of listeria.

Note that in these examples (and very typically), the name of the illness, or the bacteria, or other problem, is displaced from the logically dominant head position, to the subordinate modifier; this structural arrangement is a good indication that the real subject of discourse is not objective phenomena such as salmonella or eggs, but abstractions and subjective states such as crisis, danger, alarm. This pattern is very widespread indeed; and a single phrase will collect a large number of significant variations of topic:

(5) the salmonella outbreak [3 instances], controversy [4], warning, poisoning [8], crisis [2], epidemic [6], danger, infection [2], scare [8], cases [3], problem, scandal, threat [3], affair.

(6) the salmonella-in-eggs affair [10], scandal, scare, crisis [2], row [3].

And similarly for listeria, water pollution, environmental damage, pesticides, etc., though in smaller numbers. Structures of the kinds illustrated in (3)-(6) are formulaic: they are fixed syntactic structures – 'formulae' – which recur repeatedly throughout the corpus, in all the newspapers, with variations in the lexical items plugged into the slots provided by the syntactic frame. The 'frame-and-formula' principle can be made visible by a simple tabular presentation:

(7) Determiner	Modifier	Head
the	salmonella	crisis
the	salmonella	affair
the	salmonella-in-eggs	crisis
the	salmonella-in-eggs	affair
the	salmonella-in-eggs	scandal
the	listeria	scandal
the	water poisoning	incident
the	food poisoning	incident
the	national food poisoning	crisis

Another syntactic formula which recurs frequently reverses the order of the main elements:

(8) Determiner	Head	Modifier
the	risks	of listeria
the	poisoning and contamination	of food
—	alarm	over water safety
the	increase	in salmonella
the	threat	of salmonella

There are a few other, less common formulae based on a more complex deployment of the same syntactic and lexical components; for example:

(9) 26 official outbreaks of food poisoning related to eggs; outbreaks of food poisoning related to salmonella and listeria bacteria.

(10) Britain's worst water pollution case; Britain's worst food poisoning epidemic.

The importance of formulaic patterns in a connected body of discourse is threefold. First, formulaic patterning is cohesive in effect: recurrent patterns provide a set of stylistic 'templates', homogenizing the discourse.[2] The existence of formulae in the food poisoning (etc.) discourse, and their widespread dispersal through the language of all of the newspapers, provides a 'cue' to readers to recognize all of this as *the same discourse*.

Second, formulaic phrase patterns are generative. They are an important mechanism in facilitating the generation of new instances of 'it' in the discourse. I will discuss this generative function shortly. Just to mention the third implication of formulae, they have a levelling or equating effect, causing different matters to be perceived as instances of the same thing.

PANDORA'S BOX: GENERATING AND EQUATING NEW INSTANCES

Some newspapers were clearly aware of the journalistic opportunities provided by 'the salmonella-in-eggs affair'; the *Sunday Times*'s comment (12 February) is apt and elegant:

(11) a pandora's box of food hygiene scares that have kept the headline writers busy in an otherwise dull political winter.

This is perhaps the most accurate description of the 'it' which we have been considering: a set of ideas and emotions about food, created by and for the newspapers, defined, homogenized and sustained in discourse. In this creative process, specific linguistic structures of the kind we have been examining played a fundamental reality-constructing role. The formulation in (11) would have been impossible if the phrase 'food hygiene scares' had not, by February, attained a degree of conceptual solidity in the public imagination which had been created by the salmonella news discourse. The reality of this phrase is underpinned by the formulaic structures analysed in (3)-(8) above. The table in example (7) particularly represents an abstract pattern which offers 'slots' to be filled in with relevant words:

(12) (a) the + salmonella + X
     (b) the + Y + affair

Pandora's box works by establishing a number of conceptually appropriate fillers for the 'X' slot in (a): 'affair', 'scare', etc. This provides a substantial, but finite, repertoire of frames with the structure (12b). Now slot 'Y', unlike 'X', is open-ended: new 'Ys' can be slotted in as they are announced by experts or noticed by journalists. This generative mechanism could go on *ad infinitum*: salmonella, eggs, listeria, cheese, unpasteurized milk, aluminium, bovine spongiform encephalopathy, radon, methane, campylobacter, restaurant hygiene, kitchen hygiene, and so on. Because of its potentially infinite application, the machine is inherently hysterical in the autonomous manner discussed on p. 148, and can 'run on' out of control. The *Sunday Times* article of 12 February talks about the problem of *shutting* Pandora's box, an urgent discursive and political problem by that stage of the salmonella-in-eggs affair.

The effect of generating all the new instances that were collected over the winter of 1988–9, by slotting them into the same place in a linguistic-conceptual formula, was to level or equate them. After a while it became immaterial whether salmonella, or listeria, or anything else, was the topic. There is indeed some evidence of real blurring, as when the *Sun* (4 February) refers to 'the threat of salmonella from unpasteurized milk': this complex NP, formed by two applications of the formula underlying (8) above, illustrates what happens when the discursive machine runs automatically while the operator slumbers: 'salmonella' was written, but 'listeria' might have been intended.

Levelling is attended by generalization. This process is easily studied by scanning the data for nouns and noun phrases of more general reference, occupying the modifier 'Y' slot. General words and phrases, as distinct from their specific instances such as 'salmonella' or 'CFC', were very common in 'Y', evidencing a tendency of the discourse to represent the 'it' as a broad general phenomenon. Significantly, the *range* of such terms (the number of types, as opposed to the frequency of their tokens) was quite limited. Seven groups of terms recurred in 'Y', some with great frequency. We can therefore propose that the following concepts were deployed to categorize and link the topics of discourse:

- *Poisoning*   The word 'poisoning' itself occurs at least[3] 12 times, 'food poisoning' 49 times; variants are 'poisoned food' (twice) and 'food poison'. 'Food poisoning' seems of course to be a natural, common-sense designation for the effects of salmonella and listeria, but it also allows these illnesses to be equated with others caused by food, and therefore blurs the focus and impedes the analysis of the specific problems. The unqualified 'poisoning' diffuses attention more widely still, admitting many more types of threats to health, including (unlike salmonella) substances placed in or left in foods or drinks or their sources: pesticides, nitrates, aluminium, etc.

- *Infection* The word 'infection' (9 times) represents illness somewhat differently from 'poisoning', allowing food poisoning to be linked to hepatitis, legionnaires' disease, AIDS.
- *Contamination* 'Contamination' (7 times) is the rendering harmful of some substance by the presence within it of another. Phrase variants include 'food contamination' (4 times), 'contaminated food' (twice), 'contaminated products'. The word 'contaminated' also occurs with more specific terms, e.g. 'contaminated animal protein'.
- *Pollution* The word 'pollution' (8 times) is very close in meaning to 'contamination', but its field of reference is different, having specific application nowadays to industrial and social damaging of the environment: so in this discourse we find phrases such as 'environmental pollution', leading to a concentration, at the end of the period, on 'environmental damage', 'environmental scandals', etc. Shifting from the generalization 'contamination' to 'pollution' allowed attention to be diverted and dispersed: away from the specific food poisoning affair – which, because of government inaction, was not going to be remedied and was becoming stale news – towards world ecological health. 'Global environmental ruin', 'our world at risk', 'the darkening skies', 'the poisoning of our world': all can be generalized as 'pollution'. The health of the environment can probably not be restored, but at least the newspapers can represent it dramatically and assail our individual consciences as aerosol users; and the politicians, having failed to control the egg industry, can promise to save the ozone layer: **'Thatcher hogs the green line'** (*Observer*, 26 February).
- *Health* As can be seen from my previous sentence, 'The health of the environment . . .', the word 'health' is extremely useful for homogenizing a discourse which ranges from egg poisoning to ozone depletion. The word is very widely used in our newspaper materials, in a variety of contexts: 'health problem', 'public health', 'public health standards/agenda/problem', and so on. Such phrases allow the linking of medical concepts like 'epidemic', bureaucratic concepts like 'environmental health officers' and social concepts like 'the state of the nation's health'.
- *Safety* 'Safety' is closely associated with 'health'; the words

collocate (go habitually together) in some set phrases which are relevant to the salmonella business: 'health and safety executive'. In this material we find 'health and safety standards of food', 'food safety' (9 times), 'food safety policy'. Note that 'safety' is a euphemism: it is both vague, and positive in its connotations, allowing discourse which is finally about essentially *un*safe practices – such as over-use of pesticides, and manufacturing animal feed from infected carcasses – in an unspecific and reassuring way. Phrases giving the reverse of the picture, such as 'unwholesome or unsafe food' (*Sunday Times*, 12 February), occur very rarely.

- *Hygiene* 'Hygiene' was presented as being a concern at all stages 'from farm to dinner table': the production, distribution, retailing, preparation and service of food. It is not a particularly appropriate designation, since cleanliness was only a small part of the problem: other relevant matters include the wholesomeness of animal feed, veterinary inspection of abattoirs, storage temperature of cook-chill foods and reheating temperature, none of which are strictly speaking matters of hygiene. Yet from mid-February, the phrase 'food hygiene' appears regularly (at least 15 times in my materials); 'food and farm hygiene' is found once, 'kitchen hygiene' three times and 'home hygiene' twice. 'Hygiene', like 'safety', is a euphemism, but it has strong domestic and personal connotations. The generalization of the food poisoning episode to a matter of 'hygiene' is part of the strategy of blaming the housewife, to be discussed below.

Two final points may be made before leaving the topic of formulae. First, they are peculiarly suitable for newspaper discourse because they fit into the headline format: in the tabloids, used as a whole headline, and in the larger papers, the nuclear part of a headline. Thus they can be strongly foregrounded, offering conceptual simplicity and memorability. (See the samples on pp. 156–7.) Second, their simplicity provides a packaging of ideas with a very solid and clear outline. A phrase such as 'the great egg debate', imprecise but wholly comprehensible in terms of its discursive context, is much easier to grasp and retain than those (few) more complex phrases which actually attempt to analyse the facts behind the formulaic generalizations. I am thinking of examples such as the following:

(13) the growing danger of intensive and high technology
      methods of food production

                              (*Guardian*, 24 January)
      toxicity of chemicals in food, consumer products and the
      environment

                              (*Telegraph*, 10 February)
      changes in agriculture, food production, food technology,
      distribution, catering and handling in the home

                              (*Guardian*, 22 February)
      a possible link between feedstuffs and drugs fed to animals
      to increase yields, and salmonella and listeria

                              (*Guardian*, 23 February)

These detailed, critical wordings of hypotheses about the sources
of the problem obviously lack the rhetorical force and attractive-
ness of the simple formulae. Formulae package concepts simply
and memorably; they signify paradigms, model ideas which can
be applied to new 'instances', however remote from the original
referents. The durability of formulae as carriers of social meaning
will be illustrated below, in a postscript on the 'baby food crisis'
which flared up two months after the salmonella crisis was spent
(pp. 203–7).

'WHAT AM I?' REVISITED

In the case of the discourse under examination, what are all the
'instances', such as salmonella and aluminium in water, instances
of? When we examined the modifiers in the formulaic phrases
('Y' slot), we found generalizations such as 'poisoning' and 'contamination'. But these are not necessarily the real subject; they
are after all, syntactically, only modifiers. The heads, for which
our 'it' can be substituted in the 'X' slot, give more information,
and a number of different perspectives, on the subject of the
discourse.

• The most neutral analysis is given when the subject is felt to
  be whatever is given by the modifier ('salmonella', 'poisoning',
  etc.); some general and uninformative term occupies the head:
  'affair' (at least 15 times), 'episode' (3 times), 'business' (once);
  slightly more informatively, and negatively, 'problem' (24
  times), a euphemistic term often quoted from politicians and
  experts.

The 'problem' is specified in a number of distinct ways:

- It is often seen as an *epidemic*. The word 'epidemic' is used at least 12 times; 'outbreak' (14 times) and 'incident' (5 times) refer to poisonings of groups or sets of people; 'case' in the medical sense (19 times) occurs in estimates of the scale of the 'epidemic'.

- Another group of terms stresses *harm* to the individual or to the environment; the connotations are rather melodramatic: 'danger' (20 times), 'damage' (4 times), 'destruction' (once), 'ruin' (once). 'Risk' is a common term (24 times), implying that harm is not automatic but a matter of chance; 'hazard' (4 times) and 'peril' (3 times) carry the same suggestion, and, more dramatically, the metaphors '[food] roulette' (*Observer*, 12 February) and 'minefield' (*Sun*, 13 February). Another way of expressing the potential harm suggests a deliberate intention to harm on someone's part: 'threat' (15 times) and 'menace' (once).

- Commonly, the affair is presented in terms of *subjective reactions* rather than actual harm; these are collective reactions, often attributed to 'the public': 'confusion' (10 times) alleged by the politicians, including the Prime Minister, 'uncertainty' (once), 'dilemma' (twice), 'loss of confidence' (once), 'dissatisfaction' (once); 'interest' (once), 'awareness' (once); 'concern' (8 times), 'fears' (5 times), 'anxiety' (6 times), 'alarm' (8 times), 'alert' (once); 'panic' (4 times), 'hysteria' (4 times), 'fever' (once); by far the most common term in this set was 'scare' (27 times), the newspapers' most popular analysis of the substance of this business.

- There is a small set of terms which signify speech acts relating to the affair: 'allegation' (once), 'warning', (5 times), 'urging' (once).

- There is an alternative way of coding the salmonella-in-eggs affair which regards it not as a matter of health or public feelings but as a *political event*. 'Crisis' is a popular designation (22 times), or, emphasizing dispute and conflict, 'controversy' (13 times), 'fight' (once), 'debate' (twice), 'issue' (4 times), 'row' (13 times), 'furore' (twice). A different and more critical slant is signalled, though rarely, by 'conspiracy' (once) and 'cover-up' (twice). The whole business is sometimes condemned in the journalistic term 'scandal' (6 times); also 'chaos' (twice), 'muddle' (twice), 'riddle' (once), 'fiasco' (once), 'farce' (once). The political failure or incompetence of the government and its departments is the regular complaint of newspaper editorials and of some 'investigative' articles: see, for example, extracts (6), (7), (9) and (10) in chapter 9, pp. 161–3.

In a sense, the salmonella affair was a godsend for the Press, as the *Sunday Times* acknowledged (extract (11), p. 174). The salmonella affair was an essentially trivial matter which could however be aggrandized, diversified and prolonged. Danger and alarm were magnified, as we have seen, offering a 'scare' or a 'crisis' to the public imagination. It was a rich and productive story, well fulfilling the 'news value' criteria which we discussed in chapter 2. Whether or not the scare was well founded, political blame or praise could be handed out freely in pompous editorials: the government was wrong to minimize the risks if they were real, or wrong to allow the scare to get out of hand if the risks were not real; Mrs Currie could be praised for speaking out, or damned for speaking out ambiguously and hyperbolically. For the Tory newspapers in particular, the salmonella crisis was a gift because it allowed them to criticize the Tory government in relation to what appeared to be essentially an unimportant matter, a topic (food safety) on which the government had given no pledges, staked no honour. The Conservative Press could thus display independence and self-righteousness without doing any harm to, indeed diverting attention from, the Conservative government's major problems (inflation, education, the health service, etc.).

(Harm to the Tories was, however, a likely and unwanted outcome of the Tory Press's strategy, from the latter half of February, to steer public consciousness from the trivial dangers of salmonella and listeria to the very real problems of environmental damage. *The Times* and the *Sunday Times* were particularly vocal in identifying environmental positives and in exposing damage, specifically river pollution ('**Rivers of Shame**', *Sunday Times*, 26 February). This emphasis was met by Mrs Thatcher's sudden declaration of concern for the ozone layer. Since any claim by a Tory politician to be environment-friendly is likely to be received with scepticism, environmental critique in the Press came at the wrong time. The backfiring of Tory environmental discussions in the spring of 1989 was reflected in the remarkable success of

British Green Party candidates in the June European Parliament election: though not winning a seat, the Greens polled unexpectedly large votes throughout the country, reducing the majorities of Conservative members, or coming closer to Conservative candidates than in the previous election. This Green electoral advance was a political sign of the one positive outcome of the Press's treatment of salmonella-in-eggs and its extensions, a heightened environmental awareness.)

At the beginning of this chapter, I mentioned that my analysis of noun phrases was 'an attempt to arrive at a more precise understanding of the deep meanings of the discourse' (p. 171). I never expected to find, and was not looking for, a single referent, or group of referents, constituting the subject(s) of the salmonella discourse. Of course, salmonella poisoning and listeria poisoning were real: people fell ill, and a few died. There were some identifiable causes, including the cost-saving use of diseased poultry carcasses in the production of chicken feed. But the discourse is not really 'about' the medical and commercial realities. It is 'about' various kinds of anxiety, guilt, ideas of responsibility both political and private. I will explore some of these ideas in the final sections of this chapter.

CLOSING PANDORA'S BOX: WHAT ARE YOU GOING TO DO ABOUT IT?

Initially a good scare story, a diversion, the food hysteria was always a danger to capitalism. It was immediately a threat to the egg industry, of course, and as Pandora's box was repeatedly opened to release a succession of diverse 'food hygiene scares', a wide variety of other industrial and commercial practices were subjected to a scrutiny which was no doubt unwelcome to farmers, food producers and retailers, restaurateurs, etc. In February 1989, the field of concern was broadening uncontrollably: '**The world is dying**', proclaimed the *Sunday Times* (Magazine, 26 February). And immediately: '**What are you going to do about it?**' (cf. chapter 9, extract (11), p. 163). The lid of Pandora's box was going to be firmly shut by using a discursive strategy which followed the strategy the egg industry had wanted to deploy right from the outset: blame the consumer; more specifically, blame the housewife. That this strategy was deployed does not need proving: it is widely evident in the newspaper texts – see extracts

(6), (8) and (9) in chapter 9 (pp. 161–2) – and in other documents which were available during and after the salmonella and listeria scares. Lying around in supermarkets in the latter stages of the crisis were two little leaflets: one headed 'EGGS (The Real Truth) A MESSAGE FROM OUR EGG SUPPLIERS' and the other, nicely printed on green paper, 'THE GOOD FOOD SAFETY GUIDE', published by the 'Food Advisory Safety Centre', a public relations unit set up in response to the food scare by six supermarket chains. The opening statement in the latter leaflet summarizes the argument, moving the focus from producers and retailers to consumers:

> (14) Good food safety involves producers, distributors, retailers and customers. The six retailers supporting the Centre spend millions of pounds every year on food safety. They work closely with their suppliers to ensure good production standards. They employ food scientists and microbiologists to test food and recipes in their own laboratories. They ensure that their stores maintain good hygiene standards and that their staff are trained in handling food properly.
>
> This leaflet points to some of the actions *you* can take both in the supermarket and at home to ensure food safety.

The leaflet then lists six 'actions' which '*you* can take' 'At the Store', and no less than twenty-four that are enjoined 'At Home'. The balance of responsibility is clearly weighted to the consumer; it is a proportion which is reproduced over and again in the newspapers.

At this point, I am less concerned with the narrative of the salmonella business than with some areas of ideology, belief and value that underpin the newspapers' treatment of it. One is the ethic of personal responsibility, which is a central tenet of the political philosophy which came in the 1980s to be known as 'Thatcherism'. The second is a complex and ramified domestic stereotype of women, a conventional and much analyzed stereotype, well established long before salmonella, of course, but an essential image for the brand of Conservatism dominant in the 1980s with its call for a 'return to traditional values'. These two value-systems – personal responsibility and the domestic role of women – have a deep-seated existence independent of the salmonella affair, and it is not surprising that they should surface in the discourse concerned with this topic: it is unnecessary to believe that the newspapers were deliberately *colluding* with the food industry and with government in drawing on them. To be sure, there is some irony in that the newspapers, which claimed throughout to be supportive of 'ordinary people' and critical of food-industry bad practice and government bungling, were aware of the strategy to blame the consumer/housewife (chapter 9, extract (6), p. 161), and yet still reproduced it. This contradiction testifies to the regulative power of the paradigms: the newspaper discourse unconsciously accepts as common sense the imperative of individual responsibility and the stereotype of the housewife.

The dogma of individual responsibility was a central part of the consensual myth of the 1980s. It argued that everyone would prefer to be responsible for their own fate rather than be 'nannied by the state'. Everyone would prefer to provide their own health care, education, housing, transport, etc. In effect, 'provide' meant, of course, 'pay for', since the myth of individual responsibility is nothing other than an ideological practice designed to legitimate the curtailment of collective provisions, which are a taxation charge to the wealthy, and of costly responsibilities in relation to safe consumer products which might fall to industry and commerce. Of course the Right would deny this analysis absolutely; for a politician such as Mrs Currie, personal responsibility – keeping oneself healthy, warm and well fed – would be a matter of personal dignity, pride, vigour and perhaps social acceptability.

There is an interesting profile of Mrs Currie in the *Sunday Times* (29 January 1989), written in terms of the personal responsibility debate. It claims that, in matters of health and diet, the self-help axiom already existed in public consciousness; that Mrs Currie merely 'recognized' and 'articulated' an existing belief:

(15) Her position as junior health minister proved an ideal platform for her populism. Over the last decade and more there has been a growing popular perception of the importance of exercise, smoking and diet to one's health.

It was Mrs Currie who recognized this and became the first politician, let alone government minister, to articulate it. In this she was assisted by her remarkable ability to strike a popular chord, catch the public eye and hit the headlines. For this she has been criticized frequently, and wrongly.

It is an important quality of political leadership.

What is certainly true is that in launching her attacks on northern eating habits and calling on old people to wear warm clothes, she emphasized personal responsibility while wrongly and patronizingly ignoring the impact of material deprivation. In that she was a true Thatcherite.

But she was none the less right about the importance of individual responsibility.

We can all exercise it.

The paper goes on to speak of Mrs Currie 'recognizing the new public health agenda, the importance of diet, exercise and all that'. 'Public' relates to Mrs Currie's claimed 'populism', her ability to recognize what was in the public consciousness, and articulate it on behalf of the public; 'agenda', which becomes a frequent word in this article, seems curious until one reflects that an agenda is a formal, logical or at least organized programme of topics for public discussion. Presumably Mrs Currie articulated the public's thoughts better than they could, in a form more systematic, more amenable to debate and action.

The article then explains that she was sacked when she fell foul of the 'farming and food lobby'; interestingly, the analysis is still phrased in the discourse of 'responsibility':

(16) In drawing attention to the extraordinary extent of salmonella poisoning in eggs, she moved the focus of her attack from individual to corporate responsibility, from consumption to production.

Next, the idea of 'a new *political* agenda' (my emphasis) is introduced. It is more inclusive than the 'new *public* health agenda' of 'the importance of diet, exercise and all that' (how casual) in containing a second item:

(17) That agenda has two main parts.

First, there is the recognition of the importance of diet, exercise and smoking to health. Second, there is the concern about the health implications of intensive and high-technology methods of food production. This had been growing throughout the 1980s.

The second part of this agenda touches food production and the government's (lack of) control of it, i.e. the 'corporate' rather than 'individual' responsibility, according to the distinction the article had made earlier. But notice that the second agenda item is phrased, not in terms of facts or problems or failings of industry, but in terms of public intersubjectivity: 'concern'. It is not implied that the food industry was culpable, or had deteriorated in the 1980s, but that people had become growingly concerned about it. The author of this article is still thinking about public opinion, a consensus about food and Mrs Currie's 'populism' in recognizing it and putting it on the agenda. The next time the 'agenda' catch-phrase reappears, it has, accordingly, been reformulated away from the 'political', back to the 'public': 'that new public agenda'.

There follow six paragraphs criticizing the government, the food industry and the Labour Party for their roles in the salmonella affair: a wide-ranging critique presaging the universal condemnation which was to be meted out by the Select Committee a month later 'ALL GUILTY', *Daily Mirror*, '**Egg all over their faces**', *Daily Express*; '**They all get fried**', *Guardian* – 2 March 1989). They all got it wrong; but, according to the title of the *Sunday Times* article currently under consideration, '**Mrs Currie got it right**'.

What she got right, according to this article, was not a factual critique of the failings of the egg industry, but an accurate perception of the content of public consciousness about food production (second) and about diet (first). The six paragraphs of political criticism in this article are in effect symbolic, a ritual visiting of the faults of industry and government before returning to the real topic. The last three paragraphs attack the Labour Party for 'myopia', for being unable to see what Mrs Currie could see – and the matter not seen is not food industry bad practice or government complacency, but public belief:

(18) No doubt one reason for this myopia was that Mrs Currie was already something of a hate-figure on the left. The attacks on northern eating habits had gone down badly. Yet here again was an example of the left miscueing and failing to grasp the new public health agenda, in this case the importance of personal responsibility in matters of diet.

This newspaper article is underpinned by, and celebrates, the proposition with which it concludes: we are individually responsible for what we eat. At one point, there is even a directive to readers to act in the way indicated: 'We can all exercise [individual responsibility]' (extract (15) above). But more significant is that the writer, Martin Jacques, not only seems to subscribe to the proposition but also asserts that 'popular perception' accepts it and, what is more, is in some sense the origin of it. 'Personal responsibility' is claimed to be part of the consensus. Whether or not this claim is correct, the degree of conviction suggested by the Press discourse on this subject allows journalists to argue, or, better, presuppose, its consensual validity with plausibility, and thus persuade readers that this is what they believe. In the case of the food scares, what they are supposed to believe is that they should deal with salmonella and listeria themselves, by being careful in their choices, and watchful, 'At the Store', and hygienic 'At Home'.

BLAME THE HOUSEWIFE

(19) Meanwhile the public is going to be treated to the third phase of the Government's strategy: blame it all on the housewife. This strategy ties in nicely with the Thatcherite policy of individual responsibility.

Thus, just as Mrs Currie exhorted Northerners to eat fewer chips and pensioners to knit woolly hats, house-wives are now going to be bombarded with leaflets exhorting them to wash their hands before cooking, check that their refrigerators are working properly and cook all chickens through and through.

While all education is welcome and some conscientious citizens will no doubt sit down dutifully with their leaflet, study it assiduously and carry out its instructions to the letter, it puts the onus in the wrong place.

Surely the place to start is with the producer. Why should the housewife be expected to put up with contaminated food and put right the wrongs committed by others?
(Annabel Ferriman, '**End this food roulette**', *Observer*, 12 February 1989)

This is a rare critical analysis; and one could hardly disagree with its premises and its judgements. But exactly the strategy of which Annabel Ferriman complains was pursued by the government and the food producers and retailers, and reproduced extensively by the newspapers – despite their ostensible, and probably genuine, concern for the consumer. When listeria succeeded salmonella, the field of attention broadened to embrace, not simply an extended range of foods, but a general scrutiny of eating habits, kitchen practices, knowledge about food and cooking. From late January through February 1989, the newspapers were full of culinary advice so elementary as to suggest that people who buy and cook food were profoundly ignorant. Text (8) of chapter 9 (p. 162) is representative of a litany of advice recited repeatedly; this example is a brief text, but its content and format correspond closely to the longer lists of do's and dont's in the *Good Food Safety Guide* leaflet and the article from the *Sun* reproduced below. The short text is printed in a box right in the middle of a longish article in the *Sunday Times*, 22 January 1989. As the opening and the end of this piece show, its writers assume that 'the average household' has a total absence of culinary knowledge:

(20) **The chilling facts of safe home cooking**
   Picture the average household before their evening meal. Has mum cooked it? No, she's just come in from work – she'll get a ready-prepared meal out of the fridge just for herself. The family no longer eats together because it can rely on today's high-tech food any time they want it. The fridge is bulging with chicken tikka, lasagne, chicken supreme and ready-washed salads. Dad will take his pick when he gets home – even he has learnt how to use the microwave. As for the teenage children – if they eat at all they will want to do so quickly and conveniently, probably in front of the television. They have never learnt to cook.
   Imagine what they thought when last week's listeria scandal hit them. A hidden menace in their meals? Surrounded, as they are, by the technological trappings of the modern consumer – the oven, the microwave, the refrigerator – they are helpless. Is the problem in the food, the machinery, or both?

> All of us could be forgiven for being perplexed by the current listeria panic. . . .
>
> . . . Despite the failure of the high-tech kitchen to compensate for our low level of skills, commonsense is still a powerful corrective (see box, left).
>
> Finally, while convenience foods such as TV dinners are clearly here to stay, don't forget that the more often we cook for ourselves – with properly prepared fresh ingredients – the less risk we take.

The article asserts utter ignorance, and attributes this to dependence on high-tech foods and microwaving (and more, as we will see). A comparable article in the *Guardian*, 20 February 1989, makes the same claim about ignorance, but traces the causes one step further back, to the producers and marketers of high-tech food: '**Freedom – eat your heart out**. Increased processing of food has gone hand-in-hand with a processing of ignorance, argues Jeremy Seabrook'.

The opening two paragraphs of 'The chilling facts of safe home cooking' are stylistically marked in a most salient way. The writers offer a schematic narrative script, a diurnal scene from 'the average household', and they narrate the story from an external point of view. The imperatives 'picture' and 'imagine' direct the reader to adopt a distanced and voyeuristic site of observation; the family depicted become alienated, a third-person 'them' examined critically by writers and reader in concert. The scene is full of symbolism: stereotypes of affluence, technology, adult work and teenage idleness abound. There are significant negative connotations. The question 'Has mum cooked it?' assumes shared background knowledge to the effect that, in households, mothers do the cooking; the familiar word 'mum' has 'cook' as one of its defining values. This mother does not, going out to work instead, and the question is raised as to her qualifications to be a 'mum', her conformity with the traditional values that are being reaffirmed in the 1980s. The family is fragmented, not really a family. The text directly invokes one of the prototypical features of the stereotype 'family' by confessing that 'The family no longer eats together'. (In proverbial wisdom, the family that eats together stays together.)[4] What listeria has brought to the fore is the disintegration of family life, a breakdown for which the mother is responsible.

The family first presented distantly as 'them' is in reality 'us': it is *Sunday Times* readers – not Mrs Currie's chip-guzzling Northerners – who buy pre-cooked meals with foreign names from prestige stores. At the end of the second paragraph, a question is asked on behalf of the 'helpless' parodic family: 'Is the problem in the food, the machinery, or both?' Since 'we' could legitimately have asked the same bewildered question for ourselves in January 1989, when it seemed unclear what foods carried the danger of listeria, the transition to 'All of us can be forgiven for being perplexed' in the third paragraph is readied. The remainder of the article quotes some expert advice and opinion about listeria and cook-chill meals, and then, about two-thirds of the way through, prepares to fit the cap of guilt securely on 'our' heads:

(21) We will have to let the government investigate the food industry's methods to assess the risk. But what can we do in the meantime at home?

First, remember that chilled foods are meant to be kept below 3°C.

To whom does 'we' refer? It is the 'inclusive "we" ', logically designating the conjunction of the source and the addressee of the discourse; and the 'we' of implied consensus. This is a 'we' frequently used in newspaper editorials. The inclusiveness is phoney, however. No newspaper would propose that '*it*' has 'to let the government investigate' something; newspapers generally adopt the pose that they have the authority to tell the government what to do in such matters – and there are numerous editorials during the food scare which do just that. My intuition is that the 'we' in these two sentences is a kind of 'directive "we" ', meaning 'you': the 'directive "we" ' as used by doctors, teachers, Prime Ministers and others who occupy ascribed roles of authority. Similarly with the question-form 'what can we do?': formulating a question on behalf of the addressee is a standard strategy in pedagogic discourse. In this context of authority-differential, the imperative 'remember', the instruction at the end to 'see box' and the imperatives in the check-list within the box simply follow from the claim to the authority of superior knowledge. 'Mum' is being told what to do; her ignorance is breaking up the family.

Didacticism suffuses discourse about food and the kitchen during this period:

(22) Most refrigerators are not marked in Centigrade: if you
    want to make your fridge colder, you should check your
    owner's manual, since lowering the number means in
    some fridges that you are making your fridge warmer.

(*Guardian*, 14 February)

Note the repeated 'you/your', targeting the individual reader; and
the modal of power 'should'.

(23) Left-overs do give plenty of scope for producing imaginat-
    ive dishes. I always enjoy the chapter you find in many
    French cookery books on '*l'art d'accommoder les restes*',
    which deals with the subject quite frankly. Of course,
    you have to be careful with left-overs, as with any food
    preparation. Never just warm food through. Meat and
    fish must be thoroughly reheated to a high temperature.
    Not everything will be suitable for re-cooking. Shellfish
    spoils very quickly and should never be re-cooked. Food
    that you intend to serve again should be cooled quickly
    and refrigerated immediately. It is quite possible to follow
    sensible food hygiene guidelines and still enjoy being cre-
    ative and thrifty at the same time.

(*The Times*, 25 February 1989)

The *Times* reader is assumed to read French cookery books, or
at least understand the odd French phrase, and yet still be ignorant
about basic culinary processes. She is here treated to a helping of
'sensible food hygiene guidelines' (cf. the pamphlet), phrased in
classroom fashion, with plenty of imperatives, modals of obligation ('have to', 'must'), absolutes ('never', 'immediately'). Earlier it had been announced that a leaflet *The Recipe for Food Safety*
would 'spell out' various 'needs' in the area of food hygiene.
Note that 'spell out' denotes a most elementary, highly didactic
form of instruction, designed for someone whose level of knowledge is very low, and whose poor understanding necessitates a
simplified, itemized, breakdown of the basics. 'Spell out' describes
exactly the format of the genre of rudimentary listings of do's
and don'ts which appeared over and again in leaflets and newspapers during this period: text (8) of chapter 9 was one example,
The Good Food Safety Guide is another, the *Sun* article '**20 WAYS
TO BEAT THE KILLERS IN YOUR KITCHEN**', discussed
below, pp. 201ff. is another. The litany of do's and don'ts was

still being recited months later, e.g. in the *Observer*, 16 July 1989, on the occasion of a new listeria scare involving pâté: '**Deadly food poison that stalks our supermarkets. . . . How to reduce the risk of listeria poisoning**', then a list of eight items of standard advice about eat-by dates, re-heating, refrigerator temperature, etc. To repeat, 'spelling out', particularly if repeated so frequently, implies a profoundly ignorant consumer.

There is no doubt that the implied reader addressed by such texts is gendered as female. In extract 23, housewifely virtues are listed as 'sensible', 'thrifty', 'creative'. In many articles at the time, stereotyping phrases such as 'the housewife', 'the average housewife' recur. The naming of the stereotype implies acceptance of a package of defining features: a woman who stays at home, is totally responsible for shopping and cooking for her family, for the cleanliness of the home, for producing and caring for children, etc. She is ignorant about food science and about cooking technology, hence the patronizing didactic tone. Ignorance is of course part of the prevailing female stereotype. Note also the use of the phrase 'food hygiene', which, as I pointed out earlier, came to characterize the salmonella/listeria affair in the second half of February. Sometimes the formula occurs as 'kitchen hygiene', but the most significant variant (e.g. *The Times*, 30 January 1989, *Sun*, 13 February 1989, below) is 'personal hygiene'. The *Good Food Safety Guide*'s version is 'personal cleanliness'. The point is that 'personal hygiene' is one of the major normative components in the stereotyping of women: women have been made to feel guilty about the possibility of being unclean, or smelling, and the cosmetic-pharmaceutical industry feeds and profits from this guilt, by exhorting women to buy unnecessary 'cleansing' and 'deodorizing' products. The caterer Prue Leith, quoted in an article in *The Times*, 30 January 1989, declares that 'the average housewife would be absolutely amazed at how dirty she is'. The culturally-assigned guilt encouraged by such statements has as its unspoken central symbol the exclusively female process of menstruation, which is implied to make women unclean, and irrational and irresponsible. Not far beneath the surface of the phrase 'personal hygiene', targeted at women, is the concept of 'feminine hygiene', 'intimate hygiene', symbolized in the availability of 'feminine deodorants' for 'feminine freshness'.

In this context, the admission ' "We're all guilty" ' by another expert cited by *The Times* is a resonant confession. In the newspaper text, this complete clause, marked off by a comma, finishes at the right-hand margin of a column of print, so that until the eye goes to the next line, the clause is self-contained: potentially, 'we' are all guilty of anything women could be guilty of. The guilts which are immediately specified are in fact quite complex: shopping on the way to work rather than on the way home; ignorantly leaving 'our stuff' (note the euphemism) in a warm place so that the 'bugs' multiply; not complying with food or appliance manufacturers' instructions, through negligence or through failure to comprehend them, or both. Presupposed are a guilt about going to work (in an office, a female role) which parallels the criticism of 'mum' in text 20 above for going to work and neglecting her family.

(At this point I want to stay with the image of the housewife and her kitchen, but it could be shown that the expression of female guilt concerning women's biological and caring functions as mothers is pervasive in the salmonella/listeria discourse. Women whose babies died or were threatened by listeriosis during pregnancy were reported as being aware that, and sometimes feeling guilty that, their own eating had caused the infection. A distressing story in the *Sunday Times*, 22 January 1989, quotes one mother as feeling 'unclean', experiencing 'uncertainty and guilt', 'fearful of falling [NB the old-fashioned term with its Judaeo-Christian connotations] pregnant again': ' "I had to live with the knowledge that my very need to eat had killed our baby", she said. "I could not face the future with confidence" '; cf. two other personal stories reported in the *Independent*, 23 January. There is another area of guilt, less documented, about baby foods. The *Sunday Times*, 20 November 1988, raised the traditional thought that 'breast is best', when concern arose about levels of aluminium in powdered baby milk. Later, at the time of the scare about contaminated baby food, the *Sunday Telegraph* (30 April 1989) encoded the issue thus: 'Innocent victims: is the convenience of modern shopping too high a price to pay for babies' lives?' – again presupposed is the belief that in baby-feeding, as in shopping and cooking, nice traditional motherly practices are better than modern ways. On the same day, the *Observer* contributed the other point of view: '**Babies: Is fresh really best?**'.

Another parenthetical observation which I do not have space

to develop is that women, and specifically mothers, are frequently categorized as vulnerable and as anxious. In relation to both salmonella and to listeria, mention is frequently made of 'vulnerable groups' (*Sunday Times*, 22 January 1989) who should be careful about eggs, cheese and other suspect foods: 'pregnant women and certain other categories of people' (Mrs Thatcher, reported twice in the *Telegraph*, 15 February); 'the old, the ill and mothers worried about whether to give their children scrambled eggs' (*Telegraph*, 10 February); 'worried mothers' (*Observer*, 22 January); 'foetuses, babies, and the very elderly . . . pregnant women' (*Guardian*, 14 February); 'elderly and sick people, babies and pregnant women' (*Sunday Times*, 22 January); 'vulnerable groups like the pregnant or elderly' (*Guardian*, 2 March); 'pregnant women, young babies, and those with immune-system disorders [e.g. AIDS] . . . if you are not pregnant and haven't got an immune-system disorder', 'pregnant women, young babies and those with poor immune systems' (all *Observer*, 19 February); 'pregnant women who can miscarry, children who can contract meningitis, and the infirm' (*Sunday Telegraph*, 4 March 1989); 'pregnant women and those with a weakened immune system' (*Observer*, 16 July); and many other instances of similar categorizations, throughout the period in question. Three quick comments: notions of 'group' and 'category' are inherently belittling and de-individuating; the linking of women with pathetic or helpless stereotypes such as babies, 'the infirm' and 'the elderly' transfers prejudicial features; the 'at risk groups' are commonly contrasted with 'normal, healthy, people' – are not pregnant women normal and healthy?)

In the last few pages we have seen how the food industry and the newspapers constructed women's negative role in the salmonella/listeria crisis by invoking some crucial features of a domestic female stereotype and faulting the housewife in a demeaning and guilt-provoking way. Cleanliness and cooking procedures at home were constantly under scrutiny; and usually in a context which asserts that food producers and retailers, caterers and other 'professionals' do everything right, so it must be 'the housewife' who is at fault, in effect *causing* food poisoning. This structure of argument clearly organizes a major eight-page feature in the *Sunday Telegraph* Magazine. Published on 4 March 1989, this feature seems to have been timed immediately to follow the salmonella report of the Commons Select Committee, which appeared on 1 March and dominated the newspapers on 2 March. The cover of the magazine bills

(24) **COOK-CHILL MEALS: THE FACTS FROM THE FOOD FACTORY**

and the script for the feature is headlined inside the magazine:

(25) **THE KITCHEN REVOLUTION • COOK-CHILL FOOD HAS CHANGED THE WAY WE EAT • IT HAS ALSO RAISED THE SPECTRE OF FOOD POISONING ON A MASSIVE SCALE • WE INVESTIGATE THE PRECAUTIONS TAKEN BY ONE MAJOR MARKS AND SPENCER SUPPLIER • AND EXAMINE THE HEALTH HAZARDS YOU FACE IN YOUR OWN HOME**

On the one hand, 'precautions' in the food factory, on the other, 'health hazards', in the home. The outcome of the 'investigation' is predictable: after a reassuring review of production, seasoned with plenty of self-congratulatory quotations from company spokespersons, the cannelloni is given a clean bill of health, and the company has the final word:

(26) All our prepared salads are washed in chlorinated water which will kill listeria. All our cooked foods are .cooked to a temperature which will kill listeria – and all other bacteria. We are confident that our foods will remain completely safe.

In the short paragraph which provides the narrative link, a woman 'picks two cartons of cannelloni from the shelves'; turn the page, and there follows immediately a two-page photographic article on '**THE HAZARDS IN YOUR KITCHEN**'. A 'food inspector' reviews a nice middle-class kitchen 'to highlight the inherent threats to food hygiene posed by items of equipment found in kitchens'; but the attention of the text passes quickly from 'the appliances' to 'the habits' of 'less fastidious cooks'. The bad personal habits of the less fastidious are analysed and condemned in very much the same terms as in the 'Thought for food' piece; the food inspector concludes:

(27) If we could just convince people that washing hands is important, that temperature control is important and that

when you [who?] cook food, you must make sure it's thoroughly cooked, we could do away with food poisoning.

The *Sunday Telegraph* approved of the middle-class housewife whose kitchen it inspected: her 'appliances' passed muster; she washed her hands and did not smoke; presumably she bought her cook-chill meals from a food supplier who declared that 'We take food safety as the most important thing we do'; and so, with her help 'we could do away with food poisoning'. Not so 'the poor housewife' who was treated to some extensive advice by the *Sun* newspaper two weeks earlier. In the two pages from the same day reproduced overleaf, a complex and derogatory stereotype emerges.

In the cartoon (p. 197), the background domestic frame – 'frame' in the sense of a cultural schema (see pp. 43–4) – is as significant as the violent fantasy that threatens it. The routine breakfast scene is represented with considerable detail: cereal bowl, sugar, toast, marmalade and tea on the table, milk and sauce bottles on the work surface, with the frying pan waiting for eggs; all of these are prototypical for the English breakfast frame. The roles of the husband and wife are sharply distinguished, a division emphasized by the fact that two rooms are represented, divided by the sharp vertical of the door frame. The two rooms represent the two separate domains of activity for man and woman. With his back to the kitchen, ignoring his wife, the husband is at ease, with armchair, specs and pipe (prototypical for man's domestic role), and reads a newspaper article about listeria: his role is to acquire knowledge about food poisoning and (see the headline in his newspaper) women's fears. His aproned wife is preparing breakfast, but in fetching eggs from the fridge she is attacked. Embraced by two hairy phallic tentacles, she struggles to contain a monster inside the fridge. Her face represents fear and panic (female hysteria), her body is in violent movement, as are the tentacles. Two fictional scripts are cued by this text: invasion of the home by an alien, and a fantasy of rape by a Beast. She calls her husband, who has an old-fashioned, ordinary name, not for help, but for information: 'What does bacteria look like?' Asking a question of this type casts her in the role of the would-be instructed, like a child in a science classroom. The content of her question encodes a total ignorance: bacteria do not look like

Text of Sun editorial 13 February 1989, reproduced opposite

THE SUN SAYS

Have a heart for housewives

WHAT tough days these are for the poor housewife.
When she goes shopping for her family, she must feel as if she is entering a minefield about which foods are safe and which potentially dangerous.

If, in her dilemma, she is angry with the Government, who can blame her?

Creation

Since Edwina Currie's famous warning about eggs it has been speaking with two voices – and sometimes with no voice at all – on matters vital to the nation's health.

Agriculture Minister John MacGregor's flirtation with a ban on non-pasteurised cheese is the latest example of fumbling indecisiveness.

He does not exactly say he will forbid imports.

And he does not exactly explain why these products have suddenly become suspect.

Recruit

It is little wonder that there are now .demands for the creation of a Ministry of Consumer Affairs.

Yet there is no reason to recruit even more bureaucrats.

All that is necessary is for the Agriculture Ministry and the Health Department to carry out the task entrusted to them by the public.

They have batteries of experts. They have mountains of information and research facilities.

If they cannot do their job, if they cannot reach simple agreement, Mrs Thatcher should send them for a health cure. Permanently.

"ARTHUR! WHAT DOES BACTERIA LOOK LIKE?"

Text of Sun article 13 February 1989, reproduced on p. 200

20 WAYS TO BEAT THE KILLERS IN YOUR KITCHEN

By TESSA CUNNINGHAM

FOOD health scares have sent the nation's housewives reeling. What CAN you feed your family on without jeopardising their well-being?

But while panic reigns over the twin perils of listeria and salmonella, there are simple steps **EVERYONE** can take to combat the risk of infection.

This is The Sun's good food guide to help **YOU** minimise the hazards.

1 **DON'T** let frozen food linger in your shopping basket. Until you reach your fridge, keep it somewhere cool, like the boot of the car. **DON'T** place it near a heater – warm temperatures encourage bacteria to breed. When you get home, put it into your fridge or freezer **IMMEDIATELY**.

2 Become a health inspector when you go shopping. Check the store before buying anything. Are the shelves clean? Do the fridges register the correct temperature, 41°F (5°C) or less? Is the food on fridge shelves equally cold? Does the shop stack food above the safety line in its freezer cabinets?

3 Look closely at sell-by dates on the food. Many shops push older food to the front to tempt you. If a food's price is slashed, it may have to be eaten on the same day as purchase. Remember, food that looks perfect can still be crawling with harmful bugs.

4 Keep your kitchen clean. Disinfect kitchen working surfaces, clean utensils used on raw food, pay strict attention to personal hygiene and **NEVER** prepare food if you are suffering from a stomach upset.

5 Always store raw meat on the **BOTTOM** shelf of your fridge – well away from cooked meat. Raw meat contains bugs destroyed only by cooking. They can contaminate other foods which are not going to be heated before eating.

6 **NEVER** put frozen food in a bowl of hot water or on a radiator to speed up thawing – it allows bacteria to breed. Frozen food must be thawed thoroughly.

7 Throw out any food you cannot eat the same day if your fridge has stopped working. Freezers should be between −18°C and −23°C. That won't kill bacteria but will stop it multiplying. If you store TV dinners, the fridge temperature should be between 3°C and 5°C – lower than most domestic fridges. Buy a fridge thermometer.

8 Go back to the way your mother used to cook – from basic ingredients. Try not to stock up on pre-packed, pre-prepared food once a week. Shop daily for fresh food.

9 Kitchen hygiene is vital. When cleaning put all food away or keep it well covered. Dust and air contain bacteria which may infect food left uncovered. Don't overfill the bin so that waste and unfit foods spill over. And always wash your hands after placing refuse in dustbins.

10 Make sure cooked left-overs cool to 4°C within 30 minutes before putting them in the fridge. It is safe to reheat the food, but you must eat it within two days. Reheat the dish thoroughly – **DON'T** just warm it up in a pan.

11 Wash bought salads carefully – the listeria bug is in the soil. Ready-cut, pre-packed salads and vegetables **MUST** also be thoroughly cleaned – they are more likely than freshly-dug up produce to be infected.

12 The watery content of soft cheeses is a breeding ground for listeria. Unpasteurised cheeses can also be unsafe. Beware of some types of Canadian cheddar, traditional Cheshire, Swiss ementhal, gruyere, traditional French brie, camembert and roquefort.

13 Avoid pre-cooked chicken. Opt for fresh or frozen birds you can cook safely yourself. Experts fear 60 per cent of our chickens are infected with listeria and 80 per cent with salmonella. Cook your chicken for the maximum time at a good high temperature. If it's a frozen bird, thaw thoroughly.

14 Beware of raw eggs – they could be contaminated with salmonella. Take care with foods made from raw eggs, like mayonnaise, mousses, meringues and some ice-creams. To be safe, boil your eggs for **SEVEN** minutes or more.

15 Microwave-cooked food is safe – provided the food is cooked through properly. So follow the manufacturer's instructions. Part way through the cooking time, turn the dish and give it a stir so that all the food is thoroughly heated.

16 Apart from listeria (from salads, vegetables, soil and animals) and salmonella (from poultry and eggs), experts also warn you to watch for campylobacter (raw and poorly cooked food, including unpasteurised milk) and staphyloccus aureus (thrives on ham and bacon which other bugs find too salty).

17 Cook meat thoroughly. The surface of all meats can become contaminated with listeria but cooking will destroy the bug, even on a rare steak. But if raw meat is minced, the bacteria has spread throughout the meat – so ensure thorough cooking.

18 Cut down the risk of salmonella by giving the family no more than two or three eggs each a week. Increase your intake of fibre by eating more fresh fruit and fresh vegetables. And **WASH** everything thoroughly.

19 Be wary of cooking a stuffed chicken or turkey – it prevents heat getting to the centre of the meat and is unlikely to properly cook the stuffing. In future, cook the stuffing separately.

20 If, despite your efforts, someone in your family falls ill, these are the clues to food poisoning. **SALMONELLA:** Abdominal pain, diarrhoea and sickness. **LISTERIA:** Flu-like illness, headache, fever, muscle pain, sickness. It can even cause the brain disease meningitis. Symptoms can occur from two days to one month after food is eaten. Toddlers, the elderly and pregnant women are most at risk.

Go shopping every day for fresh food

YOUR CUT-OUT-AND-KEEP SUN SAFETY GUIDE

20 WAYS TO BEAT THE KILLERS IN YOUR KITCHEN

Esther's pony plea to Sun

Hold your oars, Cyn

EGGS

CHICKEN

CHEESE

CHEESE CAN KILL YOUR BABY

Germ war by Maggie

'COSY EGG COVER UP'

Go shopping every day for fresh food

INVESTIGATION INTO CLAPHAM JUNCTION RAILWAY ACCIDENT

The formal investigation into the Clapham Junction Railway Accident will be held before Mr. Anthony Hidden QC and will begin on Monday 20 February 1989 at 10.30 a.m. in Westminster Central Hall, Storey's Gate, Westminster, London, SW1H 9NU.

The formal investigation will be held in public. Any enquiries should be made to the Clapham Junction Secretariat on 01-276 0838.

anything, since as the newspapers have told us a hundred times, they are 'invisible', or in scare language, 'hidden'. The syntax of her question signifies ignorance as well. The word 'bacteria' is a plural count noun like 'rabbits', and generally so used by the newspapers: 'bacteria multiply/grow/invade', etc. The singular auxiliary 'does' in the wife's question treats it as a singular mass noun like 'milk', 'water'.

The cartoon is of course a gloss on the editorial. The features of woman's place encoded by the cartoon transfer to the written text. The stereotype is lexicalized – 'housewives', 'the poor house-wife' – and markedly gendered by the repeated 'she', 'her'. The reader is called to adopt a perspective separate from and external to the 'housewife', who thus becomes 'them' to our 'us'; she is to be treated to our pity. The only other point I want to draw attention to in this text is the new metaphor 'minefield' which represents a different kind of violence and danger from that offered by the beast in the fridge. Minefields are laid by men; they are hidden, indiscriminate and unpredictable.

The second page reproduced from the *Sun* is in the form of a 'litany' of instructions, an extended form of the list of do's and don'ts exemplified by text (8) of chapter 9, and very similar in scale and content to the supermarkets' *Good Food Safety Guide*; the *Sun* calls its list a 'safety guide' and a 'good food guide'. The list of advice is explicitly linked to the editorial and the cartoon by the phrases 'the killers in your kitchen' (the monster in the fridge), 'sent the nation's housewives reeling' (which would be one effect of an exploding mine, or a blow) and 'panic reigns' (the expression on the woman's face). The link ensures that the list of advice is to be read in the light of the 'housewife' stereo-type. At this stage of my exposition, only a minimal analysis is required. Ignorance is presupposed by the didactic and imperative format seen already in other texts: the syntax of command, the insistent absolutes and modals such as 'IMMEDIATELY', 'NEVER' and 'MUST'. 'Experts' and 'manufacturers' are cited as authorities whose warnings and instructions should be fol-lowed. There is the expected insistence on washing and hygiene, with the powerful cue 'personal hygiene' in paragraph 4. Paragraph 2 encourages one kind of little-girl play-acting, the busybody housewife vetting the supermarket as if she is a 'food inspector', armed with her script of interrogations. Paragraph 8 is important in invoking another model: 'Go back to the way your mother used to cook – from basic ingredients . . . fresh food.' There is the Thatcherite nostalgia for the post-war years when women were supposed to have had time to shop and cook every day; this relates to the *Sunday Times*'s critique (text (20), p. 187) of the 'mum' who goes out to work and does not cook for her family. That the *Sun* regards a return to traditional daily housewifing as desirable is stressed by the highlighting slogan at the foot of the page.

The twenty paragraphs of this 'good food guide' contain a lot more than twenty items of information that a housewife should possess, chores she should perform. The text can be read either as a digest of a comprehensive food education programme (as sometimes requested by politicians and papers), or as a schedule of duties to fill the day and keep the woman out of trouble (out of work, out of politics), or as both. But the last paragraph reminds us that the text is goal-directed. The implication of the text is that 'the housewife' can prevent food poisoning, and that 'she' (rather than the manufacturers, etc.) is therefore in some sense responsible for it. Yet food poisoning might strike:

(28) If, despite your efforts, someone in your family falls ill, these are the clues to food poisoning.

In the context, this scrap of discourse carries much significance. 'Your family' means the family that you are responsible for. 'Your efforts' means that only you are responsible for making these efforts, or that only your efforts count; nothing that another member of the family, or the manufacturers, might do counts as a relevant 'effort'. If someone falls ill, it is implied, that could happen only because your efforts are inadequate. Then you must make further efforts, diagnosing the illness and no doubt tending the sick. The text offers an opportunity for guilt, which is a major component of this stereotype and this strategy. Ending with the familiar list of 'vulnerable' groups, 'toddlers, the elderly and pregnant women', it calls for womanly pathos to reinforce the guilt.

THE PERSISTENCE OF PARADIGMS

A good Pandora's box does not easily close. 'Despite the efforts' of the Select Committee, the industry and the Press, food scares kept on coming. As I was trying to finish this chapter, in mid-July 1989, a new listeria scandal hit the headlines, this time concerning supermarket pâté. I could have written the Press coverage,[5] which rested on the same formulae that had been established months earlier: **'Deadly food poison that stalks our supermarkets'**, **'Listeria: An elusive killer'** (headings to two articles in the *Observer*, 16 July 1989). Here we had a recurrence of one of the original topics, and a reiteration of the original discourse of guilt, government inactivity, industry negligence, and so on.

But the paradigm – I mean a general way of looking at food, not just the topic of listeria – never disappeared. Throughout the spring and summer of 1989, few days went by without the newspapers invoking the paradigm. For example, quite randomly I encountered the following over three days:

(29) **Ice cream peril at beach**

(Star, 24 June)

Airline food menace

(Observer, 25 June)

The killer bug listeria   .

(Express, 26 June)

The last refers to listeria in fast food at holiday resorts. What is happening in these three headlines is that the underlying paradigm is cued by repeating the old formulaic structure, with the new content made topical as the summer holiday season, with its ice creams, hamburgers and air travel, approaches.

Often the paradigm surfaced in single news items or features such as these, with little development. However trivial the content, or brief the duration, these reiterations were important in keeping alive this particular way of representing our relationship with one part of our lives, eating and its significances. Once or twice (as with listeria in July) the full-blown paradigm appeared. I want to end by referring briefly to one such developed instance of the paradigm, the 'baby food crisis' of late April 1989.

The 'salmonella affair' in its broad sense had always contained space for discussion of baby foods and the feeding of babies, e.g. aluminium in powdered baby milk and whether 'breast is best' (see *Sunday Times*, 20 November 1989), and pesticide residues in rusks (*Guardian*, 14 March 1989). Such topics are linked to salmonella/listeria in the narrower sense through the themes of food industry practice, agricultural pollution and convenience foods. It should be clear from the discussion in the last few pages of the stereotyping of women, particularly the foregrounding and guiltifying of their maternal responsibilities, that the symbolic value of babies is very important for the discourse: they are the prototype of the utterly vulnerable, the innocent; reference to babies in this context of food poisoning and alleged maternal irresponsibility is always emotive, pathetic.

In late April 1989, the newspapers became very excited about an accumulation of reports of what can most neutrally be described as the contamination of jars of manufactured baby food. Slivers of glass, drawing pins, razor blades and other objects were found in jars of baby dinners and of dessert. The *Daily Mirror*, 26 April, prints a chronology and a map of the reported cases, and, drawing on the full power of the baby symbol, headlines the front page with the emotive question:

(30) **WHO IS TRYING TO KILL OUR BABIES?**

The *Mirror* had decided that the contamination was the malicious work of a 'baby food beast' ('maniac', 'lunatic'). On the same day, 26 April, the Home Office Minister John Patten announced that police were hunting blackmailers who were using this procedure in an attempt to extract money from the manufacturers. His language in the House of Commons, as reported in *The Times*, 27 April, summons up the emotive power of the baby symbol:

(31) 'It is difficult to imagine the twisted minds that could mount such a vicious attack on defenceless babies.' He said: 'In some cases, there have been blackmail demands. It would not be helpful for police investigations if I were to go into greater detail.

In the same article,

(32) Mr Barry Sheerman, Labour's home affairs spokesman, described the attacks as 'a horrible campaign which really attacks the most vulnerable members of our society'.

These characterizations tend to remove any ambiguity from the baby food contaminations: they are the work of deranged criminal individuals; the crime is self-evidently very deplorable because of the 'precious and vulnerable' nature of the targets (as 'Scotland Yard' put it); leave it to the police to solve the crime. The *Times* article also reports a number of recommendations to parents by Mr Patten and by the police regarding checking containers and food: the 'personal responsibility' part of the food poisoning script.

Mr Patten also offered a neat formula to categorize the crime(s) being investigated: 'consumer terrorism'. 'The Government', reported *The Times*, 'promised yesterday not to bow to "consumer terrorism".' The phrase puts the baby food contamination into the same category as airliner bombings, assassinations, etc.: the work of madmen, utterly antisocial, murderous, requiring a firm stand by the government and the police. The values packaged in the frame called 'consumer terrorism' are simple, accessible to the public and the authorities, and they disambiguate the baby food contamination in a highly specific direction.

The newspapers reported Mr Patten's offer of the 'consumer terrorism' hypothesis, and some seemed to have entertained it, at least briefly: in addition to the *Mirror*, 26 April, see also *Sunday Telegraph*, 30 April, '**How to fight the supermarket terrorists**', which makes extensive use of the analogy of airline terrorism. But there was a general tendency to deploy formulae from the salmonella discourse:

(33) Baby food panic

(*Sun*, 26 April)

Baby food crisis

(*Eastern Evening News*, 27 April; *Observer*, 30 April)

Baby scare

(*Eastern Evening News*, 28 April)

Contamination scare

(*Observer*, 30 April)

Chaos over baby food

(*Observer*, 30 April)

Blackmail hysteria

(*Observer*, 30 April)

The effect of using the salmonella/listeria discourse to refer to this new matter of baby food contamination was to preserve the ambiguity of the affair: the phrases in (33) carry no assumptions about causes, responsibilities or even the material processes producing contamination. Indeed, these formulae from the earlier (and at that time very recent) food poisoning discourse may have suggested that baby food contamination, like salmonella and listeria, was *essentially* complex, mysterious, even subjective. This implicit theory, diffuse and unfocused but potentially sophisticated, was, as it happens, more correct than Mr Patten's hardline attack on 'consumer terrorism'. The salmonella discourse, with its resonance of 'a mounting epidemic', also encouraged the affair to expand exponentially in the media and in the public consciousness. On Wednesday 26 April, the *Mirror* declared **'Spiked food maniac strikes THIRTEEN times'**; by Sunday 30 April, 'more than 250 cases of alleged contamination were reported' (*Observer*). This escalation of reporting validates the paradigm 'hysteria' rather than 'terrorism'. As with food poisoning, public consciousness that there was 'something going on' heightened awareness and imagination, hence the increase in reports. The *Observer* also claims that there had been an increase in the number of cases of ' "normal" accidents', contaminations of food during manufacture or service; a health officer is paraphrased to the effect that 'the increase of contamination goes hand in hand with the growing use of packaged convenience food in the last five years' (cf. the discussion of listeria). Finally, it had become clear by Sunday 30 April that at least some of the reports were falsely raised by members of the public 'jumping on the bandwagon', deliberately contaminating baby food in order to gain publicity or to extort compensation from the manufacturers. 'At least six people have been arrested for wasting police time over the affair.'

My point is that discussion of the baby food contamination in the terminology of the earlier food poisoning scare did actually transform baby food contamination, whatever its starting-point, into a real instance of the existing food poisoning scare. Surrounding the reporting of contamination incidents and discussion of their causes there is a substantial value-laden discourse about parental responsibility, the status of 'the vulnerable', fresh versus convenience foods, traditional and modern cooking and parenting practices, the safety of food manufacture, the effectiveness and honesty of government, and so on, all issues which as we have seen were amply debated during the salmonella affair. The baby food scare is an excellent example of a basic principle in the theory of representation: an individual event cannot be reported independently of cultural values or ideology, which already exist(s) ready to be projected on to it; if it is an event which develops, it can even become transformed to take on the characteristics of its pre-existing paradigm. Representing events changes them.

Chapter 11

Leading the people: editorial authority

Each day, newspapers print one or two separate articles, distinct from the news reporting, features and other regular daily items, claiming to speak their own point of view. These sections are variously headed or indexed as 'leading article', 'editorial', 'opinion', 'comment', 'We say', 'The *Sun* says', and so on. They have an important symbolic function, seeming to partition off the 'opinion' component of the paper, implicitly supporting the claim that other sections, by contrast, are pure 'fact' or 'report'. The firm distinction mapped out by Andrew Neil, quoted on pp. 1–2, is reflected in this differentiation of textual format. Textual symbolism is even foregrounded by layout and typography, the leader usually being printed in the same position on the same page every day, often adjacent to readers' letters, which are also categorized as (mere) opinion. Special, eye-catching type may be used, as in the *Sun* editorial reproduced in chapter 10, p. 197. A heraldic, patriotic or otherwise suggestive logo may be printed above the leader.

The present book has questioned the possibility of objective, value-free reporting. I have argued that representation in a semiotic medium such as language is inevitably a structuring process; that values and implicit propositions are continuously articulated as discourse on a subject proceeds, so that discourse is always representation from a certain point of view. This theory of structured representation is valid for any discourse: I am not saying that newspapers are particularly 'biased' (even though most have a political axe to grind); *all* texts, e.g. physics textbooks, do-it-yourself manuals, novels, children's books, biographies, histories, speeches and conversations, and naturally enough, this book too, are discursive constructions of some world. What is distinctive about newspaper editorials is not that they offer values and beliefs, but that they employ textual strategies which foreground the speech act of offering values and beliefs.

Editorials are quite diverse in their styles or textual strategies, and that is part of the point, to suggest a distinctive 'voice' for the newspaper, as the old *Times* 'thunderer', the strident interrogating of the *Mirror*, the appearance of a careful balancing of alternatives practised by the *Guardian* and the *Observer*. For this reason, the present chapter tries to be careful to avoid unwarranted generalizations; three distinct editorials are quoted, with commentaries on their discursive procedures.

All three editorials discussed come from mid-April 1986, when international news was dominated by the bombing of Libya on 15 April, and its aftermath of reprisal killings and an attempt to plant a bomb on an Israeli airliner at Heathrow Airport. More details of the chain of events were given in chapter 7, pp. 112ff. The chronological sequence of the editorials is immaterial to the points I want to make about 'leader discourse' in this chapter; the first comes from the *Express*, Friday 18 April.

(1) **Winning the war against terrorism**
Yesterday we were brutally reminded of the evil face of international terrorism. First, three of our fellow citizens were cold-bloodedly murdered in the Lebanon by Kadhafi's fanatical admirers, who were holding them hostage.

Then came the diabolical attempt to put a bomb on a Jumbo at Heathrow and blow it to bits in the air over England. Only the vigilance of El Al's security men prevented a hideous massacre.

Our hearts must go out to the loved ones of the three innocent Britons. We publish the pictures of the bodies, fully realizing that some of our readers may find them disturbing.

But we feel we have a duty to do so, to show the awful reality of terrorism which threatens the foundation of lawful and humane existence everywhere.

It is this evil against which President Reagan struck such a timely blow. And a vitally *necessary* one.

These callous killers are not bought off with soft words or by turning the other cheek.

In recent years, successive Italian Governments believed

that possible, thinking they could win their citizens immunity from terrorist attack by courting the PLO and Kadhafi. They were quickly disillusioned. But appeasing terrorists merely feeds their arrogance.

Innocent victims

Of course, the murders of the Britons – yesterday's abduction of TV cameraman John McCarthy, and the attack on our Ambassador's home in West Beirut – will be cited in support of the argument that Mrs Thatcher's backing for the US air strike against Libya has needlessly exposed British citizens to terrorist attack.

But can that really be sustained? British citizens were already targets.

The Britons mercilessly killed in Beirut became victims of terrorism the moment they were kidnapped: Alec Collett in March last year, Philip Padfield and Leigh Douglas almost three weeks ago.

They were as innocent then as they were when they were slaughtered. Policewoman Yvonne Fletcher, gunned down by one of Kadhafi's men in London two years ago yesterday, was just as innocent.

No one, least of all President Reagan, suggested that the attack on Libya would deal with Kadhafi's terrorism once and for all. The Libyan leader's fanatical friends will continue their attempts to hit back – a prospect Mrs Thatcher took into account when deciding to support any US action.

The campaign against terrorism and its sponsors must be continuous. No single blow will be enough. Terrorist reprisals must be punished in their turn.

This is the only way, in the long run, to make gangster régimes stop their training, arming and launching of terrorist killers.

We have no other choice.

A way into analysis of an editorial is to consider it in terms of three discourse participants: the *source*, the *addressee*, and the *referent(s)*: the 'I', 'you' and 'he/she/it/they'. The voice of the source is, characteristically, made more salient than it is in news report:

- *Vocabulary* is emotive, dramatizing a speaker with strong feelings and opinions. Evaluative adverbs and adjectives are prominent: 'brutally', 'evil', 'fanatical', 'diabolical', 'hideous', 'inno-cent', 'mercilessly', and so on, particularly noticeable in the opening paragraphs and sporadically maintained throughout.

- *Modality* has the insistence of a speaker who has assumed a position of authority. The authority includes a claim to know what is inevitably going to happen: 'the murders of the Britons . . . *will be* cited'; 'The Libyan leader's fanatical friends *will* continue . . .' The modal auxiliary 'must' is a crucial word in editorials, claiming that the source has the right to specify obligations: '*must be* continuous', '*must be* punished'. This modal goes with an ethical vocabulary, not particularly promi-nent here but surfacing in the word 'duty' in the fourth para-graph.

- *Generic statements* are found. These are not affirmations of obli-gation or necessity, but descriptive propositions which are sup-posedly true of any instance of the entities to which they refer: 'These callous killers are not bought off with soft words or by turning the other cheek.' Generic sentences are inevitably authoritarian, claiming total and definitive knowledge of some topic; they offer the comfort of closure as against the openness of enquiry. It is significant that the generic sentence is the most common semantic and syntactic form for proverbs – 'Birds of a feather flock together' – and that this particular generic has proverbial or biblical overtones. Proverbs encode what is taken to be common-sense wisdom.

- An editorial tends to be *argumentative*, in two senses. First, the logical and/or narrative structure of the exposition is high-lighted by 'textual signposts': 'Yesterday . . . Then . . .' Second, the editorial voice strikes a position of rebuttal in relation to other people's ideas: 'some of our readers may find them disturbing . . . *But we feel* . . . ' Often the argument is dramatized by the use of dialogic devices such as rhetorical questions: 'the murders . . . will be cited in support of the argument. . . . *But can that really be sustained?*'

What relationships does the editorial voice construct with the other discourse participants? In relation to the reader, the link is dual, and embodies a latent contradiction. On the one hand, the source claims the authority to explain an argument and to per-suade the reader of its correctness. The rhetorical and didactic form of address, though oral in tone (see chapter 4), is more like a lecture, presupposing power-difference, than a conversation, which would presuppose solidarity with the addressee. Yet, on the other hand, the editorial claims solidarity by invoking consensus. The pronouns 'we' and 'our' appear frequently: three times in the 'exclusive' sense, the 'institutional "we" ' referring to the newspaper ('We publish the pictures . . .'); most often in the 'inclusive' sense, referring to the community of values that the newspaper claims to express: 'we were brutally reminded. . . . Our hearts must go out. . . . We have no other choice.' The consensus from which the newspaper starts concerns a 'lawful and humane existence' which defines the consensual 'we' being appealed to; to that core accrete pathos, feeling, shock. The consensus is also political, in that it is represented as national: 'our fellow citizens', 'innocent Britons', 'the Britons'. The cause impressed on readers is a nationalistic one.

The *Express* puts in opposition to this 'us' two categories of 'them', the third-person referents (to turn to the third class of discourse participant mentioned above) which form the alienated topics of this editorial. They are in fact depicted in two other areas of the same page. A cartoon pictures a line of politicians (Kinnock, Heath, Steel, Mitterand and others) dressed up in imitation of 'Neville Chamberlain, Apostle of Appeasement' (of Hitler), who are declaring 'Don't provoke terrorists'. The third space on the page is taken up by a signed article on Colonel Kadhafi and his 'global army' of 'terrorists', arguing that they are well organized, widespread, heavily financed and very dangerous to 'British and American citizens'. In the editorial, the terrorists are described as 'fanatical', a word which encodes a view of 'Arab terrorists' as religious extremists, hysterical followers of the late Ayatollah Khomeini's version of Islam. They are to be regarded as beyond the pale of consensus, even of humanity: they are utterly distinct from the 'Britons' so frequently mentioned in the editorial. By association, the European politicians who reportedly advocated appeasement are non-British too: like the terrorists, they 'must be punished in their turn.'

My next text is a *Daily Mirror* editorial which was published a day earlier, Thursday 17 April 1986. The newspaper is responding to the basic story of the bombing of Tripoli, not to the 'reprisals'. But the topic is more complex, because the newspaper weaves into its response to the Libyan affair a discourse on another and quite distinct act of 'terrorism', the kidnapping and release of Mrs Jennifer Guinness, wife of a 'distant cousin of the multi-millionaire brewing family'.

(2)   **Two of a kind**
Crime, whether it is local or international, becomes rampant when it is seen to pay.

If the kidnapping of Jennifer Guinness had led to a ransom being paid, then further kidnappings were inevitable. Crime would have been handsomely rewarded. *If the terrorism of Colonel Gaddafi and his gangs had been unanswered and unpunished, then it would have continued and spread. Crime would have paid its evil dividends.*

- Does anyone doubt kidnapping is criminal?
- Does anyone doubt that terrorism is criminal?
- Does anyone doubt that they are two of a kind?

No one condemned Gaddafi more clearly, more precisely or more forcefully yesterday than Mr Neil Kinnock.

Sanctions
No one needed convincing about Gaddafi's criminality, he said. Gaddafi was a malignancy. No one could doubt his involvement in the financing and sponsoring of terrorism. Libya, he went on, was a haven for terrorists. Strong sanctions were needed to 'squeeze the very life' out of the Gaddafi regime.

There is no difference, therefore, between Mr Kinnock and Mrs Thatcher – or Mr Reagan – about Gaddafi's guilt. The only quarrel is about how to deal with him.

Sanctions would certainly be best. But Europe refused to impose them. If it changes its mind now it will be because of the bombing. That is the logic which cannot be escaped.

Many of the observations on the *Express* leader apply to this one, too. The triad of discourse participants are constituted in a similar manner. The source's voice of authority opens with a generic statement about crime and its rewards, which is intertextually related to the proverbial wisdom that 'crime doesn't pay' (the proverb is referred to again in the two sentences beginning 'Crime . . .' which end paragraphs two and three). The confidence of the leader is developed in a series of hypothetical predictions using the modal 'would' (second and third paragraphs). In the fourth paragraph, the dialogic nature of the discourse is heightened by the three rhetorical questions, in which authority is maintained by appeal to the analytic or tautologous propositions 'kidnapping is criminal' and 'terrorism is criminal': these are supposedly self-evidently true. And they are central to the consensus-forming strategy of the text; readers are implicated in the ideological position of the 'we' to the extent that they accept these propositions. It is interesting that the consensual 'we' is not actually used in this editorial; perhaps because this leader writer realizes that this form conventionally signifies, certainly in the 'quality' papers and the tabloids of the Right, a *directive* force, an instruction as to what 'we', i.e. 'you' being addressed, should think or do. Instead of 'we', the *Mirror* relies on the generic pronouns 'anyone' and 'no one'. Underlying these forms as used in questions and negations is the absolute pronoun 'everyone': 'everyone knows terrorism is criminal'; 'everyone knows about Gaddafi's criminality'. These implicit generalizations allow Labour leader Neil Kinnock and Conservative Prime Minister Margaret Thatcher to be enfolded into the 'we', leaving Colonel Gaddafi and the kidnappers of Jennifer Guinness as the sole occupiers of the referential role of 'them'.

A striking feature of the *Mirror* editorial is the salience of *logical* activity, one aspect of the 'argumentative' potential of editorials which happened not to be particularly prominent in the *Express*. The heading '**Two of a kind**', repeated in the third of the rhetorical questions at the heart of the text, announces that the editorial is concerned with classification, equivalence. The first, one-sentence, paragraph offers the general proposition that crime increases if it is 'seen to pay'. In the context of the overwhelming news story of the moment, and indeed of the main article on this page of the *Mirror*, '**THATCHER TELLS OF GADDAFI GUILT**', we assume that the opening generalization is to be read as a contribution to the debate on whether 'we' ought to have bombed Tripoli. The *Mirror* is implicitly suggesting that the action was justified, and this point of view is indeed indicated, albeit again implicitly, in the third paragraph; by contrast, the *Express* is absolutely explicit about its support for the bombing and for any further punitive action – of course, the political positions of the two newspapers are very different. The *Mirror* justifies its belief not by analysis of the Gaddafi phenomenon or the recent history of 'terrorism', but by citation of the general principle and, in the second and third paragraphs, argument by analogy. Total syntactic correspondence and lexical equivalence between the sentences in paragraphs two and three instruct the reader to analogize:

(3) If the kidnapping of Jennifer Guinness
If the terrorism of Colonel Gaddafi and his gangs

had led to a ransom being paid,
had been unanswered and unpunished

then further kidnappings were inevitable.
then it would have continued and spread.

Crime would have been handsomely rewarded.
Crime would have paid its evil dividends.

The outcome of the Jennifer Guinness kidnapping is supposed to illuminate the Tripoli bombing, but despite the equivalence of textual form between the expressions of the two sets of ideas, the logical correspondence is not very precise. Jennifer Guinness was released without payment of a ransom, and it is argued that this outcome will discourage further kidnappings because they do not (literally) pay. Alleged Libyan terrorism was 'answered' and 'punished' by the bombing of Libya, and that punishment demonstrated that terrorism will not (metaphorically) 'pay'. Despite the plea of the parallel syntax, the analogy does not work: the situations just do not correspond. The next paragraph employs parallel typography, as well as syntax and lexis, to construct a primitive syllogism based, as I said, on analyticity:

(4) kidnapping is criminal
terrorism is criminal
[therefore kidnapping and terrorism] are two of a kind.

Only in a very weak sense, of course: the propositions about the effects of payment and of punishment have been lost in the reduction.

Next Mr Kinnock is introduced, in a series of formulaic sentences based on 'No one . . .', in support of the case for 'strong sanctions' against Libya. Despite the fact that Mr Kinnock had 'denounced the use of military force' (*Mirror*, same page), the paper comes to the surprising conclusion that 'There is no difference, therefore [note the display of logical connective], between

Mr Kinnock and Mrs Thatcher . . .' Perhaps it is Kinnock and Thatcher who are 'two of a kind' – an astonishing judgement, coming from the ostensibly Left *Mirror*. The interpretation is encouraged by the reproduction, immediately adjacent to the editorial, of two passport-sized photographs of the two politicians' faces, their heads composed in exactly the same position and angle in the frame, both wearing calm and sensible expressions. Presumably this treatment is designed to resist the marginalization of the Left by suggesting that Mr Kinnock has taken a strong patriotic line. I can only comment that the *Mirror* has tried to accomplish an ideological sleight-of-hand by a spurious display of the appearances of logic. The word 'logic' appears in the concluding sentence. In effect, the editorial is confused and confusing, but is has the impressive appearance of a tightly organized argument.

We finally turn to a third treatment of this topic. The *Guardian* editorial of 16 April, the day after the bombing, is very long, occupying about a third of the large-format page. In a discursive, essayistic style, it ranges over a variety of points of view, but its opening judgement, in the very first sentence, is categorical, unequivocal:

(5) They were wrong to do it, and we were foolish to help them.

Striking is the use of pronouns. It is unusual for a text to start with pronouns which refer to entities outside the text which have not been identified. The usage makes strong assumptions about readers: that readers will already have on their minds the main news story of the day, and will automatically supply the referents of the pronouns: 'They' = 'the United States', 'do it' = 'bomb Tripoli', 'we' = 'the British government'. It is surely assumed also that *Guardian* readers, unlike readers of the *Express* or the *Mirror*, will disapprove of the bombing. No justification is offered for the judgement, and the way it is worded suggests that the judgement is the obvious point of view. The editorial then enters a dialogic relationship with its readership, constructing a devil's-advocate argument:

(6) But stick, for a moment, with the official American arguments – and the chiming sentiments of Mrs Margaret Thatcher – because they are not negligible.

Note the colloquial word 'stick', and the mundane metaphor 'chiming', both stylistic features which, as we will see, recur throughout the text, creating a familiar, matter-of-fact rhetoric entirely appropriate to the no-nonsense opening sentence. Why is this blunt, casual style adopted in writing about such a serious international topic? The answer may be that the leader writer intends an *avoidance* of any style which is hyperbolic, emotive, literary; of any style which connotes the voice of the Government, of the Right, of the Nation: any style which suggests a chauvinistic 'us' who might regard the bombing, and the obedient allegiance to the United States, as a good thing. The chosen style is that of the dissociated, pragmatic intelligence.

After its brusque opening, the editorial offers a gesture to fairness in two paragraphs reconstructing US arguments justifying the bombing of Tripoli. It then expresses scepticism about these arguments, and about the effectiveness and the propriety of the attack. Before the focus is moved to Mrs Thatcher and the British response to the United States, there is a section sarcastically dismissing President Reagan:

(7) Mad dogs (to use the easy rhetoric) cannot be cowed or trained by example. If they are murdering now, they will go on murdering. And what, pray, does the great avenger of Lakenheath do then? He presents himself at the bar of world opinion as the man who sent his bombers to pound civilians (and the French embassy in Tripoli). He didn't mean it, but it happened; inevitably so. The last high level intelligence from the White House was of Nicaragua's invasion of Honduras. Rubbish: even the Hondurans said so. The world – not just Europe, the Third World – has grown sceptical of Mr Reagan's narrow vision, and leery of the way he compensates for foreign policy revolts on Capitol Hill with risk free adventures against states which can only soak up his firepower. Ramboism without risk.

The mode appears to be oral, and the style is casual. Several of the markers of an oral model listed in chapter 4 (pp. 62–5) converge here. The syntax is broken up into short speech-like information units by frequent commas and other punctuation marks: 'He didn't mean it, but it happened; inevitably so.' There are also short, verb-less sentences: 'Ramboism without risk.' Lots of parenthetical observations, enclosed in brackets and dashes, refuse to allow the syntax to settle to the more extended rhythms of written prose. Parentheses are found throughout the editorial; not only do they help the illusion of speech syntax and intonation, they also give the impression of a speaker 'thinking on his feet' (this is a male political rhetoric), the speech not wholly pre-planned but rich with extra thoughts voiced immediately as they occur to the speaker. This style signifies a personal confidence appropriate to someone who makes total, sweeping judgements: Colonel Gadafy is 'a deranged ruler' earlier; sarcastically put, President Reagan sees himself as the deific 'great avenger of Lakenheath' (the American air base in Suffolk). The vocabulary has the casual, familiar bluntness of the 'plain speaker': 'rubbish', 'leery' and, elsewhere, 'why on earth', 'chipper', 'bind', etc.

Dialogism, an argumentative engagement with the imagined points of view of those referred to by the text, and those who read it, is highlighted by rhetorical questions: 'And what, pray . . . ?' This aspect of style will be discussed in a moment, at a point in the editorial two paragraphs later, where it is even more prominent. Let us now look at the next part of the editorial.

(8) But we are only at an interim stage as tit follows tat. Mr Reagan's judgment is that, along this road, a cowed Gadafy will sink into impotence. He will ultimately be judged – by his own electorate – on the wisdom or frailty of that judgement. Mrs Thatcher, however, is sadly exposed: girding her electorate for reprisals, defending to her people the blank cheque she gave America's bombers. And all the while there is a fatal hole in her argument.

Remember the copious evidence of Libyan terrorism she threatened to produce to the House yesterday? Did it not exist a few months ago when Britain declined to join economic sanctions against Libya? Did it not exist even on Monday when Sir Geoffrey left such sanctions out of his European package? Why on earth – if the evidence of evil is so strong – balk at peaceful reprisals by Britain? Why not even mention them today? The Bonn authorities know all about the Berlin bomb. The Paris authorities know all about the supposed massacre plot outside the Hotel Talleyrand. Why are they, too, so slow to move? European governments by their deeds – the British government high amongst them – are either derelict in any conceivable duty:

or riven by disbelief. Mrs Thatcher, by her own refusal economically to pay the modest price of isolating Libya, sets herself amongst those ranks – privately alarmed and disapproving of Washington's wild meanderings, but unwilling to make the break of an independent line.

The short transitional paragraph shifting attention to Mrs Thatcher continues the colloquialism: 'tit follows tat', a vernacular coding of the concept of reprisal which had been introduced in the first paragraph; mundane metaphors: 'girding her electorate', 'the blank cheque', 'a fatal hole'. ('Fatal hole' intertextually recalls and yet suppresses the expression 'fatal flaw' which is found in the Aristotelian theory of literary tragedy, thus pointedly denying Mrs Thatcher the dignity, the 'pity and fear', of a lofty leader about to fall.)

The second paragraph in (8), the penultimate of the editorial, brings the dialogic style to the surface of the rhetoric. The first word of the first of the series of questions, 'Remember', is a powerful cue for the construction of a set of relationships between discourse participants: it calls up an addressee (an image of the actual reader) because it is a word which, in normal usage, can only be spoken by one individual to another; it is also uttered here in a quasi-intimate style, with the auxiliary and the subject pronoun, 'do you', deleted as they would be in casual speech. Of course, this happens to be the syntax of an imperative, too, and there is a sense in which the reader is being instructed to remember. Finally, the entailment of 'remember' is important: to remember something entails that you knew it before. So the *Guardian* text is now based on a set of implicit claims as to what its readers already know: Mrs Thatcher's threat to produce copious evidence, the German and French authorities' knowledge of a bomb and of a massacre attempt. The questions apparently addressed to the reader, presupposing this information, have a dual function, querying the failure of the 'authorities' and 'governments' to agree on sanctions if this 'copious evidence' existed. The dialogic manoeuvre initiated by 'remember' sketches the parameters of an 'us/them' dichotomy without having to use those words: the *Guardian*/reader axis which is at least as highly informed as the politicians, and the European politicians who failed to act, and thereby helped precipitate the bombing. The rhetorical questions move the reader towards a judgement ('European governments

. . . the British government . . . derelict') which s/he has been made to feel qualified to join the *Guardian* in pronouncing. Towards the end of the paragraph, Mrs Thatcher is ranked with the tardy European governments, but condemned not only for tardiness, but for a contradictory stubbornness. The editorial concludes:

(9) It is that – on the issue of the use of the bases – that may so gravely damage her. Not the question of permission asked and granted. But the feeling that, in any crunch, America may insist and push aside independent British policy. Mr Kinnock was notably chipper yesterday. Who says scrapping the American bases may cost him the next election? Whilst Britain tags dumbly and miserably behind Ronald Reagan, he is right to see an opportunity, and Mrs Thatcher is adrift. Even she wouldn't try sanctions: but she condones the bombings and the loss of civilian life. It is a bleak bind, and one that may come to haunt her. But did her closest ally think of that, any more than he thought through the stages beyond the rubble of Tripoli?

The judgement of the last paragraph had been cued by the phrase 'an independent line': the final and crucial topic of the editorial is going to be Britain's servile compliance, and complicity, with US military policy in allowing the bases to be used to assist the bombing. An implied lack of independence which the *Guardian* proposes may be unacceptable to the British electorate.

By the end of the editorial, the 'them' being condemned have been comprehensively specified: Gadafy, Abu Nidal, and so on, Reagan, the European governments and, at the climax, Mrs Thatcher. The 'we' has become, not the consensual political 'Britain' of the very first sentence of this leader, that nationalistic 'we' which was present in the other two editorials, but an alignment of *Guardian* authority, the highly informed *Guardian* reader and the Labour leader Mr Kinnock sensing a political advantage in the potential damage Mrs Thatcher might have done herself by participating in the bombing of Libya. (On the evidence of the other papers, which assumed that their readers were as 'THRILLED TO BLITZ' as were the US pilots, this is an optimistic analysis.) There is a dialogically complex question at the heart of the final paragraph which further extends the range of imagined participants: 'Who says scrapping the American bases may cost him the next election?' Whoever says this – political commentators, those on the Right of the Labour Party, or whoever – is sketched as another category of 'them', and implicitly among the 'us' are a sizeable voting force who would prefer to see the end of 'our special relationship' (as the consensual view commonly puts it) with our 'closest ally' (as the *Guardian* ironizes it). On inspection, this 'Who says . . . ?' question requires a breadth of political awareness and knowledge to unpack. The editorial cleverly makes the reader do the work, thus contributing to the sense of sophistication, superiority in the way 'we' make our political judgements.

The three editorials are written in distinct styles, and articulate different points of view on the same topic, but the components of the styles are drawn from the same repertoire of textual strategies. What they have in common is a concern to highlight the judgemental character of discourse, a character which is backgrounded (but still present) in the news reporting pages. Various techniques are deployed to make salient the illusion of utterance by an authoritative speaker, addressing a particular kind of reader embraced in an 'us' relationship and taking a particular, marked stance in relation to the persons ('them') and topics referred to. These texts illustrate a discourse of institutional power in the sense that it emanates from, and in turn helps construct, the newspaper's claimed authority.

Chapter 12

Conclusion: prospects for critical news analysis

The theory of news representation on which this book is based was established in the 1970s by students of the media such as Stuart Hall, the Glasgow Media Group and the various social scientists and media specialists collected in Cohen and Young's book *The Manufacture of News*.[1] That title, and Hall's chapter title 'The social production of news', provide striking mnemonics for the basic premises of the theory. News is not a natural phenomenon emerging straight from 'reality', but a *product*. It is produced by an industry, shaped by the bureaucratic and economic structure of that industry, by the relations between the media and other industries and, most importantly, by relations with government and with other political organizations. From a broader perspective, it reflects, and in return shapes, the prevailing values of a society in a particular historical context.

I have taken the view that the basis of this account, however unpalatable to the news industry, is a very sound hypothesis. However, it is incomplete. What is missing is acknowledgement and explanation of the discursive structure of the medium itself, the power of the structural minutiae of images and words to impose a value-laden organization on news in the process of articulating it. It is discourse structure which does the work of shaping reality which is assumed by the media specialists: to show how this happens requires extra components of theory, and a more powerful technical apparatus for practical textual analysis. As far as still or moving photographic images are concerned, this analytic apparatus existed in the 1970s, and is more sophisticated today with great advances in film theory and criticism. But even admirable books like *More Bad News*, good on pictures, have little to say about verbal structure, or indeed about the relationships between words and pictures.

The linguistic gap is unnecessary, and regrettable. It is unnecessary (today anyway) because there exist the appropriate linguistic terms for analysis. In the 1970s, even the traditional grammatical terms would have been adequate to scrape through with, but since that time, advances in discourse analysis[2] and in critical linguistics[3] have developed forms of analysis which are specifically geared to explicating the structuring of signification in texts, in relation to their social and historical contexts. For some years, my own work in critical linguistics has been an attempt to develop an apparatus for this type of analysis, eclectically based but relying mostly on the functional linguistics of M. A. K. Halliday and his associates. One of the main aims of the present book is to demonstrate critical news analysis in action, guided by this specific linguistic theory and terminology.

The neglect of linguistics in early media theory was regrettable in the above sense, that there was a descriptive gap: the profoundly important linguistic structure of texts could not be accounted for adequately. But it was regrettable in a deeper sense, that the lack of connection with linguistics weakened the link with semiotics, the foundation of modern theories of representation. Saussure first showed how meanings emerge from the systematic structure of the vocabulary, not from nature.[4] My final chapter is no place to delve into semiotic theory. Let me say, however, that John Hartley's book *Understanding News* is of great importance in restoring semiotic concepts to the theory of news representation; the move makes it possible to draw support for an account of news as reality-construction through language not only from the classical tradition of Saussure and the French school but from other linguists such as Whorf and Halliday who have, like Saussure, regarded language as a structuring grid projected on to the world and intersubjectively accessible to members of a speech community. The restoration of the link with semiotics and linguistics also allows media theory and analysis to benefit from the insights of those who have worked at the interface between (literary) textual studies and linguistic semiotics. I am referring particularly to Mikhail Bakhtin, whose dialogic/monologic distinction could have been used more in the present book (see below); to the later, 'poststructuralist' thinking of Roland Barthes; to the philosopher of discourse Michel Foucault. There are other specific influences from linguistic and literary structuralism, too: in writing this book I have found myself invoking concepts such as 'foregrounding' (Mukařovský), 'defamiliarization' (Shklovsky), 'parallelism' (Jakobson), 'point of view' (Booth, Uspensky) and 'implied' or 'ideal' reader (Iser, Riffaterre).[5]

Critical news analysis has developed, for me, during the writing of this book, as an interdisciplinary project of considerable scale and complexity. In a sense it is an exemplary project, a model for how one might proceed in analysing other domains of public discourse: on the agenda might go official publications, history writing, classroom, legal or medical discourse, political speeches and writing, negotiations and bargaining, and so on. But if we return to the newspaper project, there are certain observations on what more could be done which could not be tackled in a single book.

Critical news analysis can focus on different kinds of segments of its textual materials. In ascending order of abstractness, we could consider news discourse in terms of 'stories', or of 'topics', or of 'paradigms'. I have very much relied on stories and topics to sort out my textual materials and organize my discussion. Beneath the story of Mrs Gillick's temporary victory at the Court of Appeal, there are the topics of the powerlessness of the young and the diminishing authority of professionals. More abstract still is a paradigm of young female sexuality which is experienced as problematic for the society. The Public Order White Paper story was discussed in chapter 8 for the light it cast on power-relations between state agencies and individuals; go deeper, and the story is underpinned by a contemporary paradigm of 'us' and 'them', which at a very abstract level equates female peace campers with male football hooligans. A crucial theoretical point to be made is that paradigms, frames, scripts and other such abstract schemata exist independently of the diverse stories that are made significant by them. Stereotypes of racial otherness, fanaticism, female hysteria, state benevolence, consumer power, or whatever, are expressed in countless different narratives, and in feature articles on numerous different topics. A more powerful analysis than has been possible in this preliminary study would *begin* with hypotheses about the paradigms and trace them through the pages of the newspapers, regardless of content or style: for instance, we might suppose that 'hysteria' was part of the current female stereotype, and look at how it was encoded in news stories, medical features, agony columns, letters, sports reporting, advertisements, etc. De-privileging the story or the topic as the basic principle of news organization would surely lead to greater clarity in defining the paradigms. I felt I lacked this clarity when discussing very abstract paradigms involved in, for example, 'consensus': the specific substance of the *story* distracts from a clear realization of its underlying meanings.

De-privileging story or topic would also have allowed other kinds of analysis which are under-represented in this book. Whole-page analysis, for instance, is a particularly attractive activity in the classroom, using as it does a manageable unit of text: typographical layout and the relationships between continuous text, pictures, cartoons, captions and advertisements are frequently ideologically significant. Metaphors stray from headline to headline, photographs which are meaningless in themselves become significant when juxtaposed to a piece of text – an instance in point being the two very bland small pictures of Mrs Thatcher and Mr Kinnock apparently illustrating one article in the *Mirror*, 17 April 1986, pointlessly on the surface, since everyone knew what these two politicians looked like; but juxtaposed with an editorial in which the newspaper was desperately trying to argue that they were 'two of a kind', much more meaningful. (Questions of format, typography, the use of various kinds of visuals, the juxtaposing of articles, etc., largely neglected in the present book which has concentrated on the linguistics of 'text' strictly construed, make up another important dimension of analysis to be added to critical linguistics. Indeed, thorough analysis would *have to* take on board the visual dimension; a future theoretical project would work out how to integrate it with the linguistic criticism of verbal text.)

Extending the procedure of looking at blocks of text larger than the single story or topic, we could undertake whole-issue analysis and whole-week analysis, looking for recurrent moods or themes, or conversely attempting to characterize the repertoire of varieties of textual experience presented to readers in their daily and week-long consumption of a paper.

There is a major dimension of study which requires extensive practice and systematic development: what is called in linguistics the diachronic dimension, the chronological or historical. It is a fundamental institutional fact about newspapers that their characteristic schedule of publication is daily, so that, for most readers (myself having been a long-suffering exception for the past four years), each issue is experienced as a separate, disposable text, fast fading in its impact. The sensation of autonomy is enhanced by the biological and cultural discreteness of a day's life: a day is the clearest, most marked unit of subjective time. The news values which favour the single, unambiguous event (see chapter 2) fit well with the schedules of newspaper production and consumption, and all in all, the situation disfavours accounts of development, change or constant underlying factors (as opposed to recurrent surface instances). Newspapers conceal history, presenting events as autonomous, instantaneous and rapidly erased. It would be an important critical activity to retrieve change and causation by diachronic study. Some examples of change and development in the materials I collected include the bombing of Libya, a sequence of events and changing responses over a few days; and the salmonella affair, in which, over six months, scores of reiterations of episodes and incidents, statements and statistics made the Press work hard to find significance by developing, and then attempting to remove, an underlying paradigm. I also collected an extensive sequence of texts concerning the catastrophic explosion and fire at the Chernobyl nuclear power station in Russia on 26 April 1986, an event at first treated secretly by the Russians and then gradually understood by the western Press. First, an account slowly built up of what happened at Chernobyl, and even more gradually, over weeks and months, an understanding of the global implications as radioactive debris rained down thousands of miles away. Another event with a significant development in the Press occurred in the later stages of the writing of this book: the Hillsborough football disaster on 15 April 1989, when ninety-five people were crushed to death at a Football Association Cup semi-final in Sheffield. This highly distressing event was at first presented in an extremely melodramatic and pathetic way, with shocking photographs of the dead and dying. In the two or three days following this tragedy, there were in the papers rapid revaluations of the causes: one day the event was an instance of police incompetence, the next it was transformed into an example of crowd violence and drunkenness. The diachronic development here involved rapid and radical switches of representation, as different paradigms were brought to interpret the event. Here, newspapers can be seen effectively *changing* reality.

Much more could be done on stylistic variation than I have
attempted here. Sociolinguistics demonstrates (see chapter 3, pp.
32–6) that there are complex and subtle variations of style in
utterances and texts within a community; that this variation is
systematic, rule-governed and, because systematic, capable of carrying social significances. I have not had the space to investigate
stylistic differences and similarities between newspapers and
groups of newspapers, nor to identify idiosyncrasies and explain
their functions.

Another dimension of variation which requires close study is
that of genre. The concept of genre comes from literary history,
where it refers to a set of texts with recognizable formal and
stylistic similarities, which relates to some common communication situation: 'ode', 'sonnet', 'epistolary novel', *Bildungsroman*,
'farce', etc. Now, it is intuitively obvious that there exist within
newspapers distinct genres of writing: editorials, reviews, financial reports, sports, accounts of parliamentary proceedings, etc.
Presumably, each genre employs certain textual strategies which
cue readers to expect a particular kind of discursive experience,
a particular view on some specialized portion of the represented
world. But what is intuitively obvious cannot be taken for
granted. Little is known about the characters of these genres; so
there are numerous important descriptive projects available in
these areas. It is already clear, from the preliminary look at some
editorials in the previous chapter, that there is no 'standard' form
and style for editorials: they employ many different kinds of
textual procedures, though a number of features recur (*but not all,
nor every time*): certain kinds of modality, certain pronouns, high
diction or alternatively vernacular diction, hypotaxis, syntactic
parallelism, etc. Editorials are presumably a kind of Wittgenstein-
ian family recognizable by options from a set of cues; and such
families provide a complicated descriptive task for the taxonomist
of genre.

Genre is one kind of intertextuality: a text is of a genre because
it relates to others of the type. Other kinds of intertextuality
require detailed study. There is the whole question of allusion.
In the middle-class newspapers, fragments or nuggets of allusion
– popular, literary, classical, scraps of Latin or scientific jargon –
are used frequently, particularly in editorials, to suggest breadth
of knowledge, or knowledge in some relevant specialism, thus
enhancing the appearance of authority. Although these kinds of

allusions are partly a matter of style, a display of learning, each deserves to be examined closely, for they have the function also of cueing in readers' knowledge and attitudes: they are thus both an economy, briefly inviting a ready-made point of view, and the medium of an implicit pact between source and reader, setting them above the third-person 'other' referred to by the text. The *Guardian*'s 'Ramboism without risk' (p. 217) succinctly associates Ronald Reagan with the popular myth of mindless aggression encoded in the film character, and undermines this kind of action still further with 'without risk', representing it as cowardly bullying. To cite one more example, an extremely provocative editorial in *The Times*, 30 January 1989, mocking discussion in the Church of England of gendered and ungendered language in the liturgy, was given the complexly allusive heading **'SEX AND THE SYNOD'**. My students deconstructed this initially cryptic rubric. It appears to be, on one level, a reference to the book *Sex and the Single Girl* by Helen Gurley Brown, which has been ascribed a mythical place in the history of western prurience, so to mention it in the context of a sarcastic article on language and gender is to taint the topic with a kind of voyeuristic sauciness.[6] On another level, the overall *form* of the heading refers to a formulaic 'X and Y' title for popular, including romantic, fiction, and for dirty stories, of which 'The Bishop and the Actress' is perhaps closest to the surface here. Evidently allusions convey a lot of significance in a short space; and they are important clues to the cultural assumptions a newspaper makes about its readership.

There is also a more generalized stylistic allusiveness which may almost amount to parody: some article in a newspaper may strive to sound like fiction, or scientific report, or documentary, or police investigation, legal judgement, parliamentary speech, or whatever. Conversely, an advertisement in a paper may disguise itself as a consumer journalist's report and recommendation. Especially in magazine-format sections of newspapers, whole pages may mimic the style of the newspaper itself, with only the announcement 'Advertisement' in small type at the top or bottom to give the game away. These kinds of stylistic intertextuality go far beyond the scope of this book.

If critical linguistics is concerned primarily with the ideological significances of newspaper discourse, it will be immensely important to study that discourse's relationships with its journalists' sources. We saw in chapter 2 (p. 21) that newspapers are greatly dependent on externally produced texts: speeches and debates in Parliament, Press releases from many sources, expert reports whether governmental or private, official papers, propaganda from political groups and statements and comments by privileged 'accessed voices'. Let us illustrate the last three categories.

First, 'official papers'. In 1988 and 1989 the Department of Education and Science and the National Curriculum Council published voluminous materials concerning the Education Reform Act, the National Curriculum, local financial management of schools, opting-out, etc. These papers were freely available to journalists (and somewhat less freely to parents, teachers and governors, in my experience as an instance of all three). An educational journalist consuming all of this documentation – as s/he would have to do – would have little time to read anything else in the field, and so the official papers have set the agenda and the style for newspaper discussion of educational reform. Particular intertextual studies could be made to determine the extent to which the newspapers mediated the government's ideas in the government's own terms. For instance, in June 1989 was published *English for Ages 5 to 16*, the definitive proposals for English curriculum content and attainment targets offered by the 'Cox Committee' or 'National Curriculum English Working Group'. Since 'Standard English' has become a political favourite with the British Press, the Cox proposals received wide attention in the newspapers. The *Independent*, 23 June 1989, has a whole-page article by Peter Wilby summarizing and interpreting the proposals in some detail: to what extent is the discourse of this article dependent on the language and ideas of the report, or to what extent are new paradigms called up? If there are new paradigms, what is their source? The page has two headings which seem to presuppose slightly different attitudes:

(1) **A new report says all school-leavers should have mastered the correct use of language.**
(2) **Queen's English poised to regain scholastic crown.**

Who is speaking here (to paraphrase Roland Barthes)? What are the sources, and what do those sources believe? The availability of the newspaper text and the report, not to mention the previous reports on English going back to Kingman (1988) and Bullock (1975),[7] neatly offers the possibility of a critical linguistic study.

My second category of 'intertexts' to be briefly illustrated here was 'propaganda from political groups'. I am well aware that the distinction is hard to make; I am referring here to texts which do not claim to come from government sources and which make an explicit intervention in some public debate. An example would be the series of pamphlets published by the National Union of Teachers attacking the Education Reform Act in advance of its acceptance by Parliament; to what extent did the NUT's arguments influence the discussion of educational reform in the newspapers? Another example of intertextuality between propaganda and newspaper discourse, studied some years ago by my colleague Tim Marshall and myself, concerned nuclear 'defence'. On the agenda in 1983 was the deployment of American cruise missiles in Britain, in the context of debate on the 'modernization' of 'our' 'nuclear capability'. A number of pro-nuclear organizations were active in producing literature at that time, including the 'Campaign for Defence with Multilateral Disarmament' run by the Conservative MP Winston Churchill. The leaflets produced by this organization, building on publications by the Ministry of Defence which were also available in pamphlet form, develop and crystallize a set of standard arguments in favour of nuclear armaments; these arguments, along with stock phrasings that formulate their paradigmatic forms, are extensively reproduced in the newspapers at times of crisis in the debate about nuclear defence.[8]

Finally, critical news analysis has a large area of prospective study in the newspapers' rendering of *oral* sources and other individual utterances and writings. In the papers, a large amount of report is based on speeches, statements, replies to questions and interviews. A number of institutionalized speech situations are regularly accessed by the Press: debate in the two Houses of Parliament, Press conferences, courts of law, conferences and meetings of political parties, trades unions, the Church of England and professional organizations such as the British Medical Association and the British Association for the Advancement of Science. These formats provide rich sources of personal utterance from the mouths of people who are perceived as individually important, or at least interestingly characterizable; the way their speech is presented is an important part of their public personalization. It is the same with 'personalities', 'celebrities', 'stars', particularly in the worlds of sport and entertainment: the Press is thoroughly preoccupied with what such people say. Critical analysis should pay particular attention to how what people say is transformed: there are clearly conventions for rendering speech newsworthy, for bestowing significance on it. Such conventions are little understood at the moment. As it happens, the topic of the representation of speech has in recent years been prominent in the linguistic study of literature, so there is available a methodological base to be adapted to this part of news analysis.[9]

The prospects for future news analysis sketched in the last few pages amount to an agenda of research studies: we need to find out a great deal more than is presently known about how language works in the news media. It is gratifying to report that there are a number of linguists actively involved in the analysis of news discourse. The linguistic theory of news representation is being gradually developed, and descriptive studies in books or articles may be consulted.[10] Much of this work is unashamedly 'academic' in the sense that it takes a theory and a method, and applies them to a corpus of public materials. But neither the implications nor the desired outcome of critical news analysis are purely academic: they are social, political and personal.

Critical linguistics can show that the vaunted independence of the Press is an illusion. I am not claiming that this is a new discovery: anyone who thinks about the economic position of the newspaper industry under capitalism (its dependence on consumer advertising by powerful commercial concerns), or its political intimacy with government (Press releases, the Press Lobby, access to spokespersons), will rapidly come to the conclusion that a major newspaper cannot survive unless it toes the line, reproducing established ideas or at least 'responsibly' entering debate in the areas of established ideas. Numbers of newspapers which refused such compromises have failed, most recently the short-lived socialist *News on Sunday*, 1987. The necessary norm of conformity could be predicted without any linguistics, and confirmed by simple content analysis, simple study of what topics are presented and discussed, what sources are regularly accessed and cited, what kinds of products and ideas are advertised. Critical linguistics advances this analysis by demonstrating how the detailed structure of language silently and continuously shapes the ideas presented, moulding them in the direction of established beliefs. A newspaper assumes that there is always only one reasonable point of view on any matter presented. Editorials visibly *affirm* this point of view; the news and other pages are written to assume that this point of view is natural, common sense, to be taken for granted, not needing to be asserted. Critical linguistics brings this hidden process to consciousness; the practice of analysis makes ideological structure 'tangible'.

This critical linguistic analysis is important not only academically (as, for example, confirming a content analysis hypothesis about political dependency), but also *personally*. The fact is that *readers* are implicated in the discursive articulation of values and beliefs. A reader cannot easily read through a newspaper article disinterestedly, and sit back and say 'that's biased'. The individual, processing the discourse by scanning and understanding it, has to take on board the paradigms and stereotypes that are implied: if s/he does not, the discourse will not signify. It is in this sense that newspapers *construct* readers. Discourse always has in mind an implied addressee, an imagined subject position which it requires the addressee to occupy. Newspapers are concerned – and deliberately, despite the unnoticeability of the discursive processes – to construct ideal readers: '*Times/Guardian/Sun* reader'. The *real* reader, you or I, will be comfortable with the ideological position silently offered by the particular newspaper, whether s/he notices it or not. The real reader will continue to buy the newspaper with which s/he is comfortable, keeping circulation up; sales figures are of immense importance to newspapers, because they determine advertising revenue. The comfortable individual reader will also be enrolled in an ideological mass population, holding certain views which will be useful to business and government.

At this point, I want to say that critical linguistic analysis is available as an activity that the individual in the sense of the last paragraph – the real reader – can practise; and that this practice can be a valuable intervention in the deconstruction of the all-too-comfortable 'common sense' enjoined by the newspapers. (Do I need to justify the necessity of such deconstruction?)

Viewed head-on by the lay person, critical linguistics looks like a substantial technical machinery – which, written out in fuller detail than chapter 5 provides, it actually is. Newspaper readers cannot just be provided with a do-it-yourself manual and left to follow the instructions. No 'lay reader' would be bothered to do such a thing, anyway! What we really need to plan is an educational programme in critical reading (and viewing) within which critical linguistics would be a new methodological input. The approach already has a small place in higher education, taught in some universities and polytechnics where there are linguists who are interested in the relationships between language, society and ideology. There are opportunities to extend the method to the many popular media studies courses which are on offer, and – this is a very interesting prospect – to the new English language courses which will be needed in departments of English and of Education in order to prepare teachers to cope with the new English language requirements of the National Core Curriculum for schools.[11] I have found critical news analysis extremely teachable, exciting and revealing for students of various disciplines.

Handling newspapers – current newspapers, preferably of the day of the class – has an immediacy and relevance for young people, engaging them instantly with stories and topics (and then, as they realize it, paradigms) which vitally concern them. Discussion is lively, because participants can contribute out of their knowledge of contemporary political and social life, contextualizing the analysis even if they are still learning the method and the technical linguistic jargon. And as I observed in chapter 5 (p. 70), certain parts of the model (e.g. transitivity) are extremely powerful, so that a little method goes a long way. So the amount of technical apparatus to be introduced to students can be adjusted to suit the level of technical preparedness and the goals of the class. And the method has the pedagogic advantage that it is extremely amenable to diagrammatic or tabular presentation (e.g. pp. 143, 173, above): significant structures can be displayed with great salience and clarity. This technique is effective not only for students, but also for lay people: on an open day at the University of East Anglia, there was considerable interest in blown-up wall displays based on tabular arrays prepared for this book; my colleagues and I found it very easy and satisfying to talk through these materials with visitors. Simple practical aids make ideological structures very accessible: for example, different-coloured highlighting pens reveal patterns of reference or coherence (cf. p. 105), as does collage-type editing of cut-outs tidied by photocopying. In general, the awkwardness of manipulating flimsy and irregular cuttings can be overcome by homogenizing them to A3 or A4 format on the copier; the copies are then easily sorted into categories, arranged significantly on floor or wall, and so on. Computer scrap and pencils come into their own for collecting lists of expressions (cf. chapters 9 and 10) and for roughing tables and diagrams. All in all, the teaching of critical linguistics can be managed in an engaging way, involving students in participatory practical tasks; and these tasks can be shared among a group, giving the satisfaction of co-operating towards a quickly achieved goal.

I will end the book on that practical note. For those of us who are critically interested in politics, society and the discursive moulding of individuals, it is a priority that students at all educational levels should experience these activities of analysis; that their experience of public discourse should begin to be actively critical rather than meekly receptive.

Notes

1 Introduction: the importance of language in the news

1 P. Wilsher, D. Macintyre and M. Jones, *Strike: Thatcher, Scargill and the Miners* (London: Deutsch, 1986), p. xii.

2 See Glasgow University Media Group, *Bad News* (London: Routledge & Kegan Paul, 1976); Glasgow University Media Group, *More Bad News* (London: Routledge & Kegan Paul, 1980); S. Hall, C. Crichter, T. Jefferson, J. Clarke and B. Roberts, *Policing the Crisis: Mugging, the State, and Law and Order* (London: Macmillan, 1978), and especially ch. 3, 'The social production of news'; S. Hall, D. Hobson, A. Lowe and P. Willis, *Culture, Media, Language* (London: Hutchinson, 1980); S. Cohen and J. Young (eds), *The Manufacture of News: Social Problems, Deviance and the Mass Media* (London: Constable, 1973). For a critique of the Glasgow research, see M. Harrison, *TV News: Whose Bias?* (Hermitage, Berks.: Policy Journals, 1985).

3 P. Berger and T. Luckmann, *The Social Construction of Reality* (Harmondsworth: Penguin, 1976).

4 J. Hartley, *Understanding News* (London: Methuen, 1982). For semiotics or semiology, see F. de Saussure, trans. W. Baskin and with an introduction by J. Culler, *Course in General Linguistics* (London: Fontana, 1974 [first published in French 1916]); R. Barthes, trans. A. Lavers and C. Smith, *Elements of Semiology* (London: Cape, 1967).

5 R. Barthes, trans. A. Lavers, *Mythologies* (London: Cape, 1972). For an application of Barthes-type semiological analyses to materials relevant to the present book, see J. Williamson, *Decoding Advertisements* (London: Marion Boyars, 1978).

6 E. Sapir, *Language* (New York: Harvest Books, 1949 [first published 1921]); B. L. Whorf, ed. J. B. Carroll, *Language, Thought and Reality* (Cambridge, Mass.: MIT Press, 1956); M. A. K. Halliday, *Language as Social Semiotic* (London: Edward Arnold, 1978). See also G. R. Kress and R. Hodge, *Language as Ideology* (London: Routledge & Kegan Paul, 1979).

7 For reviews, see J. B. Carroll, *Language and Thought* (Englewood Cliffs, NJ: Prentice-Hall, 1964); H. H. Clark and E. V. Clark, *Psychology and Language* (New York: Harcourt Brace Jovanovich, 1977).

8 Introductory reviews of sociolinguistics include P. Trudgill, *Sociolinguistics* (Harmondsworth: Penguin, 1974); W. Downes, *Language and Society* (London: Fontana, 1984).

9 For critical linguistics, see R. Fowler, R. Hodge, G. Kress and T. Trew, *Language and Control* (London: Routledge & Kegan Paul, 1979), especially ch. 10, 'Critical linguistics'; G. Kress, *Linguistic Processes in Sociocultural Practice* (Victoria: Deakin University Press, 1985); G. Kress, 'Discourses, texts, readers and the pro-nuclear arguments', in P. Chilton (ed.) *Language and the Nuclear Arms Debate: Nukespeak Today* (London and Dover, NH: Frances Pinter, 1985), pp. 65–87; R. Fowler, 'Notes on critical linguistics', in T. Threadgold and R. Steele (eds), *Language Topics: Essays in Honour of Michael Halliday* (Amsterdam and Philadelphia, Pa: John Benjamins, 1987), pp. 481–92; R. Fowler, 'Critical linguistics', in K. Malmkjær (ed.), *The Linguistic Encyclopaedia* (London: Routledge, forthcoming).

10 For discussion of relevant meanings of 'critique' and 'criticism', see P. Connerton (ed.), *Critical Sociology* (Harmondsworth: Penguin, 1976); J. Cook, 'Critique', in R. Fowler (ed.), *A Dictionary of Modern Critical Terms*, 2nd edn (London: Routledge & Kegan Paul, 1987), pp. 49–51.

11 See N. Chomsky, *Language and Mind* (New York: Harcourt Brace Jovanovich, 2nd edn, 1972); N. Smith and D. Wilson, *Modern Linguistics: The Results of Chomsky's Revolution* (Harmondsworth: Penguin, 1979).

2 The social construction of news

1 Glasgow University Media Group, *Bad News* (London: Routledge & Kegan Paul, 1976); Glasgow University Media Group, *More Bad News* (London: Routledge & Kegan Paul, 1980); S. Hall, C. Critcher, T. Jefferson, J. Clarke and B. Roberts, *Policing the Crisis: Mugging, the State, and Law and Order* (London: Macmillan, 1978). For a relevant American study, see H. J. Gans, *Deciding What's News* (New York: antheon, 1979).

2 G. Philo, 'Bias in the media', in D. Coates and G. Johnston (eds), *Socialist Arguments* (Oxford: Martin Robertson, 1983), pp. 130–45.

3 S. Hall, 'The social production of news', in Hall *et al.*, op. cit., p. 53.

4 Philo, op. cit., p. 135.

5 J. Galtung and M. Ruge, 'Structuring and selecting news', in S. Cohen and J. Young (eds), *The Manufacture of News: Social Problems, Deviance and the Mass Media* (London: Constable, 1973), pp. 62–72.

6 D. M. Johnson, 'The "phantom anaesthetist" of Mattoon – a field study of mass hysteria', *Journal of Abnormal and Social Psychology*, vol. 40 (April 1945); N. Z. Medalia and O. N. Larsen, 'Diffusion and belief in a collective delusion', *American Sociological Review*, vol. 23, no. 2. Brief accounts of these incidents are given in Brian Whitaker, *News Limited: Why You Can't Read All About It* (London: Minority Press Group, 1981), pp. 7–9.

7 Galtung and Ruge, op. cit., p. 65.
8 Hall *et al.*, 'The law-and-order society: the exhaustion of "consent" ', op. cit., pp. 218–72; S. Hall, 'A world at one with itself', *New Society*, 18 June 1970, pp. 1056–8, reprinted in Cohen and Young, op. cit., pp. 85–94; Hall, 'The social production of news', pp. 55–7; J. Hartley, *Understanding News* (London: Methuen, 1982), pp. 81–6.
9 For references, see chapter 3, note 28.
10 For a study of the media's treatment of nuclear affairs during April 1983, see R. Fowler and T. Marshall, 'The war against peacemongering: language and ideology', in P. Chilton (ed.), *Language and the Nuclear Arms Debate: Nukespeak Today* (London and Dover, NH: Frances Pinter, 1985), pp. 3–22.
11 Sketches of the Press and its contexts and practices may be found in Philo, op. cit., pp. 131–5; Hartley, op. cit., pp. 48–50. There is much relevant material in Cohen and Young, op. cit., and in J. Curran, M. Gurevitch and J. Woollacott (eds), *Mass Communication and Society* (London: Edward Arnold, 1977); also J. Tunstall (ed.), *Media Sociology: A Reader* (London: Constable, 1970). A standard work on the Press as an institution is J. Curran and J. Seaton, *Power without Responsibility: The Press and Broadcasting in Britain*, 3rd edn (London: Methuen, 1988). Worth reading also are: T. Baistow, *Fourth Rate Estate* (London: Comedia, 1985); A. Wesker, *Journey into Journalism* (London: Writers & Readers, 1977); K. Waterhouse, *Daily Mirror Style* (London: Mirror Books, 1981).
12 Hall, 'The social production of news', pp. 57–8; P. Rock, 'News as eternal recurrence', in Cohen and Young, op. cit., pp. 73–80.
13 Whitaker, op. cit., pp. 31–2.
14 Hartley, op. cit., pp. 109–15.
15 R. Fowler, 'Power', in T. A. van Dijk (ed.), *Handbook of Discourse Analysis*, vol. IV, *Discourse Analysis in Society* (New York: Academic Press, 1985), pp. 61–82.
16 Fowler and Marshall, op. cit.
17 I allude to the 'ideological and repressive state apparatuses' of Louis Althusser: see his *Lenin and Philosophy* (London: New Left Books, 1971).
18 Cf. the 'mass manipulative model' in Cohen and Young's characterization, op. cit., pp. 15–21.

3 Language and representation

1 Material relevant to these observations may be found in Glasgow University Media Group, *More Bad News* (London: Routledge & Kegan Paul, 1980), part III.
2 F. de Saussure, trans. W. Baskin and with an introduction by J. Culler, *Course in General Linguistics* (London: Fontana, 1974 [first published in French 1916]); L. Bloomfield, *Language* (London: Allen & Unwin, 1961 [first published 1933]). For a flavour of pre-Chomskyan American structural linguistics, see any of the textbooks published in the 1950s and 1960s, e.g. Z. S. Harris, *Structural Linguistics*

(Chicago: University of Chicago Press, 1951); A. A. Hill, *Introduction to Linguistic Structures: From Sound to Sentence in English* (New York: Harcourt Brace & World, 1958).

3 N. Chomsky, *Syntactic Structures* (The Hague: Mouton, 1957). For the idea of a 'Chomskyan revolution', see the review of *Syntactic Structures* by R. B. Lees, *Language*, no. 33 (1957), pp. 375–407; also N. Smith and D. Wilson, *Modern Linguistics: The Results of Chomsky's Revolution* (Harmondsworth: Penguin, 1979).

4 N. Chomsky, *Language and Mind*, 2nd edn (New York: Harcourt, Brace, Jovanovich, 1972), p. 1.

5 N. Chomsky, *Aspects of the Theory of Syntax* (Cambridge, Mass: MIT Press, 1965), p. 3.

6 See Bloomfield, op. cit.; E. Sapir, *Language* (New York: Harvest Books, 1949 [first published 1921]); B. L. Whorf, ed. J. B. Carroll, *Language, Thought and Reality* (Cambridge, Mass.: MIT Press, 1956). See also F. Boas, *Handbook of American Indian Languages* (first published 1911) – see P. Holder (ed.), F. Boas, *Introduction to 'Handbook of American Indian Languages'* and J. W. Powell, *Indian Linguistic Families of America North of Mexico* (Lincoln, Nebr.: University of Nebraska Press, 1966).

7 Sapir, op. cit., p. 17.

8 Whorf, op. cit., pp. 213–14.

9 E. Leach, 'Animal categories and verbal abuse', in E. H. Lenneberg (ed.), *New Directions in the Study of Language* (Cambridge, Mass.: MIT Press, 1964), p. 34.

10 For discussion of the Sapir-Whorf hypothesis and of some psycholinguistic evidence which seems to support the weaker version, see. R. Brown, *Words and Things* (New York: Free Press, 1958); J. B. Carroll, *Language and Thought* (Englewood Cliffs, NJ: Prentice-Hall, 1964); H. H. Clark and E. V. Clark, *Psychology and Language* (New York: Harcourt Brace Jovanovich, 1977), chs 13 and 14.

11 G. Orwell, 'Politics and the English language', in S. Orwell and I. Angus (eds), *The Collected Essays, Journalism and Letters of George Orwell*, vol. IV (Harmondsworth: Penguin, 1971), pp. 156–70.

12 M. A. K. Halliday, 'Linguistic function and literary style: an inquiry into the language of William Golding's *The Inheritors*', in S. Chatman (ed.), *Literary Style: A Symposium* (New York and London: Oxford University Press, 1971), pp. 332–3.

13 For discussion, see R. Fowler, *Linguistic Criticism* (Oxford: Oxford University Press, 1986).

14 Clark and Clark, op cit., ch. 14.

15 M. A. K. Halliday, 'Language structure and language function', in J. Lyons (ed.), *New Horizons in Linguistics* (Harmondsworth: Penguin, 1970), p. 142.

16 W. Labov, *Sociolinguistic Patterns* (Philadelphia, Pa: University of Pennsylvania Press, 1972); P. Trudgill, *The Social Differentiation of English in Norwich* (Cambridge: Cambridge University Press, 1974); P. Trudgill, *Sociolinguistics* (Harmondsworth: Penguin, 1974). For discussion, see N. Dittmar, trans. P. Sand, P. A. M. Seuren and K.

Whiteley, *Sociolinguistics: A Critical Survey of Theory and Application* (London: Edward Arnold, 1976); W. Downes, *Language and Society* (London: Fontana, 1984).

17 Trudgill, *The Social Differentiation of English in Norwich.*

18 J.-P. Blom and J. J. Gumperz, 'Social meaning in linguistic structures: code-switching in Norway', in J. J. Gumperz and D. Hymes (eds), *Directions in Sociolinguistics: The Ethnography of Communication* (New York: Holt, Rinehart & Winston, 1972), pp. 407–34.

19 See J. A. Fishman, 'Sociolinguistic perspective on the study of bilingualism', *Linguistics*, no. 39 (1968), pp. 21–49; J. Rubin, *National Bilingualism in Paraguay* (The Hague: Mouton, 1968); C. A. Ferguson, 'Diglossia', in P. P. Giglioli (ed.), *Language and Social Context* (Harmondsworth: Penguin, 1972), pp. 232–51.

20 R. Brown and A. Gilman, 'The pronouns of power and solidarity', in Giglioli (ed.), op. cit., pp. 252–82. Note that this study was first published in 1960; some of its observations seem somewhat quaint today.

21 M. A. K. Halliday, A. McIntosh and P. Strevens, *The Linguistic Sciences and Language Teaching* (London: Longmans, 1964), ch. 4.

22 D. H. Hymes, *Foundations in Sociolinguistics* (London: Tavistock, 1977).

23 M. A. K. Halliday, 'Sociolinguistic aspects of mathematical education', and 'Language as social semiotic', reprinted in *Language as Social Semiotic* (London: Edward Arnold, 1978), pp. 195, 111.

24 S. Hall, 'The social production of news', in S. Hall, C. Critcher, T. Jefferson, J. Clarke and B. Roberts, *Policing the Crisis: Mugging, the State, and Law and Order* (London: Macmillan, 1978), p. 61.

25 G. R. Kress, *Linguistic Processes in Sociocultural Practice* (Victoria: Deakin University Press, 1985), pp. 6–7.

26 G. R. Kress, 'Discourses, texts, readers and the pro-nuclear arguments', in P. Chilton (ed.), *Language and the Nuclear Arms Debate: Nukespeak Today* (London and Dover, NH: Frances Pinter, 1985), pp. 65–87.

27 E. H. Gombrich, *Art and Illusion* (Princeton, NJ: Princeton University Press, 1960).

28 D. E. Rumelhart, 'Schemata: the building blocks of cognition', in R. J. Spiro, B. C. Bruce and W. F. Brewer (eds), *Theoretical Issues in Reading Comprehension* (Hillsdale, NJ: Lawrence Erlbaum, 1980), pp. 33–58; M. Minsky, 'A framework for representing knowledge', in P. H. Winston (ed.), *The Psychology of Computer Vision* (New York: McGraw-Hill, 1975), pp. 211–77 (*frames*); R. C. Schank and R. P. Abelson, *Scripts, Plans, Goals and Understanding* (Hillsdale, NJ: Lawrence Erlbaum, 1977) (*scripts*); E. Rosch, 'Cognitive representations of semantic categories', *Journal of Experimental Psychology: General*, no. 104 (1975), pp. 192–233 (*prototypes*). See also references in chapter 4, note 14.

29 H. S. Cairns and C. E. Cairns, *Psycholinguistics: A Cognitive View of Language* (New York: Holt, Rinehart & Winston, 1976), ch. 6.

30 Clark and Clark, op. cit., ch. 2; J. Aitchison, *The Articulate Mammal*, 2nd edn (London: Hutchinson, 1983), ch. 10.
31 On structures of poetic language, see G. Leech, *A Linguistic Guide to English Poetry* (London: Longmans, 1969); R. Fowler, *Linguistic Criticism* (Oxford: Oxford University Press, 1986) and references.
32 ibid.

4 Conversation and consensus

1 S. Hall, 'The social production of news' in S. Hall, C. Crichter, T. Jefferson, J. Clarke and B. Roberts, *Policing the Crisis: Mugging, the State, and Law and Order* (London: Macmillan, 1978), pp. 60–1.
2 On consensus, see for example S. Hall, 'A world at one with itself', in S. Cohen and J. Young (eds), *The Manufacture of News: Social Problems, Deviance and the Mass Media* (London: Constable, 1973), pp. 85–94; J. Hartley, *Understanding News* (London: Methuen, 1982), pp. 81–3; S. Chibnall, *Law-and-Order News* (London: Tavistock, 1977), pp. 14–22.
3 See previous note.
4 G. Murdock (in Cohen and Young, op. cit.) and S. Hall (in Hall *et al.*, op. cit., p. 56) both quote a striking example from a prime ministerial broadcast by Edward Heath after the settlement of the miners' strike in February 1972:

> In the kind of country we live in there cannot be any 'we' or 'they'. There is only 'us'; all of us. If the Government is 'defeated', then the country is defeated, because the Government is just a group of people elected to do what the majority of 'us' want to see done. That is what our way of life is all about.
>
> It really does not matter whether it is a picket line, a demonstration or the House of Commons. We are all used to peaceful argument. But when violence or the threat of violence is used, it challenges what most of us consider to be the right way of doing things. I do not believe you elect any government to allow that to happen and I can promise you that it will not be tolerated wherever it occurs.

Hall suggests that 'open appeals to consensus are particularly prevalent when conflict is most visible'.
5 Chibnall, op. cit., pp. 21–2.
6 On basic-level terms, see H. H. Clark and E. V. Clark, *Psychology and Language* (New York: Harcourt Brace Jovanovich, 1977), pp. 527–30.
7 P. L. Berger and T. Luckmann, *The Social Construction of Reality* (Harmondsworth: Penguin, 1976), pp. 172ff.
8 M. A. K. Halliday, *Language as Social Semiotic* (London: Edward Arnold, 1978), pp. 160–70. Hartley, op. cit., pp. 97–8, also cites Berger and Luckmann, and Halliday.
9 Berger and Luckmann, op. cit., pp. 172–3.
10 Halliday, op. cit., p. 170.

11 Modes of discourse which seem to be deviant from 'ordinary language' are regarded by the Press as alien, indicative of false consciousness; popular and 'quality' papers are united in deriding bureaucratic 'gobbledegook', for example. Here the *Sun* (13 May 1987) ridicules an anti-sexist decree by a socialist London council:

LOONY BAN ON WIFE JOKES!

Loony left council bosses are banning staff from making jokes about their wives – in case women colleagues feel 'sexually harassed'.

Men can even face the sack for telling female colleagues they look nice . . . that's 'patronising', according to the town-hall miseries in Camden, North London . . . .

One paragraph of pure gobbledegook in the Camden charter says:

'Remarks which reflect sexist attitudes, even when not directed to a certain woman in particular, can have the effect of excluding any woman who may be present, and indicating clearly to her that, in the view of the person(s) making the remarks, women are inferior to men.'

And the *Guardian* (2 February 1988) ridicules not only EEC official jargon but also the language of an MEP's motion condemning it:

Obscuranto, the EEC's language barrier

The European Commission was accused yesterday of inventing a language, 'Obscuranto', to confuse and mislead consumers and taxpayers . . .

The consumers' body offered the most atrocious examples of 'Eurospeak' it could find.

Nuts, of the edible variety, may not be called nuts. They are officially, 'shell fruit'.

By the same logic flowers are not flowers. They are 'non-edible vegetables'. On the other hand, both sheep and goats are officially classified by the Eurocrats as 'sheepmeat' . . .

Mrs Caroline Jackson, Conservative MEP for Wiltshire, Newbury and Wantage, is demanding plain language from the commission in a motion to the European Parliament this week . . .

[T]he Lords Select Committee on the European Communities . . . complained last week that a draft directive on food inspection was so obscure and inconsistent that it should be withdrawn.

The draft directive defined food inspection as: 'The action which consists in taking note of the external phenomena by means of the senses without any further analysis.'

The commission spokesman offered this translation: 'It means you decide the quality of food by looking at it, smelling and feeling it – but would this wording stand up in a court of law?'

Mrs Jackson's motion runs to more than 20 lines and contains its own eye-glazing expressions such as 'having regard to the fact that' (twice).

12 The material in this section is adapted from my chapter 'Oral models in the Press', in M. MacLure, T. Phillips and A. Wilkinson (eds), *Oracy Matters* (Milton Keynes: Open University Press, 1988), pp. 135–46, with the permission of the publishers.
13 For representative statements, see J. V. Harari (ed.), *Textual Strategies* (London: Methuen, 1980).
14 There is a voluminous literature in cognitive psychology, particularly in the rapidly developing research fields of artificial intelligence and psycholinguistics. For an introductory survey, see P. N. Johnson-Laird, *The Computer and the Mind* (London: Fontana, 1988). Brief and accessible applications to language of 'schemas' or 'mental models' are included in R. de Beaugrande and W. Dressler, *Introduction to Text Linguistics* (London: Longman, 1981), ch. 5; G. Brown and G. Yule, *Discourse Analysis* (Cambridge: Cambridge University Press, 1983), ch. 7. Unfortunately the basic technical terminology ('frame', 'script', 'prototype', 'schema', etc.) is rather unstable. I have somewhat arbitrarily selected 'schema' as the superordinate general term for all these kinds of mental models. Others use 'schema' in more restricted senses.
15 See T. A. van Dijk, 'News schemata', in C. R. Cooper and S. Greenbaum (eds), *Studying Writing: Linguistic Approaches, Written Communication Annual*, vol. 1 (Beverly Hills, Calif.: Sage, 1986), pp. 155–85.
16 M. A. K. Halliday, A. McIntosh and P. Strevens, *The Linguistic Sciences and Language Teaching* (London: Longmans, 1964), p. 87.
17 R. A. Hudson, *Sociolinguistics* (Cambridge: Cambridge University Press, 1980), pp. 22–3.
18 For urban dialectology, see W. Labov, *Sociolinguistic Patterns* (Philadelphia, Pa.: University of Pennsylvania Press, 1972); P. Trudgill, *Sociolinguistics* (Harmondsworth: Penguin, 1974).
19 M. A. K. Halliday, 'Theme and information in the English clause', in G. Kress (ed.), *Halliday: System and Function in Language* (London: Oxford University Press, 1976), pp. 174–88.
20 See note 11.
21 John A. Searle, *Speech Acts* (Cambridge: Cambridge University Press, 1969).

5 Analytic tools: critical linguistics

1 See Glasgow University Media Group, *Bad News* (London: Routledge & Kegan Paul, 1976), ch. 1.
2 R. Fowler, R. Hodge, G. Kress and T. Trew, *Language and Control* (London: Routledge & Kegan Paul, 1979); G. Kress and T. Trew, *Language as Ideology* (London: Routledge & Kegan Paul, 1979).
3 M. A. K. Halliday, 'Linguistic structure and literary style: an inquiry into the language of William Golding's *The Inheritors*', in S. Chatman

(ed.), *Literary Style: A Symposium* (New York and London: Oxford University Press, 1971), pp. 332–4.

4 M. A. K. Halliday, *Language as Social Semiotic* (London: Edward Arnold, 1978).

5 M. A. K. Halliday, *Introduction to Functional Grammar* (London: Edward Arnold, 1985).

6 See, for example, Tony Trew's newspaper analyses in Fowler *et. al.*, *Language and Control*, chs 6 and 7; or R. Fowler, *Linguistic Criticism* (Oxford: Oxford University Press, 1986), ch. 10.

7 Halliday, *Introduction to Functional Grammar*, p. 101.

8 Transformational-generative grammar does not form an important part of the input to critical linguistics, and indeed the Chomskyan model is supposed to be theoretically and philosophically incompatible with the functional linguistics on which I draw heavily. However, critical linguistics is essentially eclectic, and I see no harm in referring to transformations for clarity of exposition of some structural relationships. The transformations used are rather old-fashioned types found in the 'classic' transformational-generative grammar of the 1960s. Two American textbooks which give detailed accounts of some major transformations are A. Akmajian and F. Heny, *An Introduction to the Principles of Transformational Syntax* (Cambridge, Mass.; MIT Press, 1975), and R. P. Stockwell, P. Schachter and B. Hall Partee, *The Major Syntactic Structures of English* (New York: Holt, Rinehart & Winston, 1973). A good modern account of generative grammar is N. Smith and D. Wilson, *Modern Linguistics: The Results of Chomsky's Revolution* (Harmondsworth: Penguin, 1979). An accessible syntax textbook which combines transformations with a more traditional account of syntactic structure is E. K. Brown and J. E. Miller, *Syntax: A Linguistic Introduction to Sentence Structure* (London: Hutchinson, 1980).

9 See J. Aitchison, *The Articulate Mammal*, 2nd edn (London: Hutchinson, 1983), pp. 200, 203 and references; H. H. Clark and E. V. Clark, *Psychology and Language* (New York: Harcourt Brace Jovanovich, 1977), p. 78 and references.

10 On sense and reference, see J. Lyons, *Semantics*, vol I (Cambridge: Cambridge University Press, 1977), ch. 7.

11 For sense-relations, see ibid., chs 8 and 9.

12 On modality, see Lyons, op. cit., vol. II, ch. 17; on the meanings of the modal auxiliaries in English, see R. Quirk, S. Greenbaum, G. Leech and J. Svartvik, *A Grammar of Contemporary English* (London: Longman, 1972), pp. 97–102.

13 J. L. Austin, *How to Do Things with Words* (Oxford: Clarendon Press, 1962); J. R. Searle, *Speech Acts* (Cambridge: Cambridge University Press, 1969); see also Lyons, op. cit., vol. II, ch. 16.

6 Discrimination in discourse: gender and power

1 There is a voluminous literature on sexism in language, and on gender-related differences in language use. J. Coates, *Women, Men*

and Language (London: Longman, 1986), is very informative on gender-related differences in language, and contains an extensive bibliography. See also C. Kramarae (ed.), *The Voices and Words of Women and Men* (Oxford: Pergamon Press, 1980), and *Women and Men Speaking* (Rowley, Mass.: Newbury House, 1981); R. Lakoff, *Language and Woman's Place* (New York: Harper & Row, 1975); D. Spender, *Man Made Language* (London: Routledge & Kegan Paul, 1980); B. Thorne, N. Henley and C. Kramarae (eds), *Language, Gender and Society* (Rowley, Mass.: Newbury House, 1983).

2 Lakoff, op. cit.; for empirical work on the differences between women's and men's speech, see Coates, op. cit..

3 After making this point, somewhat casually I admit, I came across an article 'Close-up on Winnie Mandela' by Ruth Weiss in *Marxism Today* (February 1986) which illustrates very well how much the interpretation of discourse depends on the contexts in which it is articulated and perceived. Weiss reports that 'Nomzamo Madikizela – she hates "Winnie", considering it like so many things an imposition by the white aggressor to have to carry a European name, but accepts it, because that's what she has been called for so long and so affectionately by millions – was born in the Transkei in 1934.' The black nationalist perspective and its antagonism to European names, not of course evidenced in the English newspapers which I had studied, had not occurred to me; but it was salient for a writer in a Marxist journal. Presumably, other contexts might lead to other significances; for example, the well-known dislike among blacks of diminutives and other belittling appellations such as 'boy'.

4 The popular Press recalled the young Gillick's toplessness even three years later: see *News of the World*, 7 May 1989, 'the family were rocked by scandal when her 16-year-old daughter Beattie was pictured topless with a boy on a Greek beach', an irrelevant reference in a feature on a quite different incident involving Mrs Gillick – '**MUM-OF-TEN WEPT AT CHARLES "INSULT"**'. On the general question of the popular Press's prurient interest in young women and sex, the following report in the *Guardian*, 11 August 1986, is relevant:

Sex story timing 'was grossly insensitive'

The Sun was 'grossly insensitive' to publish a sex survey with references to women's fantasies of being raped on the day the newspaper carried a front page picture of a rape victim, according to the Press Council. But in an adjudication today the council did not uphold a complaint against the Sun.

Mr Steven Bridge, of Bexley, Kent, complained that publishing a dubious sex survey was irresponsible while nationwide attention was given to rape victims.

In a feature on the 'great 1986 sex survey', reporter Roslyn Grose listed women's top sexual fantasies, the third of which was to be taken by force. In the same issue was a partly disguised front page photograph of a vicar's daughter who had been raped . . .

The Press Council said the feature appeared four days after a particularly widely reported rape and on the same day as the Sun carried the woman's picture.

Its publication of the survey on that day was grossly insensitive. The article included references to women's fantasies of being raped and of having intercourse with a group of men. There is no doubt that, with or without the coincidence or timing of its publication, many people would find it seriously offensive, tasteless and crude.

But the decision to publish it in the form he did 'lay within the editor's discretion.'

7 Terms of abuse and of endearment

1 See E. Leach, 'Animal categories and verbal abuse', in E. H. Lenneberg (ed.), *New Directions in the Study of Language* (Cambridge, Mass.: MIT Press, 1964), pp. 23–63

The following report (*Observer*, 10 August 1986) of complaints against the *Sun* shows that this paradigm of Arabs as animals, and more specifically pigs, is strongly established in the newspaper's discourse:

Sun faces charge over 'racist' cartoon
By PAUL LASHMAR

THE *Sun* is to be prosecuted for allegedly inciting racial hatred after printing a cartoon in which a group of pigs was depicted as complaining about being called Arabs.

The Attorney-General, Sir Michael Havers, has authorized a charge to be brought against the *Sun* under the Race Relations Act, 1976, after a complaint by the Arab League in London.

The cartoon by Franklin, was a response to a Press Council ruling in favour of the newspaper over an earlier complaint of racism.

Mr D. D. Jones of Northwich, Cheshire, had written to the Council over the banner headline: 'Arab pig sneaks back in' over a report that a Libyan deported at the time of the murder of WPC Yvonne Fletcher had returned to Britain. Mr Jones complained that the expression 'Arab pig' was 'intemperate, insulting and racist.'

In May, the Press Council ruled that the headline was 'intemperate,' but not racist, as it had referred to a specific person and not generally.

The next morning the *Sun* printed the cartoon showing a group of pigs outside the paper's Wapping, East London, headquarters, demonstrating over being called Arabs. [An allusion to the sacked News International print workers picketing the Wapping plant.]

That prompted the Arab League to complain to the Attorney-General. The League also wrote to Mrs Thatcher, who replied that she found the headline and cartoon 'distasteful'.

A total of 25 prosecutions for inciting racial hatred have been instigated since 1976. Last month, John Tyndall, the chairman of the British National Party, was jailed for a year for the offence.

Mr Bruce Matthews, managing director of News International, owner of the *Sun*, said yesterday it had not been informed of the prosecution.

The cartoon encodes a complex series of equivalences:

strikers ⩾ pigs ⩾ Arabs

('at least as bad as, or worse than'); while the simple expression 'Arab pig' implies

Arab ⩾ pig.

There is a linguistic point relevant to the Press Council's ruling that 'Arab pig' 'referred to a specific person and not generally'. Epithets in expressions such as this may be interpreted as either 'restrictive' or 'non-restrictive' in force. Consider 'Beautiful girls adorn the pages of the *Sun*'. This might mean 'Some girls are beautiful and just those girls adorn the pages of the *Sun*' (restrictive), or it might mean 'All girls are beautiful and girls adorn the pages of the *Sun*' (non-restrictive). Does 'Arab pig' mean 'the particular Arab who is a pig' (restrictive) or 'the particular person who is a pig because he is an Arab (because all Arabs are pigs)' (non-restrictive)? Does the popular Press characteristically use adjectives restrictively or non-restrictively?

8 Attitudes to power

1 S. Hall, 'The social production of news', in S. Hall, C. Crichter, T. Jefferson, J. Clarke and B. Roberts, *Policing the Crisis: Mugging, the State, and Law and Order*, (London: Macmillan, 1978), pp. 55–7; J. Hartley, *Understanding News* (London: Methuen, 1982), pp. 81–6.
2 The analysis which follows is adapted, with the permission of the publishers, from R. Fowler, 'Power', in Teun A. Van Dijk (ed.), *Handbook of Discourse Analysis* vol. IV, *Discourse Analysis in Society* (New York: Academic Press, 1985), pp. 61–82.
3 R. Fowler, R. Hodge, G. Kress and T. Trew, *Language and Control* (London: Routledge & Kegan Paul, 1979), pp. 40–1.
4 The newspaper industry has its own reasons for deploring 'public disorder' and supporting legislation against it. The struggle by newspaper proprietors to deploy new printing technologies against the opposition of the print unions led to conflicts between pickets and the police, notably at Warrington during picketing against Eddie Shah and his free paper the *Stockport Messenger*, and at Wapping in action by sacked employees of Rupert Murdoch's News International.

At the same time, public disorder is highly newsworthy, so the papers gain two ways when a 'riot' occurs: it provides not only saleable news but also evidence of a need for legislation which happens to serve the newspaper's interests.
5 M. Adeney and J. Lloyd, *The Miners' Strike, 1984–5: Loss without Limit* (London: Routledge & Kegan Paul, 1986); M. Crick, *Arthur Scargill* (Harmondsworth: Penguin, 1985); B. Fine and R. Millar (eds),

Policing the Miners' Strike (London: Lawrence & Wishart, 1985); G. Goodman, *The Miners' Strike* (London: Pluto, 1985); Insight Team, *Strike* (London: Coronet, 1985).

6 I discussed the following material briefly in 'The intervention of the media in the reproduction of power', in I. M. Zavala, T. A. Van Dijk and M. Diaz-Diocaretz (eds), *Approaches to Discourse, Poetics and Psychiatry*, Critical Theory Series 4 (Amsterdam and Philadelphia, Pa: John Benjamins, 1987), pp. 67–80.

7 For whatever reason, the newspapers' discussion of the White Paper pays little attention to this category of proposed offence; cf. chapter 7, note 1.

9 A Press scare: the salmonella-in-eggs affair

1 Text (10) of this chapter, from the *Sunday Times*, 29 January 1989, more fully discussed as text (15) in chapter 10, is a particularly extravagant hymn to Mrs Currie; cf. *Sunday Times*, 4 December 1988, etc. In a surprising and imaginative intervention, the American playwright Arthur Miller characterized Mrs Currie as 'a heroine for modern times', 'fighting corruption, hypocrisy and big business' like the hero of Ibsen's *Enemy of the People* (*Independent*, 5 January 1989).

2 Sources for the chronology of the earlier part of the incident, and its secret pre-public stages, include *Sunday Times*, 22 January 1989, and *Independent*, 2 February 1989.

3 See *Sunday Times*, 12 February 1989.

4 See *Sunday Times*, 22 January; *Independent*, 23 January; *Guardian*, 24 January 1989.

10 The salmonella-in-eggs affair: Pandora's box

1 See R. Barthes, trans. A. Lavers and C. Smith, *Elements of Semiology* (London: Cape, 1967), and trans. A. Lavers, *Mythologies* (London: Cape, 1972). The principle that discourse is 'about' some other topic or proposition 'underlying' the surface is methodologically enshrined in many different schools of what may be loosely called 'discourse analysis', e.g. the 'implicatures' of H. P. Grice, 'Logic and conversation', in P. Cole and J. L. Morgan (eds), *Syntax and Semantics III: Speech Acts* (New York: Academic Press, 1975), pp. 41–58; the 'general propositions' of William Labov and David Fanshel, *Therapeutic Discourse: Psychotherapy as Conversation* (New York: Academic Press, 1977).

2 See R. de Beaugrande and W. Dressler, *Introduction to Text Linguistics* (London: Longman, 1981), ch. 4.

3 'At least' acknowledges that the counting was not intended to be absolutely precise; also the fact that all of these counts are derived from my sample of 560 noun phrases: not from the material as a whole, which would have yielded vastly greater numbers.

4 A television advertisement for the *Sunday Times*, 1989, shows sections of the newspaper being shared among members of an extended family

on Sunday morning while the bonding Sunday lunch is being prepared and served.

5   'I could have written the Press coverage': when the same paradigm
recurs, existing formulae facilitate the writing, and therefore the
stereotyping, of the news. In late August 1978, Tony Trew and I
were collating manuscript copies of the final version of R. Fowler,
R. Hodge, G. Kress and T. Trew, *Language and Control* (London:
Routledge & Kegan Paul, 1979), a manual task that allowed chatting.
He remarked, 'I could write tomorrow's headlines', a reference to
the hypothetical Press coverage of the 1978 Notting Hill Carnival;
he had, in ch. 7 of that book, analysed transitivity patterns in two
reports of the last hours of the 1977 Carnival. In fact, the Carnival
reporting for 1989 could well have been written in the light of our
knowledge of the reporting of 1977:

> **INTO BATTLE!** Riot shields out as the police storm Carnival
> mob. Two hundred police carrying riot shields and truncheons
> last night charged a rioting mob of blacks youths at London's
> Notting Hill Carnival.
>
> More than 70 policemen were injured, one stabbed, before the
> Special Patrol Group officers cleared the trouble spot at Acklam
> Road – flashpoint of last year's riot in which 600 were injured.
>
> The 10-minute riot began when youths charged a police cordon.
> Hurling bottles and bricks they burst through the thin blue line.
>
> Police reformed the line and counter-charged with truncheons,
> but the weight of the crowd was too much for them.
>
> Scotland Yard's Deputy Assistant Commissioner David Helm
> gave the order that Carnival organizers had been dreading: Bring
> out the Special Patrol Group and the riot shields.
>
> The Group, held out of sight during the two day carnival, met
> a barrage of bottles and bricks.
>
> (*Sun*, 30 August 1977, quoted in
> R. Fowler *et. al.*, op. cit., pp. 120–1).

FIESTA POLICE IN RIOT BATTLE
By Nigel Freedman

SCORES of people were injured when the Notting Hill Carnival
exploded in violence last night.

Hundreds of riot police fought running battles with rampaging
youths.

The trouble flared as the West London carnival came to an end.

A gang of black teenagers started hurling flower pots down
from flats on to bobbies patrolling in Lancaster Road.

Swooped

Officers sealed off the street and the area round the notorious All
Saints Road.

As riot cops swarmed in, helicopters swooped over to pinpoint
the mobs.

Scotland Yard said several officers and bystanders were hurt by flying glass, bricks and stones.

(*Sun*, 29 August 1989)

12 Conclusion: prospects for critical news analysis

1 Full bibliographical references to this and other works in media studies are given in the notes to chapters 1 and 2.

2 G. Brown and G. Yule, *Discourse Analysis* (Cambridge: Cambridge University Press, 1983); M. Coulthard, *An Introduction to Discourse Analysis* (London: Longman, 1977); S. C. Levinson, *Pragmatics* (Cambridge: Cambridge University Press, 1983); M. Stubbs, *Discourse Analysis* (Oxford: Blackwell, 1983).

3 For references for critical linguistics, see chapter 1, note 9.

4 F. de Saussure, trans. W. Baskin and with an introduction by J. Culler, *Course in General Linguistics*, (London: Fontana, 1974).

5 For more detailed exposition of these concepts in a literary-critical context, and full references, see R. Fowler, *Linguistic Criticism* (Oxford: Oxford University Press, 1986).

6 In the course of searching for the original publication date of *Sex and the Single Girl*, Routledge discovered a wealth of formulaically related titles: *Sex and the College Girl*, *Sex and the Intelligent Teenager*, *Sex and the Man Who Used to be Single*, *Sex and the Single Man*, *Sex and the Singing Girl*, *Sex and the Single Dog*, *Sex and the Single Stewardess*, *Sex and the Single Teen*, *Sex and the Swinging Girl*, *Sex and the Teenager*.

7 *Report of the Committee of Inquiry into the Teaching of English Language*, Chairman: Sir John Kingman, FRS (London: HMSO, 1988); *A Language for Life. Report of the Committee of Inquiry*, Chairman: Sir Alan Bullock, FBA (London: HMSO, 1975).

8 The reference is in chapter 2, note 10.

9 V. N. Voloshinov, 'Reported speech', in L. Matejka and K. Pomorska (eds), *Readings in Russian Poetics* (Cambridge, Mass.: MIT Press, 1971), pp. 149–75; Brian McHale, 'Free indirect discourse: a survey of recent accounts', *Poetics and the Theory of Literature*, no. 3 (1978), pp. 249–87; A. Banfield, 'The formal coherence of represented speech and thought', *Poetics and the Theory of Literature*, no. 3 (1978), pp. 289–314; G. N. Leech and M. H. Short, *Style in Fiction* (London: Longman, 1981), ch. 10.

10 Some linguistic discussions of newspaper discourse may be found in the works cited in chapter 1, note 9. See also P. Chilton, *Orwellian Language and the Media* (London: Pluto, 1988); Teun A. Van Dijk (ed.), *Discourse and Communication: New Approaches to the Analysis of Mass Media Discourses and Communication* (Hillsdale, NJ: Lawrence Erlbaum, 1988); Teun A. Van Dijk, *News as Discourse* and *News Analysis* (both Hillsdale, NJ: Lawrence Erlbaum, 1988); R. Hodge and G. Kress, *Social Semiotics* (Oxford: Blackwell, 1988); N. Fairclough, *Language and Power* (London: Longman, 1989); D. Leith and G. Myerson, *The Power of Address* (London: Routledge, 1989); M. Montgom-

ery, *An Introduction to Language and Society* (London: Methuen, 1985); K. Richardson, 'The Mikhail and Maggie show: the British popular press and the Anglo-Soviet summit', *Multilingua*, no. 7 (1988), pp. 177–95; R. Zimmerman, 'Selling SDI to the Europeans: arguments, metaphors and adversary images', *Multilingua*, no. 7 (1988), 159–76.

11 See Kingman Report, note 7.

Index